CHILTON'S Repair and Tune-Up Guide

Barracuda
and
Challenger
1965-72

ILLUSTRATED

Prepared by the

Automotive Editorial Department

Chilton Book Company
Chilton Way
Radnor, Pa. 19089
215—687-8200

president and chief executive officer **WILLIAM A. BARBOUR;** executive vice president **RICHARD H. GROVES;** vice president and general manager **JOHN P. KUSHNERICK;** managing editor **KERRY A. FREEMAN, S.A.E.;** senior editor **RICHARD J. RIVELE;** editor **GEORGE S. RIZZO;** technical editors **JON C. JAY, ZANE C. BINDER, N. BANKS SPENCE JR, ALAN E. HOLT, III, RONALD L. SESSIONS, IVER T. ROSENLUND, JR.**

CHILTON BOOK COMPANY   RADNOR, PENNSYLVANIA

Library of Congress Cataloging in Publication Data

Chilton Book Company. Automotive Editorial Dept.
   Chilton's repair and tune-up guide for the Barracuda
and Challenger 1965–72.

   1. Barracuda automobile.   2. Challenger automobile.
I. Kelly, John D., ed.   II. Title.   III. Title:
Repair and tune-up guide for the Barracuda and
Challenger 1965–72.
TL215.B34C46   1972   629.28'7'22   72-7036
ISBN 0-8019-5721-4
ISBN 0-8019-5807-5 (pbk.)

ACKNOWLEDGMENTS

Chrysler-Plymouth and Dodge Divisions of
CHRYSLER MOTORS CORPORATION
Detroit, Michigan 48231

Contents

1 · Information and Maintenance

Introduction

Chrysler Corporation entered the personal car market with the introduction of the Plymouth Barracuda in 1965. Virtually unchanged through the 1966 model year, the first Barracuda series was moderately successful. In 1967, a completely new, and very pleasing, body style was designed for the Barracuda. This second series was very successful and was continued through 1969. Many of the 1965–69 Barracudas were equipped with the popular Formula "S" option, which included heavy-duty suspension and brakes, larger wheels and tires, and various other mechanical and trim components intended to improve the performance of the standard model. The first Formula "S" package featured the 273 cu in. engine with a special camshaft and four-barrel carburetor, which was succeeded by the 340 cu in. high-performance engine in 1968.

In 1970, as the popularity of pony cars began to wane, a third Barracuda design was introduced simultaneously with the new Dodge Challenger series. The 1970–72 Barracuda and Challenger models share the same basic body and running gear components. A wide range of engine and transmission combinations were available in the 1970 and 1971 models. Among these were the 340/440 Six Packs and the famed 426 Hemi. The 340 Six Pack was only offered in 1971 as the standard engine for the AAR 'Cuda and Challenger T/A.

Model Identification

1965 Barracuda

1966 Barracuda

1967 Barracuda

1970 'Cuda

1970 Challenger

1971 'Cuda

1971 Challenger

1972 'Cuda

1972 Challenger

Serial Number Identification

VEHICLE SERIAL NUMBERS— 1965 BARRACUDA

The vehicle serial number is located on a metal plate that is attached to the left front door hinge pillar. The serial number contains ten digits, which are interpreted as follows:

1st digit . . . . V—Barracuda
2nd digit . . . . 4—Barracuda
3rd digit . . . . 5—1965 model year
4th digit . . . . assembly plant code
1—Lynch Road   5—Los Angeles
2—Hamtramck   6—Newark, Del.
4—Belvedere   7—St. Louis
5th to 10th digits . . . . series production
  number

VEHICLE SERIAL NUMBERS— 1966–72 BARRACUDA, 1970–72 CHALLENGER

The vehicle serial numbers for the 1966 and 1967 Barracuda are located on a plate that is attached to the left front door post. Barracuda and Challenger serial number plates, from 1968 to the present, are on the left side of the dashboard and are visible through the windshield.

On 1969–72 Barracudas, the vehicle number is also stamped on a pad on the engine block. The number is located on six-cylinder engines below the no. 6 spark plug at the cylinder head joint face. On eight-cylinder engines, the number is found on the oil pan rail just to the rear of the right engine mount.

All vehicle serial numbers, since 1966, contain thirteen digits, forming a code which is interpreted as follows: make of car (1st digit), model (2nd digit), body style (3rd and 4th digits), engine displacement (5th digit), model year (6th digit), assembly plant (7th digit), and vehicle production sequence number (last six digits).

For example, the starting serial number for a 1970 340 cu in. Challenger hardtop assembled at the Hamtramck plant is JH23HOB-100001.

ENGINE SERIAL NUMBERS

The serial numbers for 170, 198, and 225 cu in. engines are stamped on the joint

Serial number plate—1965–67 Barracuda

face of the engine block, next to the no. 1 cylinder. On 273, 318, and 340 cu in. engines, the numbers are stamped on the front of the engine block, just below the left cylinder head. Serial numbers for 383, 426, and 440 cu in. engines are stamped on the oil pan rail, below the starter motor opening, at the left rear corner of the engine block.

The engine serial number consists of fourteen digits which are interpreted as follows: power train (1st and 2nd digits), cubic inch displacement (3rd, 4th, and 5th digits), low compression ratio (6th digit), manufacturing date code (7th through 10th digits), and production sequence number (11th through 14th digits).

Engine number location—170, 198, and 225 cu in. engines

Engine number location—273 cu in. engine

Vehicle Serial Number Code, 1966–72

1st Digit Make	2nd Digit Model	3rd and 4th Digits Body Style	5th Digit Engine	6th Digit Model Year	7th Digit Assembly Plant	8th–13th Digits Production Sequence Number
B—Barracuda J—Challenger	L—Low M—Medium H—High S—Special P—Premium	21—2-Dr Coupe 23—2-Dr Hardtop 27—Convertible 29—2-Dr Special	1966–69 Barracuda A—170 B—225 D—273 E—273 Hi Perf F—318 H—383 Hi Perf P—340 Hi Perf 1970–72 Barracuda and Challenger B—198 C—225 G—318 H—340 J—340 Six Pack L—383 N—383 Hi Perf R—426 U—440 Hi Perf V—440 Six Pack	5—1965 6—1966 7—1967 8—1968 9—1969 0—1970 1—1971 2—1972	1965–67 Barracuda 1—Lynch Road 2—Hamtramck 4—Belvedere 5—Los Angeles 6—Newark, Del. 7—St. Louis 9—Windsor 1968–72 Barracuda and Challenger A—Lynch Road B—Hamtramck C—Jefferson D—Belvedere E—Los Angeles F—Newark, Del. G—St. Louis H—New Stanton R—Windsor	-100001

Engine number location—318 and 340 cu in. engines

Engine number location—383, 440, and 426 cu in. engines

Manual Transmissions

Type	Model Number	Application
3 spd.	A—903	Six-cylinder models, 1965–72
3 spd.	A—745	Eight-cylinder models, 1965–69
3 spd.	A—230	Eight-cylinder models, 1970–72
4 spd.	A—833	Eight-cylinder models, 1965–72

Automatic Transmissions

Torqueflite Model Number	Application
A—904—G	Six-cylinder models, 1965–72
A—904—LA	273 cu in. models, 1965–67; 318 cu in. models
A—904—A	273 cu in. models, 1968–69
A—727—A	318 and 340 cu in. models
A—727—B	383, 426, and 440 cu in. models

NOTE: 318 cu in. models may be fitted with either A—904—LA or A—727—A transmissions.

TRANSMISSION SERIAL NUMBERS

Manual Transmissions

The serial numbers for all manual transmissions are stamped on a pad on the right side of the transmission case. Using PP 833 1861 0275 as an example, the serial number is interpreted as follows: manufacturing plant (1st and 2nd letters), transmission model number (3rd, 4th, and 5th digits), manufacturing date code (6th through 9th digits), and production sequence number (10th through 13th digits).

Automatic Transmissions

The automatic transmission identification code and serial number are cast in raised letters on the lower left side of the bellhousing.

BODY CODE PLATE

The body code plate may be located on the left front fender side shield, on the left front wheel housing, or on the left side of the upper radiator support.

The coded information includes the body production schedule date, body type, engine code, transmission code, tire code, trim code, and paint codes.

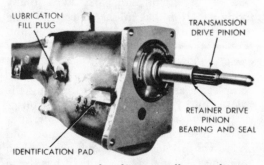

Transmission number location—all manual transmissions

Lubrication

ENGINE OIL RECOMMENDATIONS

Engine Oil Selection

For best performance and maximum engine protection, use only those lubricants that meet the requirements of the API classification "For Service SE or MS" and are of the proper SAE grade number for the expected ambient temperature range. If the proper oil is selected, additional oil additives are not usually required.

Ambient Temperature	SAE Multigrade
Where temperatures are consistently above 32°F	SAE 20W—40, SAE 10W—40, or SAE 10W—30
For year long operation where temperatures occasionally drop to —10°F	SAE 10W—30 or SAE 10W—40

	Single Grades
Where temperatures are consistently above 32°F	SAE 30
Where temperatures range between +32°F and —10°F	SAE 10W

Continuous high-speed running or rapid acceleration requires heavier-than-normal lubricating oil. For best protection under these conditions, the heaviest oil that will permit satisfactory cold starting should be used. SAE 30 and 40 are recommended. Multigrade oils SAE 20W—40 and 20W—50 may also be used.

Engine Oil Additives

In normal vehicle usage, oil additives are not necessary. However, in some instances, such as infrequent operation or short trips only, and during break-in after a major engine overhaul, the addition of antirust and antifriction materials is beneficial.

For high-performance engines equipped with four-barrel or three two-barrel carburetors, it is recommended that one pint of Chrysler Hi-Performance Oil Additive, Sulfurized Ester be added at every oil change. This additive will provide optimum engine component protection under all operating conditions.

TRANSMISSION LUBRICANT RECOMMENDATIONS

Manual Transmissions

The manufacturer recommends Dexron-type automatic transmission fluid as the proper lubricant in all three-speed and four-speed manual transmissions. However, in warm climates, the fluid may be drained from the three-speed manual transmissions and the transmission refilled with multipurpose gear lubricant SAE 90.

If excessive gear rattle occurs at idle speed in the A—833 four-speed transmission, the automatic transmission fluid may be drained and the transmission refilled with multipurpose gear lubricant SAE 140.

Automatic Transmissions

Only Dexron-type automatic transmission fluid is recommended by the manufacturer for use in all Torqueflite automatic transmissions.

REAR AXLE RECOMMENDED LUBRICANT

The manufacturer recommends that only multipurpose gear lubricant which meets the API GL—5 requirements be used in both conventional and Sure Grip differentials. Gear lubricant viscosity depends on the anticipated ambient temperature.

Anticipated Temperature Range		Viscosity Grade
Above	10°F	SAE 90
As Low As	—30°F	SAE 80
Below	—30°F	SAE 75

ENGINE OIL CHANGES

For maximum engine protection during normal operation, crankcase oil should be drained and refilled every three months or 4,000 miles. If the vehicle is driven frequently in dusty or sandy areas, more frequent oil changes may be required.

During engine break-in, the car should not be driven at speeds exceeding 50 or 60 mph for the first 300 miles. Factory installed oil should be retained for three months or 4,000 miles.

To drain the oil, place a suitable container under the rear of the oil pan. The pan drain plug is located at the rear of the oil pan sump and can be removed with a 7/8 in. wrench. Drain the oil when the engine is at normal operating temperature so that the warm oil can carry with it any foreign matter that might otherwise cling to the side of the crankcase. Remove and replace the oil filter if necessary, as discussed below.

Be sure that the oil pan is drained as completely as possible before refitting the drain plug. Fill the crankcase with oil of the recommended grade. If the oil filter has been replaced, start the engine and check the oil level. Add sufficient oil to compensate for the oil which has been drawn into the filter.

OIL FILTER CHANGES

All engines are equipped with a full-flow throwaway oil filter which should be replaced at every other oil change. Drain the oil as described above. The oil filter can be removed with a special filter wrench or by hand.

Coat the gasket of the new filter with a thin film of clean oil, place the filter in po-

Oil filter location—170, 198, and 225 cu in. engines

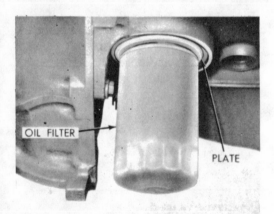

Oil filter location—318 cu in. engine

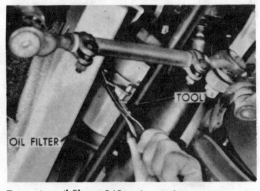

Removing oil filter—340 cu in. engine

sition on its mount, and tighten the filter by hand until the sealing gaskets just make contact. Then further tighten the filter by hand about one-half turn. *Do not use the filter wrench when tightening the filter.*

Refill the crankcase as described above.

TRANSMISSION LUBRICANT CHANGES

Manual Transmissions

Although the manufacturer does not specifically recommend periodic lubricant changes in normal service, it is suggested that the lubricant be changed at regular intervals of 36,000 miles. Regularly scheduled lubricant changes are especially recommended if the car is used in competition or to tow a trailer.

To drain the lubricant, raise the car on a hoist or jack up the front of the car and support it with suitable stands. Remove the filler plug from the right side of the transmission case. For A-745, A-230, and A-833 transmissions, position a container below the drain plug, located on the right side of the transmission case, and remove the plug, allowing the lubricant to drain into the container. A suction gun must be used on the A-903 transmission to siphon the old lubricant through the filler plug hole.

Manual transmission filler and drain plugs

After draining, replace the drain plug and fill the transmission with the proper lubricant to the correct level. Refit the filler plug and lower the car.

Automatic Transmissions

For most models in normal service, the automatic transmission fluid and filter should be changed at 36,000 mile intervals. However, for cars which are driven frequently in heavy, city traffic, fluid and filter changes should be performed every 24,000 miles. Cars powered by 426 Hemi or 340/440 Six Pack engines also require transmission fluid and filter changes at 24,000 mile intervals. For cars which are entered in competition or used for trailer towing, the recommended fluid and filter change interval is 12,000 miles.

To drain the transmission fluid, raise the car on a hoist or jack up the front of the car and support it with suitable stands. Place a container, which has a large opening, under the transmission oil pan. Loosen the pan bolts at one corner, tap the pan to break the seal, and allow the fluid to drain. Then remove the oil pan and filter. Remove the access plate from in front of the torque converter, position the container under the converter, withdraw the drain plug, and allow the fluid to drain.

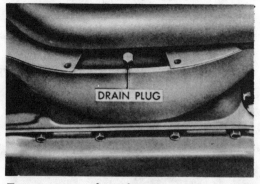

Torque converter drain plug

Refit the converter drain plug and torque to 110 in. lbs. Install the access plate. Place a new filter on the bottom of the valve body and tighten the retaining screws to 35 in. lbs. Clean the oil pan, fit a new gasket, and install the assembly. Torque the pan bolts to 150 in. lbs. Remove the container and lower the car.

Fill the transmission with six quarts of Dexron-type automatic transmission fluid. Start the engine and allow it to idle for at least two minutes. Then, with the parking brake engaged, move the selector lever momentarily to each position, ending in the Neutral position. Add enough fluid to bring the level to the "add one pint" mark on the dipstick. Road-test the vehicle to thoroughly warm up the transmission and recheck the fluid level, with the engine idling and the parking brake engaged, after the transmission is at its normal operating temperature. The fluid level should then be between the "full" and "add one pint" marks.

CAUTION: *To prevent dirt from entering the transmission, be sure that the dipstick cap is fully seated onto the filler tube.*

REAR AXLE LUBRICANT CHANGES

Regular changes of the rear axle lubricant, for both standard and Sure Grip differentials, are not recommended by the factory with the following exceptions: if the lubricant has become contaminated with water (water can enter the differential through the axle vent should the rear axle be submerged), or if the anticipated ambient temperature is much lower than average, as shown in the rear axle recommended lubricant chart. However, if the car is used in competition or is used for towing, the lubricant should be drained and refilled every 36,000 miles.

Rear Axle Identification Chart

Axle Size	Filler Plug Location	Cover Fastening	Capacity (Pints)	Lubricant Level
7¼	Cover	9 Bolts	2.0	Bottom of filler hole to ⅝ inch below
8¾	Carrier	Welded	4.4	Maintain at bottom of filler hole
9¾	Cover	10 Bolts	5.5	Bottom of filler hole to ½ inch below

Removing rear axle lubricant—8¾ in. axle

The rear axles listed in the identification chart are distinguished by their ring gear sizes: 7¼ in. for six-cylinder engines, 8¾ in. for eight-cylinder engines, and 9¾ in. heavy-duty used with the 426 Hemi engine and certain 440 cu in. engines.

To drain the axle, raise the car on a hoist. Remove the filler plug. For 7¼ and 8¾ in. axles, use a pump to siphon the old lubricant from the axle. For the 9¾ in. axle, position a container under the differential, remove the drain plug from the bottom of the differential, and drain the old lubricant into the container. Refit the drain plug.

Fill the axle with the proper grade lubricant to the level indicated in the identification chart. Refit the filler plug and lower the car.

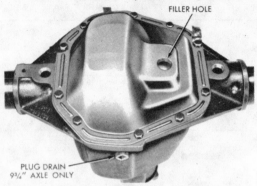

FILLER HOLE

PLUG DRAIN
9¾" AXLE ONLY

Drain and filler plug locations—9¾ in. axle

Lubrication and Maintenance Schedule

Service Interval	Item	Replace	Check Fluid Level	Inspect and/or Clean	Lubri-cate	Service
Every month	Battery		X			
	Cooling system		X			
3 months or 4,000 miles, whichever occurs first	Engine crankcase oil	X				
	Transmission		X			
	Rear axle		X			
	Universal joints			X		
Every engine oil change	Manifold heat control valve					X
	Power steering fluid		X			
	Carburetor air filter—paper					X
Every second oil change	Engine oil filter	X				
	Tire rotation					X
Every 6 months	Carburetor air filter—paper			X		
	Crankcase ventilation system			X		X
	Carburetor choke shaft			X		X
	Crankcase inlet air cleaner			X	X	
	Transmission		X			
	Rear axle		X			
	Steering Gear (manual)		X			
	Linkage			X		
	Suspension ball joints			X		
	Universal joints			X		
	Brake master cylinder		X			
	Brake hoses			X		
	Headlight aiming					X
	Hood latch and safety catch			X	X	
Every 12 months	Cooling system					X
	Crankcase ventilator valve	X				
	Carburetor air filter—paper	X				
	Throttle linkage					X

Lubrication and Maintenance Schedule

Service Interval	Item	Replace	Check Fluid Level	Inspect and/or Clean	Lubri-cate	Service
Every 12 months or 12,000 miles, which-ever occurs first	Engine performance evaluation					X
	Brakes			X		
	Front wheel bearing lubricant			X		
Every 24 months or 24,000 miles, which-ever occurs first	Carburetor air filter	X				
	Fuel filter	X				
	Brake pedal linkage bushing			X	X	
Every 36 months or 36,000 miles, which-ever occurs first	Front suspension ball joints				X	
	Steering tie rod ends				X	
	Clutch torque shaft bearings				X	
	Transmission fluid	X				
	Automatic transmission filter	X				
	Automatic transmission bands					X
	Rear axle lubricant	X				
When necessary	Distributor				X	
	Body mechanisms				X	
	Clutch drive lugs, release bear-ing sleeve, fork fingers, and pivot				X	
	Column-mounted gearshift link-age				X	
	Floor-mounted gearshift controls				X	
	Parking brake mechanism				X	
	Speedometer cable				X	

Routine Maintenance

AIR CLEANER

The paper element of the air cleaner should be inspected and cleaned every six months and replaced every two years, except on cars fitted with the Fresh Air Induction System. On models so equipped, the filter should be inspected and cleaned at every engine oil change and replaced every year. If the vehicle is driven frequently in dusty or sandy areas, more frequent filter inspections and replacements are recommended.

To remove the air cleaner, disconnect the air cleaner hose at the air cleaner and remove the cleaner from the carburetor. Remove the filter element.

Inspect the filter element. If the filter element is saturated with oil for more than one-half of its circumference, replace the element and check the rest of the crankcase ventilating system for proper functioning.

Clean the filter element with compressed air. Hold the air nozzle at least two inches from the inside screen, allowing the air to pass through the filter from the inside. *Do not use compressed air on the outside surface of the element.*

After cleaning, examine the element for punctures and discard it if the element has any pin holes.

Reassemble the air cleaner and install it on the carburetor. Refit the air cleaner hose.

FLUID LEVEL CHECKS

Engine Oil

The crankcase oil level should be checked at each fuel stop and oil should be added only when the level on the dipstick is at or below the "add oil" level.

Manual Transmission Lubricant

The lubricant level should normally be checked every six months. However, if the car is used for towing or if the transmission is otherwise highly stressed, the lubricant level should be checked at three-month or 4,000 mile intervals (at every engine oil change).

To check the lubricant level, raise the car, on a hoist or other secure support, and remove the filler plug. The correct lubricant level is at the bottom of the filler plug hole. If necessary, add the proper lubricant. Refit the filler plug and lower the car.

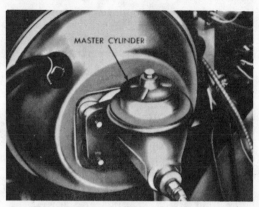

Brake master cylinder—1965–67 Barracuda

Automatic Transmission Fluid

Although the fluid level should be checked at regular, six-month intervals in normal service, it is advisable to check the fluid level more frequently, especially if the car is used in competition or for trailer towing.

The fluid level check should be made only when the engine and transmission are at their normal operating condition. Engage the parking brake and place the selector lever in the Neutral position. After the engine has idled for about two minutes, move the selector lever slowly through all the gear positions, pausing momentarily in each and ending with the lever in the Neutral position.

Before removing the transmission dipstick, wipe off the cap and the top of the filler tube to prevent dirt from dropping into the filler tube. When the fluid is hot, the fluid level should be at the "full" mark, or slightly below. Add fluid if necessary.

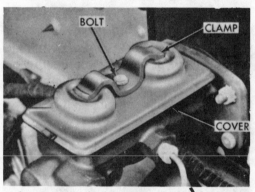

Brake master cylinder—1968–70 Barracuda and Challenger

Brake Master Cylinder

The brake master cylinder fluid level should be checked every six months. Before removing the master cylinder cover, wipe it clean to prevent foreign matter from dropping into the master cylinder.

To remove the cover from 1965–67 Barracudas, withdraw the retaining bolt and lift off the cover. For 1968–70 models, unscrew the retaining bolt, remove the securing clamp, and lift off the cover. For 1971–72 models, move the cover securing clamp to one side and lift off the cover.

If necessary, add brake fluid to within one-fourth inch of the top of the cylinder reservoir. Only brake fluid conforming to SAE requirement J1703 (70R3 type)

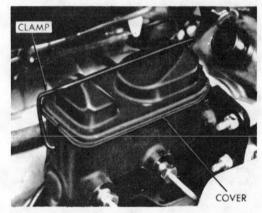

Brake master cylinder—1971–72 Barracuda and Challenger

should be used. Refit the master cylinder cover.

NOTE: *If the car is equipped with front disc brakes, the fluid level can be expected to fall as the brake pads wear. However, no noticeable drop in fluid level should occur in a car fitted with front drum brakes. A low fluid level may have been caused by a leak and the en-*

tire hydraulic system should then be inspected.

Rear Axle Lubricant

The rear axle lubricant level should be checked at every engine oil change (every 3 months or 4,000 miles). To check the level, raise the car on a hoist and remove the axle filler plug. The correct lubricant level for each axle used in Barracuda and Challenger cars is indicated in the "Rear Axle Identification" chart. If necessary, add the proper lubricant through the filler hole. Refit the filler plug and lower the car.

Manual Steering Lubricant

Although regularly scheduled lubricant changes are not necessary, the lubricant level should be checked at six-month intervals. Remove the filler plug from the steering gear housing and check to make sure that there is sufficient lubricant to cover the worm gear. If necessary, add SAE 90 multipurpose gear oil. Refit the filler plug.

Power Steering Reservoir

The fluid level in the power steering reservoir should be checked at every engine oil change (every three months or 4,000 miles). Before removing the reservoir cover, wipe the outside of the cover and case so that no dirt can drop into the reservoir.

Check the fluid level when the engine is hot. Remove the reservoir cover. If it has a dipstick, the fluid level should be at the level indicated by the marks on the dipstick. If no dipstick is fitted, the correct fluid level is approximately one-half to one inch below the top of the filler neck. If necessary for either reservoir, add power steering fluid. *Do not use automatic transmission fluid.* Replace the reservoir cover.

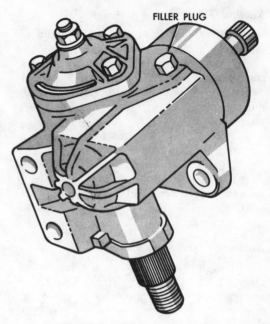

FILLER PLUG

Manual steering gear filler plug

NECK
RESERVOIR

Power steering pump reservoir

Capacities

Year	Engine No. Cyl Displacement (cu. in.)	Engine Crankcase Add 1 Qt For New Filter	Transmission Pts to Refill After Draining			Drive Axle (pts)	Gasoline Tank (gals)	Cooling System (qts) with Heater
			Manual		Automatic			
			3 Speed	4 Speed				
'65	6-170	4	6	——	17	①	18	12
	6-225	4	6	——	17	①	18	12

Capacities

Year	Engine No. Cyl Displacement (cu. in.)	Engine Crankcase Add 1 Qt For New Filter	Transmission Pts to Refill After Draining			Drive Axle (pts)	Gasoline Tank (gals)	Cooling System (qts) with Heater
			Manual					
			3 Speed	4 Speed	Automatic			
'65	8-273	4	6	7	17	①	18	12
'66	6-170	4	6.5	——	16	2	18	12
	6-225	4	6.5	——	16	2	18	13
	8-273	4	6	8	16	2	18	18
'67	6-170	4	6.5	——	16	2	18	12
	6-225	4	6.5	——	16	2	18	13
	8-273	4	6.5	8	16	2	18	19
	8-383	4	——	8	18.5	4	18	17
'68	6-170	4	6.5	——	16	2	18	12
	6-225	4	6.5	——	16	2	18	13
	8-273	4	6	8.5	16	2	18	19
	8-318	4	6.5	8.5	16	2④	18	18
	8-340	4	——	8.5	17.5	4	18	18
	8-383	4	——	8.5	17.5	4	18	17
'69	6-170	4	6.5	——	16	2	18	12
	6-225	4	6.5	——	16	2	18	13
	8-273	4	6.5	7.5	16	2⑤	18	17
	8-318	4	6	7.5	16	2④	18	17
	8-340	4	——	7.5	16	4	18	16
	8-383	4	——	7.5	16	4	18	16
'70	6-198	4	4.75	——	17	2	18	13
	6-225	4	4.75	——	17	2	18	13
	8-318	4	4.75	7.5	16	4	18	16
	8-340	4	4.75	7	16	4	18	15.5

Capacities

Year	Engine No. Cyl Displacement (cu. in.)	Engine Crankcase Add 1 Qt For New Filter	Transmission Pts to Refill After Draining			Drive Axle (pts)	Gasoline Tank (gals)	Cooling System (qts) with Heater
			Manual					
			3 Speed	4 Speed	Automatic			
'70	8-383	4	4.75	7.5	19③	4	18	14.5
	8-426	6	——	7.5	17	5.5	18	17
	8-440	6	——	7.5	19	5.5	18	17
'71	6-198	4	4.75	——	17	4.5	18	13
	6-225	4	4.75	——	17	4.5	18	13
	8-318	4	4.75	——	17	4.5	18	16
	8-340	4	4.75	7	16.3	4.5	18	15.5
	8-383	4	4.75	7.5	19③	4.5	18	14.5
	8-426	6	——	7.5	16.3	5.5	18	17
	8-440	6	——	7.5	19	5.5	18	15.5
'72	6-198	4	6.5	——	17	2	16	13
	6-225	4	4.75	——	17	2	⑧	13
	8-318	4	4.75	——	17	4.5	⑧	16
	8-340	4	4.75	7.5	16.3	4.5	⑧	15

① 7¼ in. Axle, 2.0 pts;
  8¾ in. Axle, 4.4 pts;
  9¾ in. Axle, 5.5 pts.
② Not used
③ Hi-performance—16 pts
④ Manual transmission—4 pts
⑤ 4-speed transmission—4 pts
⑥ Not used
⑦ Not used
⑧ Barracuda—16.5 gals, Challenger—18 gals
——Not applicable

TIRES

Inflation Pressures

Correct cold tire inflation pressures are listed in the "Tire and Wheel Specifications" chart and are also found, on 1967–72 models, on a tag located on the rear body pillar of the left-door. The recommended pressures have been chosen to provide a proper balance between ride comfort, handling, and tire life. Higher rear pressures are suggested for some models to ensure optimum directional stability.

Tire pressures should be checked, and adjusted, using an accurate gauge, at least once a month and before starting any long trips. *Check and adjust tire pressures only when the tires are cold.* Pressures will normally increase 2–6 psi as the tires become hot, and therefore, inflation pressures cannot be measured accurately under these conditions. *Under no circumstances should the inflation pressures of warm tires be reduced.* Always replace the tire valve caps or valve extensions after the inflation pressures have been checked and adjusted.

Tire Rotation

Tires should be rotated no later than every second oil change. Tires should be inspected at every oil change and if uneven tire wear is evident, the tires should then be rotated.

Refer to the diagrams shown for four and five-tire rotation. Be sure to adjust the inflation pressures after the tires have been rotated.

Radial Tires

Although these cars have been designed for bias-belted or cross-bias tires, radial ply tires can be used. Driving habits may have to be adjusted when radial tires are fitted because of their different ride and handling characteristics. If radial tires are desired, use the maximum allowable size.

Radial tires should be used in sets of four or five (to permit correct tire rotation) and never should be used on the front only. If conventional snow tires are used, do not use radial tires on the front wheels. *The safest policy is: never intermix radial ply tires with bias-belted or cross-bias tires.*

Wide-Tread 70 and 60 Series Tires

On cars which are not fitted with 70 or 60 Series wide-tread tires as original equipment, these tires may be used as replacements, provided that there is adequate clearance for correct suspension

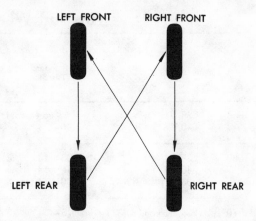

Tire rotation diagram—four tires

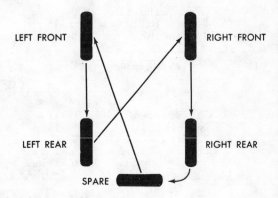

Tire rotation diagram—five tires

travel and steering movement when these tires are mounted on the car.

Wide-tread tires should be used only in sets of four or five and never should be used on the front only. If snow tires are fitted, they must also be of the same wide-tread size as the front tires. *Do not intermix 70 or 60 Series tires with other designs.*

Tire and Wheel Specifications

Year	Model	Standard Tire Size	Optional Tire Sizes ①	Cold Tire Pressures (psi)				Radial Ply Tires	Standard Rim Size
				Average Load		Maximum Load ②			
				Front	Rear	Front	Rear		
1965–66	170, 225 cu in.	6.50—13③	7.00—13	24	26	30	32		4½J
	273 cu in.	7.00—13③		24	26	30	32		4½J
	273 cu in. Hi Perf	6.95—14		24	24	30	30		5½J
1967	225, 273 cu in.	6.95—14	D70—14	24	24	28	28	185—14	4½J
	273 cu in. Hi Perf	D70—14	E70—14	24	24	28	30	185—14	5½J

Tire and Wheel Specifications

| Year | Model | Standard Tire Size | Optional Tire Sizes ① | Cold Tire Pressures (psi) | | | | Radial Ply Tires | Standard Rim Size |
| | | | | Average Load | | Maximum Load ② | | | |
				Front	Rear	Front	Rear		
1968	225, 318 cu in.	6.95—14	D70—14	24	24	30④	30④	185—14	4½J
	340, 383 cu in.	E70—14		24	24	30④	30④	185—14	5½J
1969	225, 318 cu in.	6.95—14	D70—14	26	26	32	32	185—14	4½J
	340 cu in.	D70—14	E70—14	26	26	30④	30④	185—14	5½J
	383 cu in.	E70—14		26	26	28④	28④	185—14	5½J
1970	225, 318 cu in.	E78—14	E70—14, F70—14	24	28	26⑤	30⑤	185—14	5J
	383 cu in.	F78—14	F70—14	24	28	25	28	195—14	5½JJ, 6JJ⑥
	383, 440 cu in. Hi Perf	F70—14		24	28	25⑦	28⑦	195—14	6JJ⑥
	340 cu in. Hi Perf	E60—15		26	28	28	32	185—15	7JJ⑥
	426 cu in. Hemi	F60—15		24	28	28	32	195—15	7JJ⑥
1971	198, 225, 318 cu in.	E78—14	F78—14, F70—14	See tire information tag located on car	26	30		185—14	5J
	383 cu in.	F78—14	F70—14		28	32		195—14	5½JJ, 6JJ⑥
	383, 440 cu in. Hi Perf	F70—14			28	32		195—14	6JJ⑥
	340 cu in. Hi Perf	E60—15			28	32		185—15	7JJ⑥
	426 cu in. Hemi	F60—15			28	28		195—15	7JJ⑥
	340 cu in. Six Pack	E60—15 Front G60—15 Rear			24	28			7JJ⑥
1972	225, 318 cu in.	7.35—14	F78—14	See tire information tag located on car				195—14	5J, 5½JJ
	340 cu in.	F70—14						195—14	5½JJ

①—Should be mounted on cars equipped with air conditioning or used for trailer towing; note that optional tires may require wider-than-standard wheel rims.
②—Unless otherwise noted, use maximum load tire pressures for trailer towing.
③—With front disc brakes, 6.95—14 standard.
④—For trailer towing, 32 psi front and rear.
⑤—For trailer towing, 28 psi front and 32 psi rear.
⑥—6JJ and 7JJ rims require 11 in. drum or disc brakes.
⑦—For trailer towing or for 440 cu in. with air conditioning, 28 psi front and 32 psi rear.

FUEL FILTER

A disposable, inline-type fuel filter is used in the fuel line between the fuel pump and the carburetor. In normal service, the filter should be replaced every two years or 24,000 miles. If the car is frequently operated under dusty or sandy conditions, the filter should be replaced more often.

Follow the replacement filter manufacturer's instructions for removing the old filter and installing the new unit. After the new filter has been installed, start the engine and run it for several minutes to check for any leaks at the filter and fuel line connections.

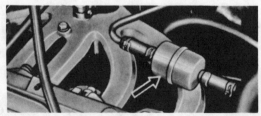

Fuel filter location—170, 198, and 225 cu in. engines

Fuel filter location—273, 318, and 340 cu in. engines

Fuel filter location—383, 440, and 426 cu in. engines

BATTERY

Check the battery electrolyte level once a month. Use only distilled or de-ionized water to maintain the liquid level to ⅜ in. above the battery plates. *Do not overfill.*

Check the specific gravity of the battery electrolyte, using a reliable hydrometer,

every twelve months or 12,000 miles, or more often if there is excessive use of water. Refer to the "Battery Care" section in chapter 3. Clean the battery posts and cable terminals and tighten the cable connections. Coat the connections with a thin film of petroleum jelly to prevent corrosion.

Pushing, Towing, and Jump Starting

Do not attempt to start a car that is equipped with an automatic transmission by pushing it. A car with a manual transmission can be push-started in the following manner: depress the clutch pedal, place the gearshift lever in high gear, push the car, and as the car speed reaches 10 mph, slowly release the clutch pedal.

A disabled vehicle can be towed by placing the gear selector lever in Neutral, providing that the distance to be traveled is less than 15 miles and the towing speed does not exceed 30 mph. If the transmission is not operative, or the car is to be towed more than fifteen miles, the drive shaft must be disconnected; or the car can be towed from the rear, with the rear wheels off the ground.

If no ignition key is available for a car that is fitted with an ignition lock, the car can be towed from the front by placing a dolly under the rear wheels and lifting the front of the car.

When using the battery of one car to jump-start another vehicle, be sure that the jumper cables are connected correctly between the battery terminals of each vehicle, positive to positive and negative to negative. Otherwise, serious damage to the vehicle electrical systems may occur.

2 · Tune-Up and Troubleshooting

Tune-Up Specifications

When analyzing compression test results, look for uniformity among cylinders rather than specific pressures.

Year	ENGINE No. Cyl Displacement (cu in.)	hp	SPARK PLUGS Type §	Gap (in.)	DISTRIBUTOR Point Dwell (deg)	Point Gap (in.)	IGNITION TIMING ▲ (deg) ● Man Trans	Auto Trans	Valves Intake Opens ■ (deg) ●	Fuel Pump Pressure (psi)	IDLE SPEED (rpm) ▲ Man Trans	Auto Trans
'65	6-170	101	N-14Y	0.035	40–45	0.020	2½B	2½B	8	3½–5	550	550
	6-225	145	N-14Y	0.035	40–45	0.020	2½B	2½B	8	3½–5	550	550
	8-273	180	N-14Y	0.035	28–33	0.017	5B	10B	14	5–7	550	550
	8-273	235	N-9Y	0.035	27–31①	0.017	10B	10B	14	5–7	650	650
'66	6-225	145	N-14Y	0.035	43	0.020	2½B(5A)	2½B(5A)	10	3½–5	550(650)	550(650)
	8-273	180	N-14Y	0.035	30	0.017	5B(5A)	10B(5A)	14	6–7½	500(700)	550(650)
	8-273	225	N-9Y	0.035	29①	0.017	10B(5A)	10B(5A)	14	5–7	600(700)	600(650)

18

Tune-Up Specifications

When analyzing compression test results, look for uniformity among cylinders rather than specific pressures.

Year	No. Cyl Displacement (cu in.)	hp	Type §	Gap (in.)	Point Dwell (deg)	Point Gap (in.)	Man Trans	Auto Trans	Valves Intake Opens ■ (deg) ●	Fuel Pump Pressure (psi)	Man Trans	Auto Trans
'67	6-255	145	N-14Y	0.035	43	0.020	5B(TDC)	5B(TDC)	10	3½–5	550(650)	550(650)
	8-273	180	N-14Y	0.035	30	0.017	5B(5A)	10B(5A)	14	5–7	500(750)	500(650)
	8-273	235	N-10Y	0.035	29①	0.017	10B(5A)	10B(5A)	14	5–7	600(700)	600(650)
'68	6-225	145	N-14Y	0.035	43	0.020	5B(TDC)	5B(TDC)	10	3½–5	550(650)②	550(650)②
	8-318	230	N-14Y	0.035	31	0.017	5B(5A)	10B(2½A)	10	5–7	650	600
	8-340	275	N-9Y	0.035	30③	0.017	TDC	5B	26④	3½–5	700	650
	8-383	300	J-11Y	0.035	31	0.017	TDC	5B	18	3½–5	650	600
'69	6-225	145	N-14Y	0.035	45	0.020	TDC	TDC	10	3½–5	700	650
	8-318	230	N-14Y	0.035	33	0.017	TDC	TDC	10	5–7	700	650
	8-340	275	N-9Y	0.035	30③	0.017	TDC	5B	22	5–7	750	700
	8-383	330	J-11Y	0.035	30③	0.017	TDC	5B	21	3½–5	700	650
'70	6-225	145	N-14Y	0.035	44	0.020	TDC	TDC	10	3½–5	700	650
	8-318	230	N-14Y	0.035	32	0.017	TDC	TDC	10	5–7	750	700
	8-340	275	N-9Y	0.035	30③	0.017	5B	5B	22	5–7	900	900
	8-383	290	J-14Y	0.035	30½	0.019	TDC	2½B	18	3½–5	750	650
	8-383	330	J-11Y	0.035	30½	0.019	TDC	2½B	18	3½–5	750	700
	8-383	335	J-11Y	0.035	30½	0.019	TDC	2½B	21	3½–5	750	750
	8-426	425	N-10Y	0.035	30③	0.017	TDC	2½B	36	7–8½	900	900
	8-440	375	J-11Y	0.035	30½	0.019	TDC	2½B	21	3½–5	900	800
	8-440	390	J-11Y	0.035	30③	0.017	5B	5B	21	6–7½	900	900
'71	6-198	125	N-14Y	0.035	44	0.020	2½B	2½B	16	3½–5	800	800
	6-225	145	N-14Y	0.035	44	0.020	TDC(2½B)	TDC(2½B)	16	3½–5	750	750
	8-318	230	N-14Y	0.035	32	0.017	TDC	TDC	10	5–7	750	700
	8-340	275	N-9Y	0.035	32③	0.017	5B	5B	22	5–7	900	900
	8-383	275	J-14Y	0.035	30½	0.019	TDC	2½B	18	3½–5	750	700
	8-383	300	J-11Y	0.035	30½	0.019	TDC	2½B	21	3½–5	900	800
	8-426	425	N-10Y	0.035	30	0.017	TDC	2½B	36	7–8½	950	950
	8-440	385	J-11Y	0.035	30	0.017	5B	5B	21	6–7½	900	900

Tune-Up Specifications

When analyzing compression test results, look for uniformity among cylinders rather than specific pressures.

Year	ENGINE No. Cyl Displacement (cu in.)	hp	SPARK PLUGS Type §	Gap (in.)	DISTRIBUTOR Point Dwell (deg)	Point Gap (in.)	IGNITION TIMING ▲ (deg) ● Man Trans	Auto Trans	Valves Intake Opens ■ (deg) ●	Fuel Pump Pressure (psi)	IDLE SPEED (rpm) ▲ Man Trans	Auto Trans
'72	6-225	110	N-14Y	0.035	44	0.020	TDC(2½B)	TDC(2½B)	16	2½–5	750(700)	750(700)
	8-318	150	N-13Y	0.035	32	0.017	TDC	TDC	10	5–7	750	750(700)
	8-340	240	N-9Y	0.035	Electronic		TDC(2½B)	2½B	22	5–7	900(850)	750

▲ See text for procedure
● Figure in parentheses indicates California engine
■ All figures Before Top Dead Center
§ All spark plug listings are Champion original equipment numbers
① Adjust both sets of points to this figure. With both sets connected, the total reading should be 38 degrees.
② A/C on
③ Adjust both sets of points to this figure. With both sets connected, the total reading should be 40 degrees.
④ For vehicles with automatic transmission, adjust to 22 degrees Before Top Dead Center
A After Top Dead Center
B Before Top Dead Center

TDC Top Dead Center
—— Not applicable

Mechanical Valve Lifter Clearance

Year	Engine	Intake (Hot) In.	Exhaust (Hot) In.
1965–1972	All 6 cylinders	0.010	0.020
1966–1967	273 V8	0.013	0.021

Tune-Up Procedures

SPARK PLUGS AND WIRING

After removing the spark plugs, carefully inspect them for cracked or broken porcelain and loose electrodes. Spark plugs with minor carbon and oxide deposits (porcelain should be light tan or medium gray in color) can be cleaned, adjusted, and reinstalled.

Clean the plugs in a sandblasting machine or by hand with a fine wire brush, being careful not to scratch the porcelain. Use compressed air to blow off the dust.

Set the electrode gap by bending the outside electrode to the proper clearance. Never bend the center electrode. Some spark plugs have platinum electrodes which require the greatest care when being handled.

Spark plugs should not be reset more than once because the range heat changes as the center electrode wears back toward the insulator.

Carefully install each spark plug and tighten each to 30 ft lbs. When installing new spark plugs on a slant-six engine, do not use the metal gaskets supplied with the plug. If a rubber gasket is used on the spark plug, replace it with a new gasket when installing new plugs.

Label each spark plug cable and its corresponding terminal on the distributor cap according to the number of the cylinder to which it is connected. Remove the cables and clean them with a kerosine-moistened cloth. Wipe the cables dry and inspect them for brittle, cracked, gummy, or otherwise deteriorated insulation. Defective or old wiring should be replaced because it may cause engine misfires and/or cross-firing. Inspect and clean wire terminals, spark plug terminals, and distributor cap sockets to ensure perfect electrical contact.

BREAKER POINTS AND CONDENSER

Single Point Distributor

Use the procedure described below to remove, install, and gap a single contact point set.

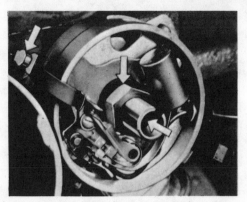

Breaker points and condenser. Arrows indicate distributor lubrication points

1. Pull back the spring clips and lift off the distributor cap. Remove the rotor.

2. Loosen the terminal screw nut and remove the primary and condenser leads.

3. Remove the stationary contact lockscrew and remove the contact point set.

4. Remove the condenser retaining screw and lift out the condenser.

5. Install the new condenser and tighten its retaining screw.

6. Install the new point set but do not fully tighten its lockscrew.

7. Connect the condenser and primary leads.

8. If necessary, align the contacts by bending the stationary contact bracket only. *Never bend the movable contact arm to correct alignment.*

9. Attach a remote starter switch to the electrical system according to the switch manufacturer's instructions. Use this switch to crank the engine, rotating the distributor cam until the rubbing block of the movable contact arm rests on a peak of the cam lobe.

10. Insert the proper thickness feeler gauge between the contact points. If necessary, increase or decrease the gap by inserting a screwdriver in the vee notch of the stationary contact base and using the screwdriver to move the stationary contact.

11. Tighten the lockscrew and recheck the gap setting. Reset if necessary.

12. Install the new rotor and refit the distributor cap. Check the point dwell.

Dual Point Distributor

Removal and installation of dual contact points is the same as for a single point set.

However, adjustment of dual points is slightly different because one set of contacts must be blocked open with a clean insulator while the opposite points set is adjusted to specifications, using the single point set adjustment procedure. When adjusted correctly, tighten the lockscrew. Then block open this contact set and adjust the other set in the same manner as for the first. Check the point dwell. If the contacts have been installed and adjusted correctly, the dwell angle should be as specified for both contact sets.

DWELL ANGLE

If the contact points have been installed and gapped correctly the dwell angle should be within specifications.

1. Disconnect the vacuum line at the distributor.

2. Connect the dwell meter leads to the distributor terminal of the coil and ground.

3. Start the engine and run it at idle speed.

4. Note the dwell meter reading. If it is not within specifications, the point gap may be incorrect or the movable contact arm may be distorted. Readjust the contact points and recheck the dwell. Be sure that the correct point set has been installed.

IMPORTANT: *Dwell and point gap must both be within their specification limits at the same time. If this cannot be accomplished, probably the wrong contacts are installed, the rubbing block or cam lobes are badly worn, or the movable contact is distorted. A dwell variation test may be performed to check for distributor wear.*

Dwell Variation

Excessive wear of the distributor mechanical parts may cause variations in dwell that affect ignition timing. The following is the procedure for a dwell variation test.

1. Disconnect the vacuum line at the distributor, connect the dwell meter, and run the engine at its idle speed.

2. Slowly increase engine speed to 1,500 rpm, and then slowly reduce to idle speed while noting the dwell meter reading.

If the dwell reading varies more than two degrees, wear in the distributor shaft, bushings, or breaker plate is probably excessive. The distributor will have to be removed for a complete inspection and test.

NOTE: *Dwell variation at speeds above 1,500 rpm does not necessarily indicate distributor wear.*

IGNITION TIMING

To obtain maximum engine performance, the distributor must be correctly positioned on the engine to give proper ignition timing. Ignition timing must be checked only when the engine is hot and running at its correct idle speed.

1. Clean the timing indicator and the circumference of the vibration damper. Paint the correct timing mark on the indicator and the timing mark on the damper with white or luminescent (day-glo) paint.

2. Disconnect the vacuum line at the distributor.

3. Connect a stroboscopic timing light according to the manufacturer's instructions.

4. Start the engine and adjust the idle speed to specification with the *transmission in Neutral.*

5. Loosen the distributor hold-down screw so the housing can be rotated.

6. Check the ignition timing by aiming the strobe light at the timing indicator and the vibration damper. If the timing is correct, the painted mark on the damper will appear opposite the timing indicator painted mark. If necessary, advance or retard the timing by rotating the distributor housing, until the correct timing is obtained.

7. Tighten the distributor hold-down screw and connect the vacuum line. Stop the engine and disconnect the timing light.

dealer. A special test instrument is required to properly service this system.

The electronic ignition system can be easily identified by the double primary wire from the distributor, the dual ballast resistor mounted on the firewall, and the control unit which is located on either the firewall or left front inner fender panel. The ignition timing can be checked and adjusted in the normal manner but, because there are no ignition breaker points, there is no point gap or dwell angle to measure and adjust.

VALVE LASH

Mechanical Tappets

170, 198, 225, AND 273 CU IN. ENGINES

The six-cylinder engines and the 273 cu in. V8 engine used in various Barracuda and Challenger models have mechanical valve tappets (lifters) and adjustable rocker arms. Therefore, the valve lash or valve clearance, can be checked and adjusted to the specified values listed in the "Tune-Up Specifications" chart in the conventional manner for mechanical tappets which is described below. The valve lash adjustment should be performed on these engines only when the engine is hot and running.

1. Warm up the engine until it reaches its normal operating temperature (water temperature of about 185° F).

2. Set the engine idle speed to 550 rpm and run the engine at this speed for five minutes.

3. Remove the valve cover (two on V8) by withdrawing its securing bolts. Be careful of the hot oil which will splash off the

Ignition Timing Marks

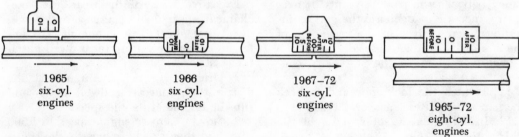

| 1965 six-cyl. engines | 1966 six-cyl. engines | 1967–72 six-cyl. engines | 1965–72 eight-cyl. engines |

ELECTRONIC IGNITION

Barracuda and Challenger models with the Chrysler Electronic Ignition System require special tune-up procedures which are best performed by an authorized

rocker assembly when the cover is removed.

4. Using the proper thickness feeler gauge, measure the clearance between the

valve stem tip and the end of the rocker arm adjusting screw at each valve. If necessary, turn the adjusting screw to obtain the correct valve clearance.

5. After all of the valves have been checked and adjusted, stop the engine and replace the valve cover, using a new gasket between the cover and cylinder head when necessary. If much oil was lost during the valve adjustment procedure, check the oil level in the crankcase.

Hydraulic Tappets

318, 340 4-BBL, 383, and 440
Cu In. Engines

Because these engines are fitted with hydraulic tappets which are self-adjusting, there are no provisions for manual valve lash adjustment.

340 Six Pack and 426 Hemi Engines

Although engines with hydraulic valve tappets usually have no provisions for valve lash adjustment, the 340 Six Pack and 426 Hemi engines are equipped with adjustable rocker arms and special hydraulic tappets. Valve lash adjustment on these two engines must be performed when the engine is cold and using only the procedure described below.

1. Remove the valve covers by withdrawing their securing bolts.

2. Because it is very important that each tappet be at the lowest point of the camshaft (on the base circle) when adjusting the valves, *this procedure must be carried out exactly in the order described.*

3. Position the crankshaft as indicated below and adjust only the valves listed at each position. Each rocker arm has an ad-

Ignition Timing and Crankshaft Setting	Adjust Tappets	
	Intake	Exhaust
A. Adjust ignition timing to TDC, chalk-mark TDC and 180° opposite TDC on front crankshaft damper.	2 and 7	4 and 8
B. Set the crankshaft so no. 1 cylinder is at TDC (compression stroke, points opening).	2 and 7	4 and 8
C. Turn the crankshaft in its running direction until points open for no. 4 cylinder.	1 and 8	3 and 6
D. Turn the crankshaft an additional 180° until points open for no. 6 cylinder.	3 and 4	5 and 7
E. Turn the crankshaft an additional 180° until points open for no. 7 cylinder.	5 and 6	1 and 2

justing screw which is secured by a locknut. Adjust each valve by loosening the locknut and setting the rocker arm adjusting screw so that there is no clearance (zero lash) in the system. Then turn the screw into the rocker arm one and one-half turns. Torque the locknut to 25 ft lbs.

4. After all of the valves have been adjusted, reset the ignition timing to the correct specifications. Install the valve covers, using new gaskets between the cover and cylinder when necessary.

CARBURETOR

Since 1965, Barracuda and Challenger models have used many different types of carburetors. However, the adjustment procedure for all these carburetors, with a few exceptions, is the same. Some 1966–67 and all 1968 and later carburetors incorporate modifications to reduce engine exhaust emissions. Carburetor modifications for 1966–69 are part of Chrysler's Cleaner Air Package, and 1970 and later models are part of the Cleaner Air System.

The 426 Hemi and the 340 and 440 engines are available with multiple carburetor options. The 426 Hemi is equipped with two Carter AFB carburetors. Both of these carburetors have complete idle systems which must be adjusted and synchronized to obtain a satisfactory engine idle. The 340 and 440 Six Pack engines are equipped with three Holley 2300 two-venturi carburetors. Only the center carburetor on these engines is equipped with an idle system and the inboard and outboard carburetors contain no idle adjustments.

Idle speed and mixture adjustment procedures are described below. See the fuel system service section for other carburetor adjustments.

Idle Speed and Mixture Adjustment

1965–67 Barracuda without CAP
(Cleaner Air Package)

Adjust the idle speed (curb idle) and fuel mixture with the air cleaner installed.

1. Run the engine at fast idle to stabilize its operating temperature and then check the ignition timing. If necessary, adjust the timing to specification.

2. Be sure that the choke plate is fully released.

3. Connect an accurate ignition tachometer to the engine according to the manufacturer's instructions.

4. On models with six-cylinder engines, turn the headlights on high beam.

5. If the car is equipped with air conditioning, turn on the air conditioner.

6. Adjust the carburetor idle screw (see illustrations) to obtain a curb idle speed of 500 rpm (550 rpm if equipped with air conditioner).

7. Turn the idle mixture screws in or out to obtain the highest rpm possible. After obtaining the highest rpm, turn each idle mixture screw clockwise until the engine speed starts to drop, then turn the mixture screw counterclockwise just enough to regain the lost rpm.

8. If the mixture adjustment has changed the curb idle speed, adjust the idle to compensate.

1966–72 Barracuda and Challenger with CAP or CAS

The recommended adjustment procedure for these emission-controlled engines requires the use of an exhaust gas analyzer to accurately determine the air/fuel mixture ratio. This procedure is basic and applies to all 1966–72 engines except the 426 Hemi. Adjust the idle speed (curb idle) and fuel mixture with the air cleaner installed.

1. Run the engine at fast idle to stabilize its operating temperature and then check the ignition timing. If necessary, adjust the timing to specification.

2. On models with automatic transmissions, place the gear selector lever in the Neutral position (not in Park).

3. Connect an accurate ignition tachometer to the engine, according to the manufacturer's instructions.

4. On models with six-cylinder engines, turn the headlights on high beam.

5. If the car is equipped with air conditioning, turn off the air conditioner.

6. Insert the probe of the exhaust gas analyzer into the tailpipe as far as possible (minimum distance of two feet). On cars with dual exhausts, insert the probe into the left tailpipe as this is the side without the heat riser valve. If a garage exhaust system is used to conduct the exhaust gases away, a plenum chamber or other means must be used to reduce the exhaust system's vacuum to one-half inch of water or less.

7. Connect the exhaust gas analyzer,

warm it up, and calibrate it according to the manufacturer's instructions.

8. Use the engine idle speed adjustment screw and/or the electric solenoid throttle positioner adjustment to set the idle speed to the specified value for each engine transmission combination. Then adjust the curb idle screw until it just touches the stop on the carburetor body and back out the adjusting screw one full turn.

9. Adjust the fuel mixture, using the exhaust analyzer and the carburetor mixture screws, as follows:

IMPORTANT: *When adjusting the mixture screws to obtain the specified air/fuel ratio, do not turn the mixture screw more than 1/16 turn at a time. The exhaust analyzer is so sensitive that the ratio must be changed by small increments if accurate readings are to be obtained. The analyzer meter reads in air/fuel ratio so that a higher reading indicates a leaner mixture and vice versa.*

a. Adjust each mixture screw 1/16 turn richer (counterclockwise) and wait ten seconds before reading the analyzer reading.

b. If necessary, repeat step "a" until the analyzer meter indicates a definite increase in the richness of the mixture.

NOTE: *This step is very important because a carburetor that is set too lean will cause the exhaust analyzer to give a false reading, indicating a rich mixture. Because of this, the carburetor must first be known to have a rich mixture to verify the reading of the exhaust analyzer.*

c. After verifying the analyzer meter reading, adjust the mixture screws to obtain an air/fuel ratio of 14.2:1. Turn the mixture screws clockwise (leaner) to raise the meter reading or counterclockwise (richer) to lower the reading.

d. If the curb idle speed changes as the mixture screws are adjusted, reset the idle speed to specification and readjust the fuel mixture as required so that the 14.2:1 air/fuel mixture ratio is obtained at the specified idle speed.

Rough Idle and Low-Speed Surge

Rough idle and low-speed surge may be a problem on 1968–71 models using the one and one-half inch Ball & Ball, Carter AVS, or Holley 4160 carburetors, and on

1972 models using the one and one-fourth inch Ball & Ball or Carter Thermo-Quad carburetors. This is the result of improper idle setting balance between the carburetor bores and can be corrected by using the procedure below.

IMPORTANT: *These carburetors are fitted with either plugs or plastic caps on the mixture screws to limit fuel mixture adjustment in compliance with federal and state emission requirements. The plugs or caps must be removed during the adjustment procedure and will be broken in the process. Therefore, it will be necessary to obtain new plugs or caps from an authorized dealer as any attempt to refit the original parts will damage the mixture screws.*

1. Remove the lead plugs or the plastic caps from the mixture screws in the bases of the Ball & Ball and Carter carburetors. The best way to remove the lead plugs is with a small drill and easy-out. On Holley carburetors, remove the cup plugs or plastic caps from the mixture screws in the sides of the primary metering block. Use a sharp punch to remove the cup plugs.

2. Follow steps 1 through 8 of the idle speed and mixture adjustment procedure. Then stop the engine.

NOTE: *On 1968–69 engines with the Carter AVS carburetor, turn the single off idle mixture adjustment screw counterclockwise (richer) until it is seated, then turn it clockwise (lean) three-quarters of a turn. Do not disturb this adjustment during the remainder of this procedure.*

3. Turn both mixture adjustment screws clockwise until they are lightly seated. On some carburetors, the screws have a prevailing torque feature which causes the screws to become more difficult to turn as they approach the seated position.

4. Turn both mixture screws one and one-half turns counterclockwise on Ball & Ball carburetors and two to three turns counterclockwise on Carter and Holley carburetors. Use these positions as starting points. Experience may indicate more or less turns as a rough setting, but both screws should be turned equally.

5. Start the engine and follow step 9 of the idle speed and mixture adjustment procedure to obtain the correct 14.2:1 air/fuel ratio.

NOTE: *In order to obtain a smooth idle,*

it is important that both mixture adjustment screws be turned the same amount at each adjustment so that, at the final setting, both adjusting screws are the same number of turns from the seated position.

6. Install *new* lead plugs, cup plugs, or plastic caps on the mixture screws.

426 HEMI

Because each carburetor is equipped with a complete idle system, an accurate balance of the idle speed between the carburetors is very important. Correct idle speed balance will also ensure proper carburetor throttle synchronization. The air cleaner must be removed to adjust the carburetors.

1. Run the engine at fast idle to stabilize its operating temperature and then check the ignition timing. If necessary, adjust the timing to specification.

2. On cars with automatic transmissions, place the gear selector lever in the Neutral position (not in Park).

3. Connect an accurate ignition tachometer to the engine, according to the manufacturer's instructions.

4. If the engine is equipped with a hot idle compensator valve, make sure that it is fully seated in the closed position.

5. Use the engine idle speed adjustment screw and/or the electric solenoid throttle positioner adjustment to set the idle speed to the specified value for the particular engine transmission combination. Adjust the curb idle screw until it just touches the stop on the carburetor body, then back out the adjusting screw one full turn.

6. Adjust each idle mixture screw to obtain the highest rpm possible. Repeat this operation until all four mixture adjustment screws have been properly adjusted and balanced.

7. If the idle mixture adjustment procedure has changed the engine idle speed, adjust the idle to compensate.

After this adjustment has been completed, road-test the car for at least five miles and then recheck and rebalance the carburetors as required.

Balancing Multiple Carburetor Installations

426 HEMI

There is no actual adjustment of the external carburetor linkage to synchronize the twin carburetors. Proper balancing of the carburetor idle speeds as described in the idle speed and mixture adjustment procedure for the 426 Hemi will ensure correct carburetor synchronization.

340 AND 440 SIX PACKS

Because only the center carburetor has provisions for adjusting the engine idle speed and fuel mixture, these adjustments are performed using the procedure for single carburetor installations. However, the throttle rods which connect each outboard carburetor to the center carburetor can be adjusted for correct throttle synchronization using the procedure below.

1. Remove the air cleaner.
2. Remove the outboard throttle rod securing clips and disengage the front and rear rods from the throttle levers.
3. Be sure that the ignition switch is turned off. (This de-energizes the fast curb idle solenoid so that clearance can be obtained between the plunger and the fast curb idle adjusting screw.)
4. Close the throttle valve of all three carburetors and hold them in the closed position.
5. Shorten or lengthen the front and rear connector rods by turning each rod into or out of the threaded sleeve until the rod end can be inserted into the hole in the throttle lever smoothly.
6. Fit each throttle connector rod into its corresponding throttle lever and secure each rod with a clip.

Engine Tune-Up

Engine tune-up is a procedure performed to restore engine performance, deteriorated due to normal wear and loss of adjustment. The three major areas considered in a routine tune-up are compression, ignition, and carburetion, although valve adjustment may be included.

A tune-up is performed in three steps: *analysis*, in which it is determined whether normal wear is responsible for performance loss, and which parts require replacement or service; *parts replacement or service*; and *adjustment*, in which engine adjustments are returned to original specifications. Since the advent of emission control equipment, precision adjustment has become increasingly critical, in order to maintain pollutant emission levels.

Analysis

The procedures below are used to indicate where adjustments, parts service or replacement are necessary within the realm of a normal tune-up. If, following these tests, all systems appear to be functioning properly, proceed to the Troubleshooting Section for further diagnosis.

—Remove all spark plugs, noting the cylinder in which they were installed. Remove the air cleaner, and position the throttle and choke in the full open position. Disconnect the coil high tension lead from the coil and the distributor cap. Insert a compression gauge into the spark plug port of each cylinder, in succession, and crank the engine with

Maxi. Press. Lbs. Sq. In.	Min. Press. Lbs. Sq. In.	Max. Press. Lbs. Sq. In.	Min. Press. Lbs. Sq. In.
134	101	188	141
136	102	190	142
138	104	192	144
140	105	194	145
142	107	196	147
146	110	198	148
148	111	200	150
150	113	202	151
152	114	204	153
154	115	206	154
156	117	208	156
158	118	210	157
160	120	212	158
162	121	214	160
164	123	216	162
166	124	218	163
168	126	220	165
170	127	222	166
172	129	224	168
174	131	226	169
176	132	228	171
178	133	230	172
180	135	232	174
182	136	234	175
184	138	236	177
186	140	238	178

Compression pressure limits
(C) Buick Div. G.M. Corp.)

the starter to obtain the highest possible reading. Record the readings, and compare the highest to the lowest on the compression pressure limit chart. If the difference exceeds the limits on the chart, or if all readings are excessively low, proceed to a wet compression check (see Troubleshooting Section).

—Evaluate the spark plugs according to the spark plug chart in the Troubleshooting Section, and proceed as indicated in the chart.

—Remove the distributor cap, and inspect it inside and out for cracks and/or carbon tracks, and inside for excessive wear or burning of the rotor contacts. If any of these faults are evident, the cap must be replaced.

—Check the breaker points for burning, pitting or wear, and the contact heel resting on the distributor cam for excessive wear. If defects are noted, replace the entire breaker point set.

—Remove and inspect the rotor. If the contacts are burned or worn, or if the rotor is excessively loose on the distributor shaft (where applicable), the rotor must be replaced.

—Inspect the spark plug leads and the coil high tension lead for cracks or brittleness. If any of the wires appear defective, the entire set should be replaced.

—Check the air filter to ensure that it is functioning properly.

Parts Replacement and Service

The determination of whether to replace or service parts is at the mechanic's discretion; however, it is suggested that any parts in questionable condition be replaced rather than reused.

—Clean and regap, or replace, the spark plugs as needed. Lightly coat the threads with engine oil and install the plugs. CAUTION: *Do not over-torque taper-seat spark plugs, or plugs being installed in aluminum cylinder heads.*

—If the distributor cap is to be reused, clean the inside with a dry rag, and remove corrosion from the rotor contact points with fine emery cloth. Remove the spark plug wires one by one, and clean the wire ends and the inside of the towers. If the boots are loose, they should be replaced.

If the cap is to be replaced, transfer the wires one by one, cleaning the wire ends and replacing the boots if necessary.

—If the original points are to remain in service, clean them lightly with emery cloth, lubricate the contact heel with grease specifically designed for this purpose. Rotate the crankshaft until the heel rests on a high point of the distributor cam, and adjust the point gap to specifications.

When replacing the points, remove the original points and condenser, and wipe out the inside of the distributor housing with a clean, dry rag. Lightly lubricate the contact heel and pivot point, and install the points and condenser. Rotate the crankshaft until the heel rests on a high point of the distributor cam, and adjust the point gap to specifications. NOTE: *Always replace the condenser when changing the points.*

—If the rotor is to be reused, clean the contacts with solvent. Do not alter the spring tension of the rotor center contact. Install the rotor and the distributor cap.

—Replace the coil high tension lead and/or the spark plug leads as necessary.

—Clean the carburetor using a spray solvent (e.g., Gumout Spray). Remove the varnish from the throttle bores, and clean the linkage. Disconnect and plug the fuel line, and run the engine until it runs out of fuel. Partially fill the float chamber with solvent, and reconnect the fuel line. In extreme cases, the jets can be pressure flushed by inserting a rubber plug into the float vent, running the spray nozzle through it, and spraying the solvent until it squirts out of the venturi fuel dump.

—Clean and tighten all wiring connections in the primary electrical circuit.

Additional Services

The following services *should* be performed in conjunction with a routine tune-up to ensure efficient performance.

—Inspect the battery and fill to the proper level with distilled water. Remove the cable clamps, clean clamps and posts thoroughly, coat the posts lightly with petroleum jelly, reinstall and tighten.

—Inspect all belts, replace and/or adjust as necessary.

—Test the PCV valve (if so equipped), and clean or replace as indicated. Clean all crankcase ventilation hoses, or replace if cracked or hardened.

—Adjust the valves (if necessary) to manufacturer's specifications.

Adjustments

—Connect a dwell-tachometer between the distributor primary lead and ground. Remove the distributor cap and rotor (unless equipped with Delco externally adjustable distributor). With the ignition off, crank the engine with a remote starter switch and measure the point dwell angle. Adjust the dwell angle to specifications. NOTE: *Increasing the gap decreases the dwell angle and*

vice-versa. Install the rotor and distributor cap.

—Connect a timing light according to the manufacturer's specifications. Identify the proper timing marks with chalk or paint. NOTE: *Luminescent (day-glo) paint is excellent for this purpose.* Start the engine, and run it until it reaches operating temperature. Disconnect and plug any distributor vacuum lines, and adjust idle to the speed required to adjust timing, according to specifications. Loosen the distributor clamp and adjust timing to specifications by rotating the distributor in the engine. NOTE: *To advance timing, rotate distributor opposite normal direction of rotor rotation, and vice-versa.*

—Synchronize the throttles and mixture of multiple carburetors (if so equipped) according to procedures given in the individual car sections.

—Adjust the idle speed, mixture, and idle quality, as specified in the car sections. Final idle adjustments should be made with the air cleaner installed. CAUTION: *Due to strict emission control requirements on 1969 and later models, special test equipment (CO meter, SUN Tester) may be necessary to properly adjust idle mixture to specifications.*

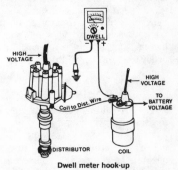

Dwell meter hook-up

Trouble-shooting

The following section is designed to aid in the rapid diagnosis of engine problems. The systematic format is used to diagnose problems ranging from engine starting difficulties to the need for engine overhaul. It is assumed that the user is equipped with basic hand tools and test equipment (tach-dwell meter, timing light, voltmeter, and ohmmeter).

Troubleshooting is divided into two sections. The first, *General Diagnosis*, is used to locate the problem area. In the second, *Specific Diagnosis*, the problem is systematically evaluated.

General Diagnosis

PROBLEM: Symptom	Begin diagnosis at Section Two, Number ——
Engine won't start:	
Starter doesn't turn	1.1, 2.1
Starter turns, engine doesn't	2.1
Starter turns engine very slowly	1.1, 2.4
Starter turns engine normally	3.1, 4.1
Starter turns engine very quickly	6.1
Engine fires intermittently	4.1
Engine fires consistently	5.1, 6.1
Engine runs poorly:	
Hard starting	3.1, 4.1, 5.1, 8.1
Rough idle	4.1, 5.1, 8.1
Stalling	3.1, 4.1, 5.1, 8.1
Engine dies at high speeds	4.1, 5.1
Hesitation (on acceleration from standing stop)	5.1, 8.1
Poor pickup	4.1, 5.1, 8.1
Lack of power	3.1, 4.1, 5.1, 8.1
Backfire through the carburetor	4.1, 8.1, 9.1
Backfire through the exhaust	4.1, 8.1, 9.1
Blue exhaust gases	6.1, 7.1
Black exhaust gases	5.1
Running on (after the ignition is shut off)	3.1, 8.1
Susceptible to moisture	4.1
Engine misfires under load	4.1, 7.1, 8.4, 9.1
Engine misfires at speed	4.1, 8.4
Engine misfires at idle	3.1, 4.1, 5.1, 7.1, 8.4

PROBLEM: Symptom	Probable Cause
Engine noises: ①	
Metallic grind while starting	Starter drive not engaging completely
Constant grind or rumble	*Starter drive not releasing, worn main bearings
Constant knock	Worn connecting rod bearings
Knock under load	Fuel octane too low, worn connecting rod bearings
Double knock	Loose piston pin
Metallic tap	*Collapsed or sticky valve lifter, excessive valve clearance, excessive end play in a rotating shaft
Scrape	*Fan belt contacting a stationary surface
Tick while starting	S.U. electric fuel pump (normal), starter brushes
Constant tick	*Generator brushes, shreaded fan belt
Squeal	*Improperly tensioned fan belt
Hiss or roar	*Steam escaping through a leak in the cooling system or the radiator overflow vent
Whistle	*Vacuum leak
Wheeze	Loose or cracked spark plug

①—It is extremely difficult to evaluate vehicle noises. While the above are general definitions of engine noises, those starred (*) should be considered as possibly originating elsewhere in the car. To aid diagnosis, the following list considers other potential sources of these sounds.

Metallic grind:
Throwout bearing; transmission gears, bearings, or synchronizers; differential bearings, gears; something metallic in contact with brake drum or disc.

Metallic tap:
U-joints; fan-to-radiator (or shroud) contact.

Scrape:
Brake shoe or pad dragging; tire to body contact; suspension contacting undercarriage or exhaust; something non-metallic contacting brake shoe or drum.

Tick:
Transmission gears; differential gears; lack of radio suppression; resonant vibration of body panels; windshield wiper motor or transmission; heater motor and blower.

Squeal:
Brake shoe or pad not fully releasing; tires (excessive wear, uneven wear, improper inflation); front or rear wheel alignment (most commonly due to improper toe-in).

Hiss or whistle:
Wind leaks (body or window); heater motor and blower fan.

Roar:
Wheel bearings; wind leaks (body and window).

Specific Diagnosis

This section is arranged so that following each test, instructions are given to proceed to another, until a problem is diagnosed.

INDEX

Group		Topic
1	*	Battery
2	*	Cranking system
3	*	Primary electrical system
4	*	Secondary electrical system
5	*	Fuel system
6	*	Engine compression
7	**	Engine vacuum
8	**	Secondary electrical system
9	**	Valve train
10	**	Exhaust system
11	**	Cooling system
12	**	Engine lubrication

*—The engine need not be running.
**—The engine must be running.

SAMPLE SECTION

Test and Procedure	Results and Indications	Proceed to
4.1—Check for spark: Hold each spark plug wire approximately ¼″ from ground with gloves or a heavy, dry rag. Crank the engine and observe the spark.	If no spark is evident:	4.2
	If spark is good in some cases:	4.3
	If spark is good in all cases:	4.6

DIAGNOSIS

Test and Procedure	Results and Indications	Proceed to
1.1—Inspect the battery visually for case condition (corrosion, cracks) and water level.	If case is cracked, replace battery:	1.4
	If the case is intact, remove corrosion with a solution of baking soda and water (CAUTION: *do not get the solution into the battery*), and fill with water:	1.2
1.2—Check the battery cable connections: Insert a screwdriver between the battery post and the cable clamp. Turn the headlights on high beam, and observe them as the screwdriver is gently twisted to ensure good metal to metal contact. **Testing battery cable connections using a screwdriver**	If the lights brighten, remove and clean the clamp and post; coat the post with petroleum jelly, install and tighten the clamp:	1.4
	If no improvement is noted:	1.3

Test and Procedure		Results and Indications	Proceed to
1.3—Test the state of charge of the battery using an individual cell tester or hydrometer.		If indicated, charge the battery. NOTE: *If no obvious reason exists for the low state of charge (i.e., battery age, prolonged storage), the charging system should be tested:*	1.4

Spec. Grav. Reading	Charged Condition
1.260-1.280	Fully Charged
1.230-1.250	Three Quarter Charged
1.200-1.220	One Half Charged
1.170-1.190	One Quarter Charged
1.140-1.160	Just About Flat
1.110-1.130	All The Way Down

State of battery charge

The effect of temperature on the specific gravity of battery electrolyte

Test and Procedure	Results and Indications	Proceed to
1.4—Visually inspect battery cables for cracking, bad connection to ground, or bad connection to starter.	If necessary, tighten connections or replace the cables:	2.1

Tests in Group 2 are performed with coil high tension lead disconnected to prevent accidental starting.

Test and Procedure	Results and Indications	Proceed to
2.1—Test the starter motor and solenoid: Connect a jumper from the battery post of the solenoid (or relay) to the starter post of the solenoid (or relay).	If starter turns the engine normally:	2.2
	If the starter buzzes, or turns the engine very slowly:	2.4
	If no response, replace the solenoid (or relay).	3.1
	If the starter turns, but the engine doesn't, ensure that the flywheel ring gear is intact. If the gear is undamaged, replace the starter drive.	3.1
2.2—Determine whether ignition override switches are functioning properly (clutch start switch, neutral safety switch), by connecting a jumper across the switch(es), and turning the ignition switch to "start".	If starter operates, adjust or replace switch:	3.1
	If the starter doesn't operate:	2.3
2.3—Check the ignition switch "start" position: Connect a 12V test lamp between the starter post of the solenoid (or relay) and ground. Turn the ignition switch to the "start" position, and jiggle the key.	If the lamp doesn't light when the switch is turned, check the ignition switch for loose connections, cracked insulation, or broken wires. Repair or replace as necessary:	3.1
	If the lamp flickers when the key is jiggled, replace the ignition switch.	3.3

Checking the ignition switch "start" position

Test and Procedure	Results and Indications	Proceed to
2.4—Remove and bench test the starter, according to specifications in the car section.	If the starter does not meet specifications, repair or replace as needed:	3.1
	If the starter is operating properly:	2.5
2.5—Determine whether the engine can turn freely: Remove the spark plugs, and check for water in the cylinders. Check for water on the dipstick, or oil in the radiator. Attempt to turn the engine using an 18″ flex drive and socket on the crankshaft pulley nut or bolt.	If the engine will turn freely only with the spark plugs out, and hydrostatic lock (water in the cylinders) is ruled out, check valve timing:	9.2
	If engine will not turn freely, and it is known that the clutch and transmission are free, the engine must be disassembled for further evaluation:	Next Chapter

Tests and Procedures	Results and Indications	Proceed to
3.1—Check the ignition switch "on" position: Connect a jumper wire between the distributor side of the coil and ground, and a 12V test lamp between the switch side of the coil and ground. Remove the high tension lead from the coil. Turn the ignition switch on and jiggle the key.	If the lamp lights:	3.2
	If the lamp flickers when the key is jiggled, replace the ignition switch:	3.3
	If the lamp doesn't light, check for loose or open connections. If none are found, remove the ignition switch and check for continuity. If the switch is faulty, replace it:	3.3

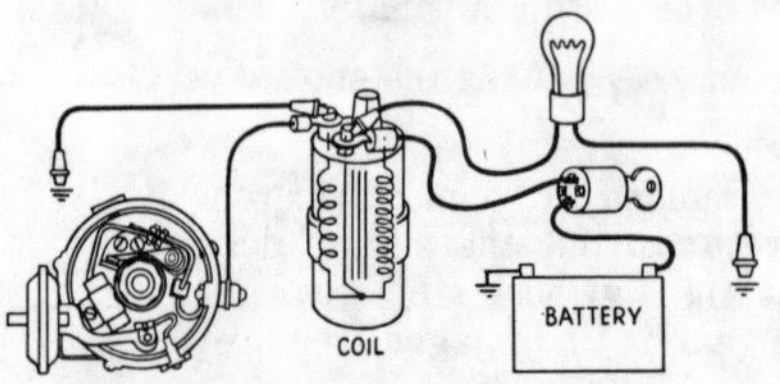

COIL   BATTERY

Checking the ignition switch "on" position

3.2—Check the ballast resistor or resistance wire for an open circuit, using an ohmmeter.	Replace the resistor or the resistance wire if the resistance is zero.	3.3
3.3—Visually inspect the breaker points for burning, pitting, or excessive wear. Gray coloring of the point contact surfaces is normal. Rotate the crankshaft until the contact heel rests on a high point of the distributor cam, and adjust the point gap to specifications.	If the breaker points are intact, clean the contact surfaces with fine emery cloth, and adjust the point gap to specifications. If pitted or worn, replace the points and condenser, and adjust the gap to specifications: NOTE: *Always lubricate the distributor cam according to manufacturer's recommendations when servicing the breaker points.*	3.4
3.4—Connect a dwell meter between the distributor primary lead and ground. Crank the engine and observe the point dwell angle.	If necessary, adjust the point dwell angle: NOTE: *Increasing the point gap decreases the dwell angle, and vice-versa.*	3.6
	If dwell meter shows little or no reading:	3.5

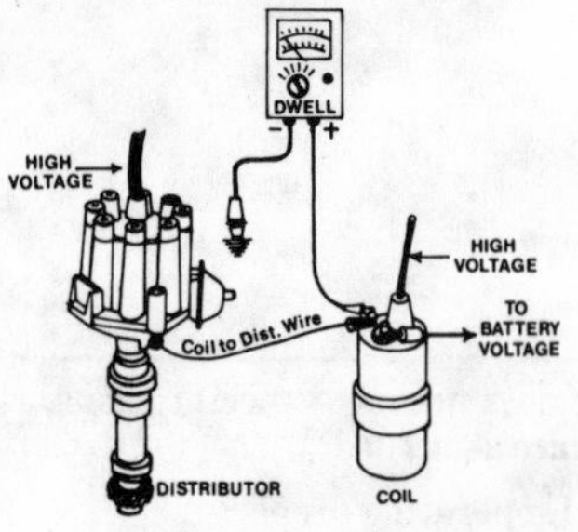

DWELL

HIGH VOLTAGE

HIGH VOLTAGE

Coil to Dist. Wire

TO BATTERY VOLTAGE

DISTRIBUTOR   COIL

Dwell meter hook-up

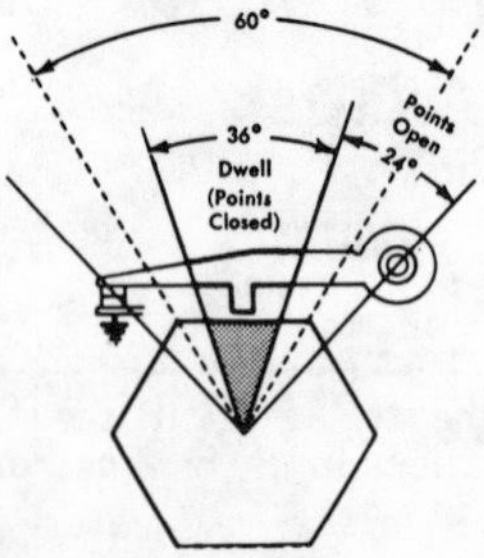

60°

36° Dwell (Points Closed)

Points Open 24°

Dwell angle

| 3.5—Check the condenser for short: Connect an ohmmeter across the condenser body and the pigtail lead. | If any reading other than infinite resistance is noted, replace the condenser: | 3.6 |

Checking the condenser for short

OHMMETER

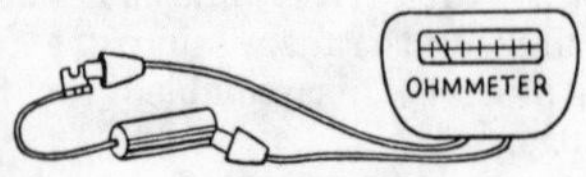

Test and Procedure	Results and Indications	Proceed to
3.6—Test the coil primary resistance: Connect an ohmmeter across the coil primary terminals, and read the resistance on the low scale. Note whether an external ballast resistor or resistance wire is utilized.	Coils utilizing ballast resistors or resistance wires should have approximately 1.0Ω resistance; coils with internal resistors should have approximately 4.0Ω resistance. If values far from the above are noted, replace the coil:	4.1

Testing the coil primary resistance

Test and Procedure	Results and Indications	Proceed to
4.1—Check for spark: Hold each spark plug wire approximately $\frac{1}{4}''$ from ground with gloves or a heavy, dry rag. Crank the engine, and observe the spark.	If no spark is evident:	4.2
	If spark is good in some cylinders:	4.3
	If spark is good in all cylinders:	4.6
4.2—Check for spark at the coil high tension lead: Remove the coil high tension lead from the distributor and position it approximately $\frac{1}{4}''$ from ground. Crank the engine and observe spark. CAUTION: *This test should not be performed on cars equipped with transistorized ignition.*	If the spark is good and consistent:	4.3
	If the spark is good but intermittent, test the primary electrical system starting at 3.3:	3.3
	If the spark is weak or non-existent, replace the coil high tension lead, clean and tighten all connections and retest. If no improvement is noted:	4.4
4.3—Visually inspect the distributor cap and rotor for burned or corroded contacts, cracks, carbon tracks, or moisture. Also check the fit of the rotor on the distributor shaft (where applicable).	If moisture is present, dry thoroughly, and retest per 4.1:	4.1
	If burned or excessively corroded contacts, cracks, or carbon tracks are noted, replace the defective part(s) and retest per 4.1:	4.1
	If the rotor and cap appear intact, or are only slightly corroded, clean the contacts thoroughly (including the cap towers and spark plug wire ends) and retest per 4.1: If the spark is good in all cases: If the spark is poor in all cases:	 4.6 4.5
4.4—Check the coil secondary resistance: Connect an ohmmeter across the distributor side of the coil and the coil tower. Read the resistance on the high scale of the ohmmeter.	The resistance of a satisfactory coil should be between $4K\Omega$ and $10K\Omega$. If the resistance is considerably higher (i.e., $40K\Omega$) replace the coil, and retest per 4.1: NOTE: *This does not apply to high performance coils.*	4.1

Testing the coil secondary resistance

Test and Procedure	Results and Indications	Proceed to
4.5—Visually inspect the spark plug wires for cracking or brittleness. Ensure that no two wires are positioned so as to cause induction firing (adjacent and parallel). Remove each wire, one by one, and check resistance with an ohmmeter.	Replace any cracked or brittle wires. If any of the wires are defective, replace the entire set. Replace any wires with excessive resistance (over 8000Ω per foot for suppression wire), and separate any wires that might cause induction firing.	4.6
4.6—Remove the spark plugs, noting the cylinders from which they were removed, and evaluate according to the chart below.	See below.	See below.

	Condition	Cause	Remedy	Proceed to
	Electrodes eroded, light brown deposits.	Normal wear. Normal wear is indicated by approximately .001″ wear per 1000 miles.	Clean and regap the spark plug if wear is not excessive: Replace the spark plug if excessively worn:	4.7
	Carbon fouling (black, dry, fluffy deposits).	If present on one or two plugs: Faulty high tension lead(s). Burnt or sticking valve(s).	Test the high tension leads: Check the valve train: (Clean and regap the plugs in either case.)	4.5 9.1
		If present on most or all plugs: Overly rich fuel mixture, due to restricted air filter, improper carburetor adjustment, improper choke or heat riser adjustment or operation.	Check the fuel system:	5.1
	Oil fouling (wet black deposits)	Worn engine components. NOTE: *Oil fouling may occur in new or recently rebuilt engines until broken in.*	Check engine vacuum and compression: Replace with new spark plug	6.1
	Lead fouling (gray, black, tan, or yellow deposits, which appear glazed or cinderlike).	Combustion by-products.	Clean and regap the plugs: (Use plugs of a different heat range if the problem recurs.)	4.7

Condition	Cause	Remedy	Proceed to
Gap bridging (deposits lodged between the electrodes).	Incomplete combustion, or transfer of deposits from the combustion chamber.	Replace the spark plugs:	4.7
Overheating (burnt electrodes, and extremely white insulator with small black spots).	Ignition timing advanced too far.	Adjust timing to specifications:	8.2
	Overly lean fuel mixture.	Check the fuel system:	5.1
	Spark plugs not seated properly.	Clean spark plug seat and install a new gasket washer: (Replace the spark plugs in all cases.)	4.7
Fused spot deposits on the insulator.	Combustion chamber blow-by.	Clean and regap the spark plugs:	4.7
Pre-ignition (melted or severely burned electrodes, blistered or cracked insulators, or metallic deposits on the insulator).	Incorrect spark plug heat range.	Replace with plugs of the proper heat range:	4.7
	Ignition timing advanced too far.	Adjust timing to specifications:	8.2
	Spark plugs not being cooled efficiently.	Clean the spark plug seat, and check the cooling system:	11.1
	Fuel mixture too lean.	Check the fuel system:	5.1
	Poor compression.	Check compression:	6.1
	Fuel grade too low.	Use higher octane fuel:	4.7

Test and Procedure	Results and Indications	Proceed to
4.7—Determine the static ignition timing: Using the flywheel or crankshaft pulley timing marks as a guide, locate top dead center on the *compression* stroke of the No. 1 cylinder. Remove the distributor cap.	Adjust the distributor so that the rotor points toward the No. 1 tower in the distributor cap, and the points are just opening:	4.8
4.8—Check coil polarity: Connect a voltmeter negative lead to the coil high tension lead, and the positive lead to ground (NOTE: *reverse the hook-up for positive ground cars*). Crank the engine momentarily. **Checking coil polarity**	If the voltmeter reads up-scale, the polarity is correct:	5.1
	If the voltmeter reads down-scale, reverse the coil polarity (switch the primary leads):	5.1

Test and Procedure	*Results and Indications*	Proceed to
5.1—Determine that the air filter is functioning efficiently: Hold paper elements up to a strong light, and attempt to see light through the filter.	Clean permanent air filters in gasoline (or manufacturer's recommendation), and allow to dry. Replace paper elements through which light cannot be seen:	5.2
5.2—Determine whether a flooding condition exists: Flooding is identified by a strong gasoline odor, and excessive gasoline present in the throttle bore(s) of the carburetor.	If flooding is not evident:	5.3
	If flooding is evident, permit the gasoline to dry for a few moments and restart.	
	If flooding doesn't recur:	5.6
	If flooding is persistant:	5.5
5.3—Check that fuel is reaching the carburetor: Detach the fuel line at the carburetor inlet. Hold the end of the line in a cup (not styrofoam), and crank the engine.	If fuel flows smoothly:	5.6
	If fuel doesn't flow (NOTE: *Make sure that there is fuel in the tank*), or flows erratically:	5.4
5.4—Test the fuel pump: Disconnect all fuel lines from the fuel pump. Hold a finger over the input fitting, crank the engine (with electric pump, turn the ignition or pump on), and feel for suction.	If suction is evident, blow out the fuel line to the tank with low pressure compressed air until bubbling is heard from the fuel filler neck. Also blow out the carburetor fuel line (both ends disconnected):	5.6
	If no suction is evident, replace or repair the fuel pump:	5.6
	NOTE: *Repeated oil fouling of the spark plugs, or a no-start condition, could be the result of a ruptured vacuum booster pump diaphragm, through which oil or gasoline is being drawn into the intake manifold (where applicable).*	
5.5—Check the needle and seat: Tap the carburetor in the area of the needle and seat.	If flooding stops, a gasoline additive (e.g., Gumout) will often cure the problem:	5.6
	If flooding continues, check the fuel pump for excessive pressure at the carburetor (according to specifications). If the pressure is normal, the needle and seat must be removed and checked, and/or the float level adjusted:	5.6
5.6—Test the accelerator pump by looking into the throttle bores while operating the throttle.	If the accelerator pump appears to be operating normally:	5.7
	If the accelerator pump is not operating, the pump must be reconditioned. Where possible, service the pump with the carburetor(s) installed on the engine. If necessary, remove the carburetor. Prior to removal:	5.7
5.7—Determine whether the carburetor main fuel system is functioning: Spray a commercial starting fluid into the carburetor while attempting to start the engine.	If the engine starts, runs for a few seconds, and dies:	5.8
	If the engine doesn't start:	6.1

Test and Procedures	Results and Indications	Proceed to
5.8—Uncommon fuel system malfunctions: See below:	If the problem is solved: If the problem remains, remove and recondition the carburetor.	6.1

Condition	Indication	Test	Usual Weather Conditions	Remedy
Vapor lock	Car will not restart shortly after running.	Cool the components of the fuel system until the engine starts.	Hot to very hot	Ensure that the exhaust manifold heat control valve is operating. Check with the vehicle manufacturer for the recommended solution to vapor lock on the model in question.
Carburetor icing	Car will not idle, stalls at low speeds.	Visually inspect the throttle plate area of the throttle bores for frost.	High humidity, 32-40° F.	Ensure that the exhaust manifold heat control valve is operating, and that the intake manifold heat riser is not blocked.
Water in the fuel	Engine sputters and stalls; may not start.	Pump a small amount of fuel into a glass jar. Allow to stand, and inspect for droplets or a layer of water.	High humidity, extreme temperature changes.	For droplets, use one or two cans of commercial gas dryer (Dry Gas) For a layer of water, the tank must be drained, and the fuel lines blown out with compressed air.

Test and Procedure	Results and Indications	Proceed to
6.1—Test engine compression: Remove all spark plugs. Insert a compression gauge into a spark plug port, crank the engine to obtain the maximum reading, and record.	If compression is within limits on all cylinders:	7.1
	If gauge reading is extremely low on all cylinders:	6.2
	If gauge reading is low on one or two cylinders: (If gauge readings are identical and low on two or more adjacent cylinders, the head gasket must be replaced.)	6.2

Testing compression
(© Chevrolet Div. G.M. Corp.)

Compression pressure limits
(© Buick Div. G.M. Corp.)

Maxi. Press. Lbs. Sq. In.	Min. Press. Lbs. Sq. In.	Maxi. Press. Lbs. Sq. In.	Min. Press. Lbs. Sq. In.	Max. Press. Lbs. Sq. In.	Min. Press. Lbs. Sq. In.	Max. Press. Lbs. Sq. In.	Min. Press. Lbs. Sq. In.
134	101	162	121	188	141	214	160
136	102	164	123	190	142	216	162
138	104	166	124	192	144	218	163
140	105	168	126	194	145	220	165
142	107	170	127	196	147	222	166
146	110	172	129	198	148	224	168
148	111	174	131	200	150	226	169
150	113	176	132	202	151	228	171
152	114	178	133	204	153	230	172
154	115	180	135	206	154	232	174
156	117	182	136	208	156	234	175
158	118	184	138	210	157	236	177
160	120	186	140	212	158	238	178

Test and Procedure	Results and Indications	Proceed to
6.2—Test engine compression (wet): Squirt approximately 30 cc. of engine oil into each cylinder, and retest per 6.1.	If the readings improve, worn or cracked rings or broken pistons are indicated:	Next Chapter
	If the readings do not improve, burned or excessively carboned valves or a jumped timing chain are indicated:	7.1
	NOTE: *A jumped timing chain is often indicated by difficult cranking.*	
7.1—Perform a vacuum check of the engine: Attach a vacuum gauge to the intake manifold beyond the throttle plate. Start the engine, and observe the action of the needle over the range of engine speeds.	See below.	See below

	Reading	Indications	Proceed to
	Steady, from 17-22 in. Hg.	Normal.	8.1
	Low and steady.	Late ignition or valve timing, or low compression:	6.1
	Very low	Vacuum leak:	7.2
	Needle fluctuates as engine speed increases.	Ignition miss, blown cylinder head gasket, leaking valve or weak valve spring:	6.1, 8.3
	Gradual drop in reading at idle.	Excessive back pressure in the exhaust system:	10.1
	Intermittent fluctuation at idle.	Ignition miss, sticking valve:	8.3, 9.1
	Drifting needle.	Improper idle mixture adjustment, carburetors not synchronized (where applicable), or minor intake leak. Synchronize the carburetors, adjust the idle, and retest. If the condition persists:	7.2
	High and steady.	Early ignition timing:	8.2

Test and Procedure	Results and Indications	Proceed to
7.2—Attach a vacuum gauge per 7.1, and test for an intake manifold leak. Squirt a small amount of oil around the intake manifold gaskets, carburetor gaskets, plugs and fittings. Observe the action of the vacuum gauge.	If the reading improves, replace the indicated gasket, or seal the indicated fitting or plug:	8.1
	If the reading remains low:	7.3
7.3—Test all vacuum hoses and accessories for leaks as described in 7.2. Also check the carburetor body (dashpots, automatic choke mechanism, throttle shafts) for leaks in the same manner.	If the reading improves, service or replace the offending part(s):	8.1
	If the reading remains low:	6.1
8.1—Check the point dwell angle: Connect a dwell meter between the distributor primary wire and ground. Start the engine, and observe the dwell angle from idle to 3000 rpm.	If necessary, adjust the dwell angle. NOTE: *Increasing the point gap reduces the dwell angle and vice-versa.* If the dwell angle moves outside specifications as engine speed increases, the distributor should be removed and checked for cam accuracy, shaft end-play and concentricity, bushing wear, and adequate point arm tension (NOTE: *Most of these items may be checked with the distributor installed in the engine, using an oscilloscope*):	8.2
8.2—Connect a timing light (per manufacturer's recommendation) and check the dynamic ignition timing. Disconnect and plug the vacuum hose(s) to the distributor if specified, start the engine, and observe the timing marks at the specified engine speed.	If the timing is not correct, adjust to specifications by rotating the distributor in the engine: (Advance timing by rotating distributor opposite normal direction of rotor rotation, retard timing by rotating distributor in same direction as rotor rotation.)	8.3
8.3—Check the operation of the distributor advance mechanism(s): To test the mechanical advance, disconnect all but the mechanical advance, and observe the timing marks with a timing light as the engine speed is increased from idle. If the mark moves smoothly, without hesitation, it may be assumed that the mechanical advance is functioning properly. To test vacuum advance and/or retard systems, alternately crimp and release the vacuum line, and observe the timing mark for movement. If movement is noted, the system is operating.	If the systems are functioning:	8.4
	If the systems are not functioning, remove the distributor, and test on a distributor tester:	8.4
8.4—Locate an ignition miss: With the engine running, remove each spark plug wire, one by one, until one is found that doesn't cause the engine to roughen and slow down.	When the missing cylinder is identified:	4.1

Test and Procedure	Results and Indications	Proceed to
9.1—Evaluate the valve train: Remove the valve cover, and ensure that the valves are adjusted to specifications. A mechanic's stethoscope may be used to aid in the diagnosis of the valve train. By pushing the probe on or near push rods or rockers, valve noise often can be isolated. A timing light also may be used to diagnose valve problems. Connect the light according to manufacturer's recommendations, and start the engine. Vary the firing moment of the light by increasing the engine speed (and therefore the ignition advance), and moving the trigger from cylinder to cylinder. Observe the movement of each valve.	See below	See below

Observation	Probable Cause	Remedy	Proceed to
Metallic tap heard through the stethoscope.	Sticking hydraulic lifter or excessive valve clearance.	Adjust valve. If tap persists, remove and replace the lifter:	10.1
Metallic tap through the stethoscope, able to push the rocker arm (lifter side) down by hand.	Collapsed valve lifter.	Remove and replace the lifter:	10.1
Erratic, irregular motion of the valve stem.*	Sticking valve, burned valve.	Recondition the valve and/or valve guide:	Next Chapter
Eccentric motion of the pushrod at the rocker arm.*	Bent pushrod.	Replace the pushrod:	10.1
Valve retainer bounces as the valve closes.*	Weak valve spring or damper.	Remove and test the spring and damper. Replace if necessary:	10.1

*—When observed with a timing light.

Test and Procedure	Results and Indications	Proceed to
9.2—Check the valve timing: Locate top dead center of the No. 1 piston, and install a degree wheel or tape on the crankshaft pulley or damper with zero corresponding to an index mark on the engine. Rotate the crankshaft in its direction of rotation, and observe the opening of the No. 1 cylinder intake valve. The opening should correspond with the correct mark on the degree wheel according to specifications.	If the timing is not correct, the timing cover must be removed for further investigation:	

Test and Procedure	Results and Indications	Proceed to
10.1—Determine whether the exhaust manifold heat control valve is operating: Operate the valve by hand to determine whether it is free to move. If the valve is free, run the engine to operating temperature and observe the action of the valve, to ensure that it is opening.	If the valve sticks, spray it with a suitable solvent, open and close the valve to free it, and retest. If the valve functions properly: If the valve does not free, or does not operate, replace the valve:	10.2 10.2
10.2—Ensure that there are no exhaust restrictions: Visually inspect the exhaust system for kinks, dents, or crushing. Also note that gasses are flowing freely from the tailpipe at all engine speeds, indicating no restriction in the muffler or resonator.	Replace any damaged portion of the system:	11.1
11.1—Visually inspect the fan belt for glazing, cracks, and fraying, and replace if necessary. Tighten the belt so that the longest span has approximately ½″ play at its midpoint under thumb pressure.	Replace or tighten the fan belt as necessary:	11.2

Checking the fan belt tension
(© Nissan Motor Co. Ltd.)

Test and Procedure	Results and Indications	Proceed to
11.2—Check the fluid level of the cooling system.	If full or slightly low, fill as necessary: If extremely low:	11.5 11.3
11.3—Visually inspect the external portions of the cooling system (radiator, radiator hoses, thermostat elbow, water pump seals, heater hoses, etc.) for leaks. If none are found, pressurize the cooling system to 14-15 psi.	If cooling system holds the pressure: If cooling system loses pressure rapidly, reinspect external parts of the system for leaks under pressure. If none are found, check dipstick for coolant in crankcase. If no coolant is present, but pressure loss continues: If coolant is evident in crankcase, remove cylinder head(s), and check gasket(s). If gaskets are intact, block and cylinder head(s) should be checked for cracks or holes. If the gasket(s) is blown, replace, and purge the crankcase of coolant: NOTE: *Occasionally, due to atmospheric and driving conditions, condensation of water can occur in the crankcase. This causes the oil to appear milky white. To remedy, run the engine until hot, and change the oil and oil filter.*	11.5 11.4 12.6

Test and Procedure	Results and Indication	Proceed to
11.4—Check for combustion leaks into the cooling system: Pressurize the cooling system as above. Start the engine, and observe the pressure gauge. If the needle fluctuates, remove each spark plug wire, one by one, noting which cylinder(s) reduce or eliminate the fluctuation. **Radiator pressure tester** (© American Motors Corp.)	Cylinders which reduce or eliminate the fluctuation, when the spark plug wire is removed, are leaking into the cooling system. Replace the head gasket on the affected cylinder bank(s).	
11.5—Check the radiator pressure cap: Attach a radiator pressure tester to the radiator cap (wet the seal prior to installation). Quickly pump up the pressure, noting the point at which the cap releases. **Testing the radiator pressure cap** (© American Motors Corp.)	If the cap releases within ± 1 psi of the specified rating, it is operating properly: If the cap releases at more than ± 1 psi of the specified rating, it should be replaced:	11.6 11.6
11.6—Test the thermostat: Start the engine cold, remove the radiator cap, and insert a thermometer into the radiator. Allow the engine to idle. After a short while, there will be a sudden, rapid increase in coolant temperature. The temperature at which this sharp rise stops is the thermostat opening temperature.	If the thermostat opens at or about the specified temperature: If the temperature doesn't increase: (If the temperature increases slowly and gradually, replace the thermostat.)	11.7 11.7
11.7—Check the water pump: Remove the thermostat elbow and the thermostat, disconnect the coil high tension lead (to prevent starting), and crank the engine momentarily.	If coolant flows, replace the thermostat and retest per 11.6: If coolant doesn't flow, reverse flush the cooling system to alleviate any blockage that might exist. If system is not blocked, and coolant will not flow, recondition the water pump.	11.6 —
12.1—Check the oil pressure gauge or warning light: If the gauge shows low pressure, or the light is on, for no obvious reason, remove the oil pressure sender. Install an accurate oil pressure gauge and run the engine momentarily.	If oil pressure builds normally, run engine for a few moments to determine that it is functioning normally, and replace the sender. If the pressure remains low: If the pressure surges: If the oil pressure is zero:	— 12.2 12.3 12.3

Test and Procedure	Results and Indications	Proceed to
12.2—Visually inspect the oil: If the oil is watery or very thin, milky, or foamy, replace the oil and oil filter.	If the oil is normal:	12.3
	If after replacing oil the pressure remains low:	12.3
	If after replacing oil the pressure becomes normal:	—
12.3—Inspect the oil pressure relief valve and spring, to ensure that it is not sticking or stuck. Remove and thoroughly clean the valve, spring, and the valve body.	If the oil pressure improves:	—
	If no improvement is noted:	12.4

Oil pressure relief valve
(© British Leyland Motors)

Test and Procedure	Results and Indications	Proceed to
12.4—Check to ensure that the oil pump is not cavitating (sucking air instead of oil): See that the crankcase is neither over nor underfull, and that the pickup in the sump is in the proper position and free from sludge.	Fill or drain the crankcase to the proper capacity, and clean the pickup screen in solvent if necessary. If no improvement is noted:	12.5
12.5—Inspect the oil pump drive and the oil pump:	If the pump drive or the oil pump appear to be defective, service as necessary and retest per 12.1:	12.1
	If the pump drive and pump appear to be operating normally, the engine should be disassembled to determine where blockage exists:	Next Chapter
12.6—Purge the engine of ethylene glycol coolant: Completely drain the crankcase and the oil filter. Obtain a commercial butyl cellosolve base solvent, designated for this purpose, and follow the instructions precisely. Following this, install a new oil filter and refill the crankcase with the proper weight oil. The next oil and filter change should follow shortly thereafter (1000 miles).		

3 · Engine and Engine Rebuilding

Engine Electrical

DISTRIBUTOR

Removal

1. Disconnect the vacuum advance line at the distributor.

2. Disconnect the primary wire at the coil.

3. Unfasten the distributor cap retaining clips and lift off the cap.

4. Mark the distributor body and the engine block to indicate the position of the body in the block. Scribe a mark on the edge of the distributor housing to indicate the position of the rotor on the distributor. These marks can be used as guides when installing the distributor in a correctly timed engine.

5. Remove the distributor hold-down clamp screw and clamp.

6. Carefully lift the distributor out of the block.

Installation

If the crankshaft has not been rotated while the distributor was removed from the engine, installation is the reverse of the removal procedure. (See step 2 or 3 of the procedure below.) Use the reference marks that were made before removal to correctly position the distributor in the block. Check the point gap and, before connecting the vacuum advance line, adjust the ignition timing. (See the "Tune-Up Procedures" section.)

If the crankshaft has been rotated or otherwise disturbed (as during engine rebuilding) after the distributor was removed, proceed as follows to install the distributor.

1. Bring the no. 1 piston to top dead center (TDC). By removing the no. 1 spark plug and inserting a finger into the hole, while rotating the crankshaft, the compression pressure can be felt as the no. 1 piston approaches TDC. The TDC timing mark on the crankshaft vibration

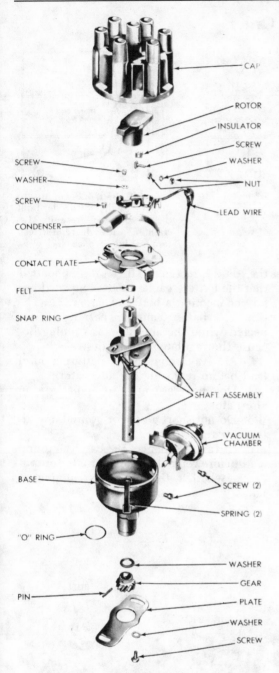

CAP
ROTOR
INSULATOR
SCREW
SCREW
WASHER
WASHER
SCREW
NUT
CONDENSER
LEAD WIRE
CONTACT PLATE
FELT
SNAP RING
SHAFT ASSEMBLY
VACUUM CHAMBER
BASE
SCREW (2)
SPRING (2)
"O" RING
WASHER
GEAR
PIN
PLATE
WASHER
SCREW

Exploded view of distributor—six-cylinder engines

damper should now be opposite the indicator on the timing chain case.

2. *For six-cylinder engines:* Note the position of the distributor cap (which should be connected to the engine by the spark plug cables). Hold the distributor so that the rotor will be in position *just ahead* of the distributor cap terminal for the no. 1 spark plug when the distributor is installed. Now lower the distributor into its

engine block opening, engaging the distributor gear with the camshaft drive gear. Be sure that the rubber O-ring seal is in the groove in the distributor shank. When the distributor is properly seated, the rotor should be under the no. 1 distributor cap terminal with the contact points just opening. Proceed with step 4.

3. *For eight-cylinder engines:* Clean the top of the engine block around the distributor opening to ensure a good seal between the distributor base and the block. Note the position of the distributor cap (which should be connected to the engine by the spark plug cables). Hold the distributor so that the rotor will be in position *directly under* the distributor cap terminal for the no. 1 spark plug when the distributor is installed. Now lower the distributor into its engine block opening, engaging the tongue of the distributor shaft with the slot in the distributor and oil pump drive gear. Proceed with step 4.

4. Install the distributor hold-down clamp and tighten its retaining screw finger-tight.

5. Check the point gap and refit the distributor cap. Connect the primary wire to the coil.

6. Check and adjust the point dwell and the ignition timing using the procedures described in the tune-up section.

7. Connect the vacuum advance line to the distributor.

ALTERNATOR

The alternator is basically an alternating current (AC) generator with solid state rectifiers which convert AC current to DC current (direct current) for charging the battery. The solid state rectifiers are located between the battery alternator coil

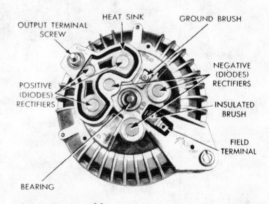

OUTPUT TERMINAL SCREW
HEAT SINK
GROUND BRUSH
POSITIVE (DIODES) RECTIFIERS
NEGATIVE (DIODES) RECTIFIERS
INSULATED BRUSH
FIELD TERMINAL
BEARING

Alternator assembly

Firing Order

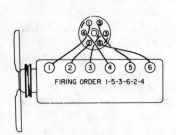

170, 198, and 225 cu in. engines

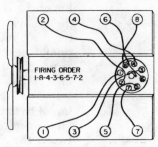

273, 318, and 340 cu in. engines

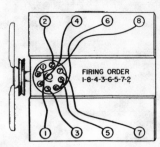

383, 440, and 426 cu in. engines with Chrysler-built distributor. For Prestolite distributor, each distributor cap terminal is one space clockwise

and, since they are one-way current flow devices, the rectifers eliminate any need for a cutout relay in the charging circuit.

Be sure to read and follow the "Alternator Service Precautions" before servicing the vehicle charging system.

Alternator Service Precautions

Because the alternator design is unique, special care must be taken when servicing the charging system.

1. Battery polarity should be checked before any connections, such as jumper cables or battery charger leads, are made. Reversed battery connections will damage the diode rectifiers. It is recommended that the battery cables be disconnected before connecting a battery charger.

2. The battery must *never* be disconnected while the alternator is running because the regulator will be destroyed.

3. Always disconnect the battery ground lead before replacing the alternator.

4. Do not attempt to polarize an alternator.

5. Do not short across or ground any alternator terminals.

6. Always disconnect the battery ground lead before removing the alternator output cable, whether the engine is running or not.

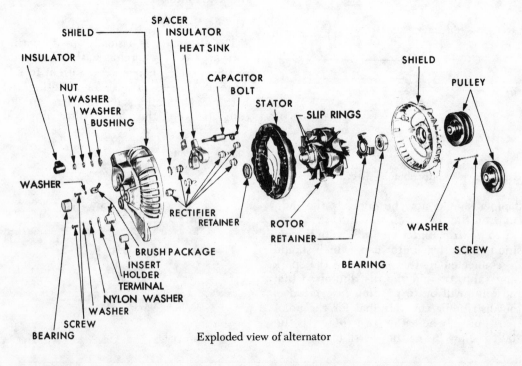

Exploded view of alternator

7. If electric arc welding has to be done on the car, first disconnect the battery and alternator cables. Never start the car with the welding unit attached.

Removal and Installation

1. Disconnect the battery ground cable at the battery negative terminal.

2. Disconnect the alternator output (BAT) and field (FLD) leads, and disconnect the ground wire.

3. Remove the alternator mounting bracket bolts and remove the alternator.

4. Installation is the reverse of the above. Adjust the alternator drive belt tension. Check the alternator and regulator circuits and perform any necessary adjustments.

Belt Tension Adjustment

Alternator and other accessory drive belts can be adjusted using the torque method procedure. Torque requirements for various components are listed in the "Accessory Belt Tension Torque Specifications" chart. The procedure below describes the alternator belt adjustment but it can also be applied to the other accessory drive belts if the accessory bracket has a square hole.

1. Loosen the alternator mounting bracket bolts.

2. Position the alternator on its mounting bracket until there is no slack in the drive belt.

3. Using a suitable adaptor, attach a torque wrench to the ribbed section of the alternator rectifier end shield. While applying the specified torque to the alternator, tighten the alternator mounting bracket bolts.

Alternator System Tests

The charging system can be checked while the alternator is mounted on the car if the following equipment is available: a DC voltmeter, a 0–75 ampere scale DC ammeter, and a carbon pile rheostat.

If an alternator malfunction is detected, perform the necessary adjustments. Be sure to test the voltage regulator. If the malfunction continues after all possible adjustments have been made, it is recommended that the alternator be removed and replaced with a new or reconditioned unit.

FIELD CIRCUIT RESISTANCE TEST

Excessive resistance in the circuit can be detected by this test. *Fluctuation of the instrument panel ammeter may be caused by excessive resistance in the regulator wiring circuit.* Refer to the field circuit resistance test illustration.

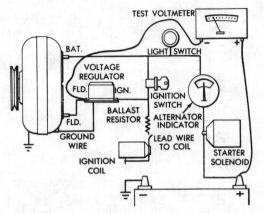

Field circuit resistance test

1. Disconnect the ignition wire at the coil side of the ballast resistor. Connect the positive lead of the test DC voltmeter to the battery positive post and connect the voltmeter negative lead to the voltage regulator field (FLD) terminal. Be sure that all lights and accessories are turned off.

2. Turn on the ignition switch. Switch the voltmeter to its low-voltage scale (if so equipped). The voltage reading should not exceed 0.55 volt. A reading in excess of 0.55 volt indicates high resistance in the field circuit between the battery and the voltage regulator field terminal.

3. If high resistance is indicated, move the negative voltmeter lead to each connection along the circuit (see illustration) toward the battery. A sudden drop in voltage indicates a loose or corroded connection between that point and the last point tested. To test the terminal for tightness, attempt to move the terminal while observing the voltmeter. Any movement of the meter pointer indicates looseness.

4. Turn off the ignition switch, disconnect the voltmeter, and reconnect the ignition primary wire at the coil side of the ballast resistor.

CHARGING CIRCUIT RESISTANCE TEST

This test will indicate excessive resistance in the charging circuit.

Accessory Belt Tension Torque Specifications (ft lbs)

Accessory Bracket	Model Year	New Belt						Used Belt ①					
		170	198	225	273	318 340	383 440 426	170	198	225	273	318 340	383 440 426
Power Steering Pump	1965–68	80	—	80	85	85	90②	45	—	45	50	50	55②
	1969–70	—	—	80	—	85	120	—	—	45	—	50	70
	1971–72	—	90	90④	—	50	120	—	50	50③	—	35	90
Alternator with A/C	1965–66	20	—	20	50	—	—	15	—	15	30	—	—
without A/C	1965–66	20	—	20	50	—	—	15	—	15	30	—	—
with A/C (Single Belt)	1967–70	—	—	20	55	55	70	—	—	15	40	40	45
with A/C (Dual Belt)	1967–70	—	—	—	—	50	40	—	—	—	—	35	25
without A/C	1967–70	—	—	20	55	55	60	—	—	15	40	40	40
with A/C	1971–72	—	15	15	—	100	120	—	10	10	—	70	80
without A/C	1971–72	—	15	15	—	35	70	—	10	10	—	25	40

Engine Displacement (cu in.)

Accessory Belt Tension Torque Specifications (ft lbs)

Accessory Bracket	Model Year	Used Belt ①						New Belt					
		Engine Displacement (cu in.)						Engine Displacement (cu in.)					
		170	198	225	273	318 340	383 440 426	170	198	225	273	318 340	383 440 426
A/C Idler	1965–66	25	—	25	55	—	—	35	—	35	75	—	—
	1967–70	—	—	25	45	45	—	—	—	35	60	60⑤	—
	1971–72	—	15	15	—	—	—	—	25	25	—	—	—
Fan Idler	1965–70	—	—	—	—	—	40	—	—	—	—	—	65
	1971–72	—	—	—	—	20	20	—	—	—	—	35	30
Air Pump with A/C	1972	—	—	20	—	—	—	—	—	35	—	—	—
without A/C	1972	—	—	25	—	—	—	—	—	40	—	—	—

①—Any bolt that has operated for a minimum of one-half hour is considered to be used.
②—45 ft lbs for self-tightening bracket.
③—20 ft lbs for power steering and air pump bracket.
④—On 1972 models with air pump, 35 ft lbs for power steering and air pump bracket.
⑤—65 ft lbs for 1968–70 318 and 340 cu in. engine.

Charging System Service Diagnosis

Condition	Possible Cause	Correction
Alternator Fails to Charge (No Output)	(a) Blown fusible wire in voltage regulator	(a) Locate and correct cause of the fuse blowing. Install new voltage regulator.
	(b) Alternator drive belt loose	(b) Adjust drive belt for specifications.
	(c) Worn brushes and/or slip rings	(c) Replace alternator.
	(d) Sticking brushes	(d) Replace alternator.
	(e) Open field circuit	(e) Test all the field circuit connections and correct as required.
	(f) Open charging circuit	(f) Inspect all connections in charging circuit and correct as required.
	(g) Open circuit in stator windings	(g) Replace alternator.
	(h) Open rectifiers	(h) Replace alternator.
Low, Unsteady Charging Rate	(a) Alternator drive belt loose	(a) Adjust alternator drive belt.
	(b) High resistance at battery terminals	(b) Clean and tighten battery terminals.
	(c) High resistance in charging circuit	(c) Test charging circuit resistance. Correct as required.
	(d) High resistance in body-to-engine ground lead	(d) Tighten ground lead connections. Install new ground lead if necessary.
	(e) Open stator winding	(e) Replace alternator.
Low Output and a Low Battery	(a) High resistance in charging circuit	(a) Test charging circuit resistance and correct as required.
	(b) Low regulator setting	(b) Reset voltage regulator to specifications.
	(c) Shorted rectifier / Open rectifier	(c) Perform current output test. Replace alternator if necessary.
	(d) Grounded stator windings	(d) Replace alternator.
Excessive Charging Rate to a Fully Charged Battery	(a) Regulator set too high	(a) Reset voltage regulator to specifications.
	(b) Regulator contacts stuck	(b) Install new voltage regulator.
	(c) Regulator voltage winding open	(c) Install new voltage regulator.
	(d) Regulator base improperly grounded	(d) Connect regulator base to a good ground.
	(e) Faulty ignition switch	(e) Install new ignition switch.
	(f) Faulty voltage regulator (transistorized)	(f) Test voltage regulator. Replace as necessary.
Regulator Contacts Burned *	(a) High regulator setting	(a) Reset voltage regulator to specifications.
	(b) Shorted rotor field coil windings	(b) Test rotor field coil current draw. If excessive, replace alternator.
Regulator Contact Points Stuck *	(a) Poor ground connection between alternator and regulator / Open resistor element	(a) Correct ground connection. Install new regulator. Test regulator setting and reset if necessary.
Noisy Alternator	(a) Alternator mounting loose	(a) Properly install and tighten alternator mounting.
	(b) Worn or frayed drive belt	(b) Install a new drive belt and adjust to specifications.
	(c) Worn bearings	(c) Replace alternator.
	(d) Interference between rotor fan and stator leads or rectifiers	(d) Replace alternator.
	(e) Rotor or rotor fan damaged	(e) Replace alternator.
	(f) Open or shorted rectifier	(f) Replace alternator.
	(g) Open or shorted winding in stator	(g) Replace alternator.
Excessive Ammeter Fluctuation	(a) High resistance in the field circuit to the alternator or an improperly set voltage regulator	(a) Clean and tighten all connections as necessary. Adjust voltage regulator as necessary.

* Mechanical voltage regulator only.

1. Disconnect the battery ground cable.

2. Disconnect the BAT lead at the alternator output terminal.

3. Connect a 0–75 ampere scale DC ammeter in series between the alternator BAT terminal and the disconnected BAT (see illustration).

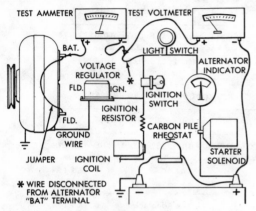

Charging circuit resistance test

4. Connect the positive lead of the test voltmeter to the disconnected BAT lead. Connect the voltmeter negative lead to the battery positive post.

5. Disconnect the FLD lead from the alternator.

6. Connect a jumper lead from the alternator FLD terminal to ground.

7. Connect an engine tachometer according to the manufacturer's instructions. Connect the battery ground cable.

8. Connect a carbon pile rheostat to the battery terminals. (See illustration.)

9. Start the engine and, *immediately after starting, reduce the engine speed to idle.*

10. Adjust the engine speed and rheostat to obtain 10 amperes (20 amperes for transistorized voltage regulators) flowing in the circuit. Observe the voltmeter reading. The reading should not exceed 0.3 volt (0.7 volt for transistorized voltage regulators). If higher voltage reading is indicated, you must inspect, clean, and tighten all connections in the charging circuit. A voltage drop test may be performed at each connection to locate the connection with excessive resistance.

11. When the test is completed, reduce the engine speed, turn off the rheostat, and switch off the ignition. Leave all of the

other connections intact and continue with the current output test.

Current Output Test

Internal malfunctions of the alternator will be indicated by this test. After completing the charging circuit resistance test, continue with the procedure below.

1. Start the engine and, *immediately after starting, reduce the engine speed to idle.*

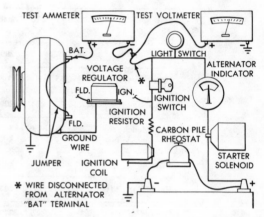

Current output test

2. Adjust the rheostat and the engine speed in increments until an engine speed of 1,250 rpm and a voltmeter reading of 15 volts is obtained.

CAUTION: *Incremental increases in engine speed should not be large enough to allow voltage to go above 16 volts.*

3. Observe the ammeter reading. The output current should be within the limits listed in the "Alternator and Regulator Specifications" chart. If the output is slightly less (5 to 7 amperes) than specified, it may be an indication of an "open" rectifier or other alternator internal problems. If the output is considerably lower than that specified, it may be an indication of a possible "shorted" rectifier or other internal problems. In either case, it is recommended that the alternator be removed and replaced with a new or reconditioned unit.

4. When this test is completed, adjust the idle speed to specification, turn off the rheostat, and switch off the ignition.

5. Disconnect the battery ground cable.

6. Disconnect and remove the ammeter, voltmeter, tachometer, and rheostat.

7. Remove the jumper from between the

Alternator and Regulator Specifications

Year	Alternator			Regulator						
	Part No. or Manufacturer	Field Current @ 12 V	Output (amps)	Part No. or Manufacturer	Field Relay			Regulator		
					Air Gap (in.)	Point Gap (in.)	Volts to Close	Air Gap (in.)	Point Gap (in.)	Volts @ 75°
'65	2098835	2.38–2.75	30	2098300	0.050	0.014	13.8	0.050	0.015	13.2–14.2
	2098830	2.38–2.75	35	2098300	0.050	0.014	13.8	0.050	0.015	13.2–14.2
	2098850	2.38–2.75	46	2098300	0.050	0.014	13.8	0.050	0.015	13.2–14.2
	2444599	2.38–2.75	46	2098300	0.050	0.014	13.8	0.050	0.015	13.2–14.2
'66–'69	6 Cyl Models	2.38–2.75	26	2098300①	0.050①	0.014	13.8	0.050	0.015	13.8–14.4
	8 Cyl Std.	2.38–2.75	35	2098300①	0.050①	0.014	13.8	0.050	0.015	13.8–14.4
	Heavy Duty, A/C	2.38–2.75	44	2098300①	0.050①	0.014	13.8	0.050	0.015	13.8–14.4
	Special Equip.	2.38–2.75	51	2098300①	0.050①	0.014	13.8	0.050	0.015	13.8–14.4
'70–'71	6 Cyl Models	2.38–2.75	26	3438150	Not Adjustable					13.8–14.4
	8 Cyl Std.	2.38–2.75	34②	3438150	Not Adjustable					13.8–14.4
	Heavy Duty, A/C	2.38–2.75	45	3438150	Not Adjustable					13.8–14.4
	Special Equip.	2.38–2.75	51	3438150	Not Adjustable					13.8–14.4
'72	6 Cyl Models	2.5–3.1	39	3438150	Not Adjustable					13.8–14.4
	8 Cyl Std.	2.5–3.1	41	3438150	Not Adjustable					13.8–14.4
	Heavy Duty, A/C	2.5–3.1	50	3438150	Not Adjustable					13.8–14.4
	Special Equip.	2.5–3.1	60	3438150	Not Adjustable					13.8–14.4

① Essex wire regulator, #2444980, used interchangeably. Air gap setting is 0.032–0.042 in., all other dimensions are identical with #2098300
② '71 models use a standard 44 amp alternator

alternator FLD terminal and ground. Connect the FLD lead to the alternator FLD terminal.

8. Connect the battery ground cable.

VOLTAGE REGULATOR

The only function of the voltage regulator is to limit the output voltage by controlling the flow of current in the alternator rotor field coil which, in effect, controls the strength of the rotor magnetic field. On Barracuda and Challenger models, the output voltage is limited by two different types of voltage regulators.

Some Barracuda models (1965–69) use a mechanical voltage regulator, i.e., the regulator has contact points which are adjustable. Barracuda and Challenger cars from 1970 to 1972 are equipped with a solid state (silicon transistor) voltage regulator which is not adjustable. Test procedures for each type of regulator and adjustments for the mechanical unit are described under the heading for the particular regulator.

Removal and Installation

Both types of voltage regulators can be removed and installed by using the same procedure.

1. Disconnect the cables from the battery posts.

2. Label and disconnect each electrical lead from the voltage regulator.

3. Remove the regulator by withdrawing its securing screws.

4. Installation is the reverse of the above. Be sure that the electrical leads are connected to the correct terminals and that all connections are clean and tight. If possible, test the voltage regulator to be sure that the output is correct.

Mechanical Voltage Regulator

Barracuda models from 1965 to 1969 use a voltage regulator manufactured by Chrysler, which is the same regulator used on other Plymouth cars in those model years. Because these other Plymouth models also used a voltage regulator manufactured by Essex (identified by an adjusting screw in the regulator cover) interchangeably with the Chrysler-built unit, it is possible that an Essex unit was installed in a Barracuda. If this is the case, it is recommended that the original unit be removed and replaced with a Chrysler voltage regulator.

Normally, when the voltage regulator is suspected of being the cause of a vehicle charging system problem, the procedure is to remove the old unit and replace it with a new or reconditioned regulator. However, since these regulators are adjustable, it is advisable to perform the regulator tests and adjustments (if the necessary test equipment is available) before removing the old unit. If the problem cannot be corrected easily by adjusting the voltage regulator and if no other possible causes of the problem can be found, the old regulator should then be replaced. In addition, the regulator testing and adjustment procedures can be used when installing a new regulator to check to make sure that the voltage setting is correct.

Upper Contacts Voltage Test— Chrysler-Built

This test procedure requires the use of an on-off switch such as the factory unit shown in the illustration. Fabricate this switch using the factory parts as shown. (Chrysler part numbers are indicated in the illustration.) Otherwise, use similar parts that are available elsewhere.

1. With the ignition switched off, disconnect the wire at the ignition side of the voltage regulator and install the on-off switch and wire in series with the regulator and the wire which was disconnected from the regulator. (See diagram.)

2. Connect the test voltmeter positive lead to the switch terminal (no. 1704562 in switch illustration) and connect the meter negative lead to a good ground on the car body.

3. Disconnect the BAT lead at the alternator BAT terminal.

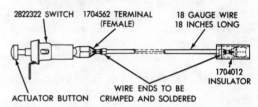

Voltage regulator test on-off switch

4. Connect the test ammeter in series between the alternator BAT terminal and the disconnected BAT lead.

CAUTION: *If the field circuit is grounded on the field terminal side of the regulator circuit when removing or installing the lead, while the ignition is on, the fuse wire in the regulator circuit will be blown and the regulator may be damaged.*

5. Start and operate the engine at 1,250 rpm. Connect the carbon pile rheostat used in the alternator test to the battery posts. Adjust the rheostat to obtain a reading of 15 amperes on the test meter. No current reading indicates either a low regulator setting or a blown fuse wire inside the voltage regulator. Correct this situation before continuing with the procedure by making a preliminary contacts adjustment as described in the "Voltage Regulator Adjustments" procedures. If this adjustment does not improve the current reading, the regulator should be removed and replaced with a new or reconditioned unit. Continue this test as follows:

6. Operate the engine at this speed and load (1,250 rpm and 15 amperes) for 15 minutes to make sure that the entire system is temperature-normalized.

7. Readjust the engine speed to 1,250 rpm and the rheostat to maintain a 15 amperes reading on the test ammeter.

8. Measure and record the temperature

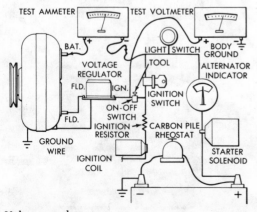

Voltage regulator test

at the regulator by holding a reliable thermometer one-fourth inch from the regulator cover.

9. Flash the voltage regulator circuit by momentarily opening and closing the on-off switch several times.

10. Observe the test voltmeter. The voltmeter now indicates the setting of the Chrysler-built regulator upper contacts. Refer to the "Alternator and Regulator Specifications" chart.

11. If the regulator operates within specifications, proceed to the next test procedure. If the voltage setting is incorrect, refer to the proper adjustment procedure to adjust the Chrysler-built regulator upper contacts. After the adjustment is completed, proceed to the next test.

Lower Contacts Voltage Test— Chrysler-Built

CAUTION: *Be sure that the battery negative post is always connected to ground. Incorrect battery polarity may result in damage to the vehicle wiring harness and/or the alternator rectifiers. Do not ground the alternator field circuit as this may damage the voltage regulator.*

1. Increase the engine speed to 2,200 rpm.

2. Adjust the rheostat to decrease the current reading to 7 amperes on the test ammeter. (The voltage should increase as the amperage decreases.)

3. Measure the temperature again (as in step 8 of the procedure above) to make sure that it is the same as it was during the previous test.

4. Flash the voltage regulator circuit by momentarily opening and closing the on-off switch several times.

5. Observe the test voltmeter and note the exact amount that the voltage has increased above the reading observed in the previous test. The voltage increase should not be less than 0.2 volt or more than 0.7 volt. If the voltage increase is not within these limits, it is an indication that the air gap and/or contact clearance is in need of adjustment. Refer to the proper adjust procedure to adjust the Chrysler-built regulator lower contacts or the Essex-built regulator upper contacts.

6. After the test and necessary adjustments are completed, reduce the engine speed to idle, stop the engine, and disconnect all test leads and adaptors. Be sure that all of the electrical cables and wiring connections are secure before restarting the engine.

Voltage Regulator Adjustments— Chrysler-Built

Adjust the *upper contact* voltage setting as follows:

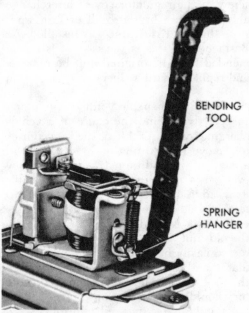

Adjusting mechanical voltage regulator

1. Remove the regulator cover.

2. Use an insulated tool (see illustration) to adjust the upper contact voltage as necessary by bending the regulator lower spring hanger *down* to *increase* the voltage setting or *up* to *decrease* the voltage setting.

3. Refit the regulator cover.

Adjust the *lower contact* voltage setting as follows:

1. Remove the regulator cover.

2. Measure the lower contact point gap

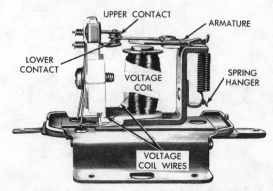

Mechanical voltage regulator (cover removed)

with a feeler gauge. The lower contact gap should be 0.014 in. plus or minus 0.002 in. If necessary, adjust the contact gap by bending the lower stationary contact bracket while making sure that the contacts remain in alignment.

3. If the voltage reading is now correct, refit the regulator cover. If the lower contact gap is correct but the voltage reading is still outside the 0.2–0.7 volt increase, continue this procedure to adjust the lower contacts air gap.

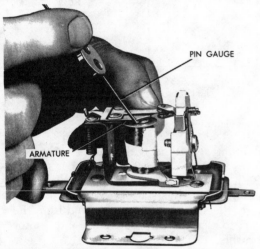

Testing air gap on mechanical voltage regulator

4. Connect a small dry cell and test lamp in series with the IGN and FLD terminals of the voltage regulator.

5. Insert a 0.048 in. wire gauge between the regulator armature and the core of the voltage coil next to the stop pin on the armature.

6. Press down on the armature (not on the contact reed) until the armature contacts the wire gauge. The upper contacts should just open and the test lamp should be dim.

7. Insert a 0.052 in. wire gauge between the armature and the voltage coil core, next to the stop pin on the armature.

8. Press down on the armature until it contacts the wire gauge. The upper contacts should remain closed and the test lamp should remain bright.

9. To obtain the correct difference of 0.2–0.7 volt increase of the lower contact voltage over the upper contact voltage, adjust the lower contacts air gap by loosening the stationary contact bracket screw and moving the bracket up or down to obtain the proper air gap setting as follows:

If the difference is above 0.7 volt, reduce the air gap to a minimum of 0.045 in. with the contacts open and the test lamp dim. At 0.048 in., the contacts should close and the test lamp should be bright.

If the difference is below 0.2 volt, increase the air gap to a maximum of 0.055 in. with the contacts closed and the test lamp bright. At 0.052 in., the contacts should be open and the test lamp should be dim.

Be certain that the air gap is measured with the stationary contact bracket attaching screw fully tightened.

10. When all adjustments are complete, refit the regulator cover.

Transistorized Voltage Regulator

This voltage regulator maintains correct charging voltage by varying the duty cycle of a series of pulses to the alternator field. The pulse frequency is controlled by the ignition frequency of the engine. The regulator has no moving parts and requires no adjustment after it is set internally at the factory. If the unit is found to be defective, it must be removed and replaced with a new regulator.

VOLTAGE REGULATOR TEST

1. Clean the battery terminals and check the specific gravity of the battery electrolyte. (See "Battery Care" procedures.) If the specific gravity is below 1.200, charge the battery before performing the voltage regulator test as it must be above 1.200 to allow a prompt, regulated voltage check.

2. Connect the positive lead of the test voltmeter to the ignition number one (1) terminal of the ballast resistor (the end with one or two blue wires connected to it).

3. Connect the voltmeter negative lead to a good body ground.

4. Start and operate the engine at 1,250 rpm with all lights and accessories switched off. Observe the voltmeter reading. The regulator is working properly if the voltage readings are in accordance with the following chart.

Ambient Temp Near Regulator	Voltage Range
Below 20° F	14.3–15.3
80° F	13.8–14.4
140° F	13.3–14.0
Above 140° F	Less than 13.8

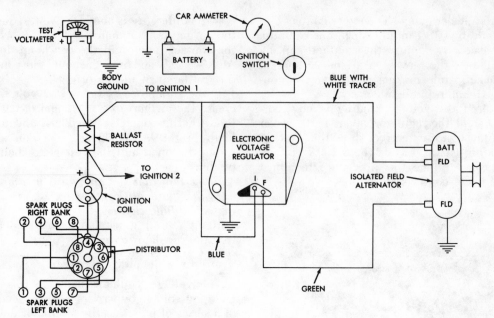

Transistorized voltage regulator test

5. If the voltage reading is below the specified limits, check for a good voltage regulator ground. Using the low voltage scale of the test meter, check for a voltage drop between the regulator cover and body.

If the reading is still low, switch off the ignition and disconnect the voltage regulator connector. Switch on the ignition but do not start the car. Check for battery voltage at the wiring harness terminal connected to the blue and green leads. *Disconnect the wiring harness from the voltage regulator when checking the leads.* Switch off the ignition. If there is no voltage at either lead, the problem is in the vehicle wiring or alternator field circuit. If voltage is present, change the voltage regulator and repeat step 4.

6. If the voltage reading is above the specified limits, check the ground between the voltage regulator and the vehicle body, and between the vehicle body and the engine. Check the ignition switch circuit between the switch battery terminal and the voltage regulator. If the voltage reading is still high (more than one-half volt above the specified limits), change the voltage regulator and repeat step 4.

7. Remove the test voltmeter.

STARTER

Barracuda and Challenger models are equipped with two types of starters: a re-

duction gear type with a 3.5:1 reduction gear set, or a direct drive type starter. Both types have solenoids which are mounted on the starter assembly. Therefore, the starter must be removed from the car to service the solenoid and motor brushes.

Removal and Installation

1. Disconnect the ground cable at the battery.

2. Remove the cable from the starter.

3. Disconnect the solenoid leads at their solenoid terminals.

4. Remove the starter securing bolts and withdraw the starter from the engine flywheel housing. On some models with automatic transmissions, the oil cooler tube bracket will interfere with starter removal. In this case, remove the starter securing bolts, slide the cooler tube bracket off the stud, and then withdraw the starter.

5. Installation is the reverse of the above. Be sure that the starter and flywheel housing mating surfaces are free of dirt and oil.

Solenoid and Brush Service

REDUCTION GEAR STARTER

1. Remove the starter from the car and support the starter gear housing in a vise with soft jaws. DO NOT CLAMP.

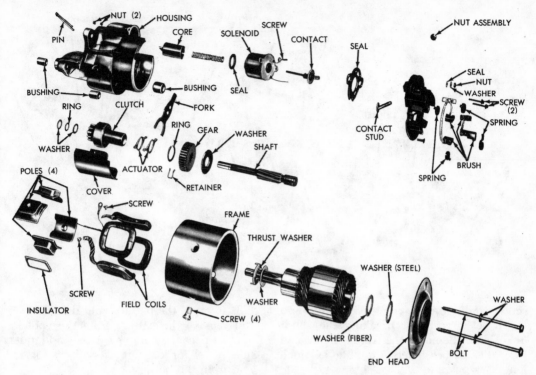

Reduction gear starter—exploded view

2. Remove the two thru-bolts and the starter end assembly.

3. Carefully pull the armature up and out of the gear housing and the starter frame and field assembly.

4. Carefully pull the frame and field assembly up just enough to expose the terminal screw (which connects the series field coils to one pair of motor brushes) and support it with two blocks.

5. Support the terminal by placing a finger behind the terminal and remove the terminal screw.

6. Unwrap the shunt field coil lead from the other starter brush terminal. Unwrap the solenoid lead wire from the brush terminal.

7. Remove the steel and fiber thrust washer.

8. Remove the nut, steel washer, and insulating washer from the solenoid terminal.

9. Straighten the solenoid wire and remove the brush holder plate with the brushes and solenoid as an assembly.

10. Inspect the starter brushes. Brushes that are worn more than one-half the length of new brushes or are oil-soaked, should be replaced.

11. Assemble the starter using the reverse of the above procedure. When resoldering the shunt field and solenoid leads, make a strong, low-resistance connection using a high-temperature solder and resin flux. *Do not break the shunt field wire units when removing and installing the brushes.*

DIRECT-DRIVE STARTER

1. Remove the starter from the car and support it in a vise with soft jaws. DO NOT CLAMP.

2. Remove the thru-bolts and tap the commutator and head from the field frame.

3. Remove the thrust washers from the armature shaft.

4. Lift the brush holder springs and remove the brushes from the brush holders. Remove the brush plate.

5. Disconnect the field coil leads at the solenoid connector.

6. Inspect the starter brushes. Brushes that are worn more than one-half the length of new brushes or are oil-soaked should be replaced. To replace the brushes, continue this procedure as follows.

7. Remove the ground brush terminal

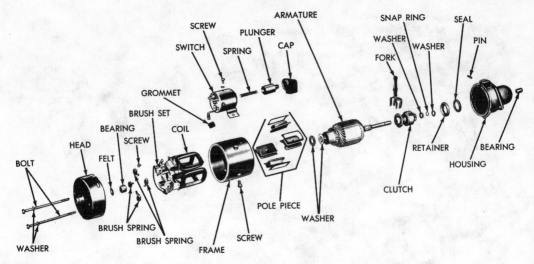

Direct drive starter—exploded view

screw and carefully remove the ground brush set to prevent breaking the shunt field lead. Remove the shunt field lead from the old brush set to provide as much length as possible.

8. Remove the field terminal plastic covering and remove the old brushes. Use side cutters to break the weld by rolling the stranded wire off the terminal.

9. Drill a 0.174–0.184 in. hole in the series coil terminal $3/16$ of an inch from the top of the terminal to the centerline of the hole (use a number 16 drill).

CAUTION: *Do not damage the field coil during the drilling operation.*

10. Attach the insulated brush set to the series field terminal with a flat washer and number 8 self-tapping screw. Attach the shunt field lead to the new ground brush set by making a loop around the terminal and soldering the lead to the terminal with resin core solder.

11. Attach the ground brush terminal to the field frame with the securing screw. Fold the extra shunt field lead back along the brush lead and secure it with electrical tape.

12. Assemble the starter using the reverse of steps 1 through 5.

BATTERY

Removal and Installation

1. Protect the paint finish with fender covers.

2. Disconnect the battery cables at the battery terminal posts.

3. Remove the battery hold-down clamp and remove the battery from the vehicle.

4. Inspect the battery carrier and fender side panel for damage caused by loss of acid from the battery.

5. If the battery is to be reinstalled, clean the top of the battery with a solution of clean warm water and baking soda. Scrub heavily deposited areas with a stiff-bristled brush, being careful not to scatter corrosion residue. Finally, wipe off the top of the battery with a cloth that has been moistened with ammonia or baking soda in water. *Keep the cleaning solution out of the battery cells.* Examine the battery case and cover for cracks.

6. Clean the battery posts and cable connectors with a wire brush or special cleaning tool. Replace any damaged or frayed cables.

7. Install the battery in the car and tighten the hold-down clamp nuts. Connect the cables to their correct battery posts and, after tightening the cable connectors, coat all connections with petroleum jelly to prevent corrosion. If the electrolyte level is low, fill to the recommended level with distilled or de-ionized water.

Battery Care

Batteries should be checked periodically for adequate electrolyte level, proper output, and good connections. Add nothing but distilled water and fill, when necessary, to about $3/8$ in. above the plates.

Inspect the battery case for cracks and

weakness. A leaky battery should be replaced. Check the specific gravity of the
battery electrolyte with a hydrometer.
Readings from a fully charged battery de-
pend on the make but will be in the range
of 1.260–1.310 times as heavy as pure
water at 80° F.

NOTE: *All cells should produce nearly
equal readings. If one or two cell readings
are considerably lower, they are defective, and if they continue to be low
after charging, the battery must be replaced.*

As a battery releases its charge, sulphate
ions in the electrolyte become attached to
the plates, reducing the density of the
fluid. The specific gravity of the electrolyte
varies not only with the percentage of acid
in the liquid but also with the temperature. As temperature increases, the electrolyte expands, so that specific gravity is reduced in this second way. As temperature
drops, the electrolyte contracts and gravity
increases. To correct readings for temperature variation, add 0.004 to the hydrometer
reading for every 10° F that the electrolyte
is above 80° F, and subtract 0.004 for
every 10° F that the electrolyte is below

80° F. The drawing shows the total correction to make for any temperature above or
below 80° F.

The state of charge of the battery can be
determined roughly from the following
specific gravity readings:

Hydrometer Readings	Condition
1.260–1.310	Fully charged
1.230–1.250	¾ charged
1.200–1.220	½ charged
1.170–1.190	¼ charged
1.140–1.160	Almost discharged
1.110–1.130	Fully discharged

Make a light-load voltage test to detect
weak cells. First draw off the transient surface charge by operating the starter for
three seconds and then turning on the
low-beam lights. After one minute, test
each cell (with lights still on) with the
voltmeter. A fully charged battery has no
cell voltage difference of more than 1.95
volts. A greater variation at full charge indicates a defective cell.

Another check for a 12 volt battery in-
volves connecting a charger for three minutes under 40 amperes. Read the battery
voltage with the charger still operating.
Voltage over 15.5v indicates a defective
battery. If battery voltage is under this
limit and individual cell readings are
within 0.1 volts, the battery is usable.

Charging a weak battery is best done by
a slow-charge method. If quick-charging is
attempted, check the cell voltages and the
color of the electrolyte a few minutes after
the charge is started. If cell voltages are
not uniform or if the electrolyte is dis-
colored with brown sediment, quick-charging should be stopped in favor of a slow
charge. In either case, do not let electrolyte temperature exceed 120° F.

If a high electrical circuit voltage is suspected, the voltage regulator might be cutting in abnormally because of corroded or
loose battery connections. The symptoms
are hard starting, full ammeter charge, and
brightly flaring lights. After cleaning, coat
the battery terminals with petroleum jelly
to prevent recurrence of the problem.

Overcharging the battery is a common
cause of battery failure. A symptom of
overcharging is a frequent need for the addition of water to the battery. The generat-
ing system should be corrected immediately to prevent internal battery
damage.

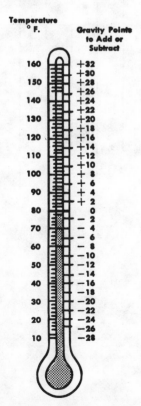

**Temperature
° F.**

**Gravity Points
to Add or
Subtract**

Temperature ° F.	Gravity Points to Add or Subtract
160	+32
	+30
150	+28
	+26
140	+24
	+22
130	+20
	+18
120	+16
	+14
110	+12
	+10
100	+ 8
	+ 6
90	+ 4
	+ 2
80	0
	− 2
70	− 4
	− 6
60	− 8
	−10
50	−12
	−14
40	−16
	−18
30	−20
	−22
20	−24
	−26
10	−28

Hydrometer reading correction chart

Battery and Starter Specifications

| Year | Engine Displacement (cu in.) | Battery | | | Starters | | | | | | Brush Spring Tension (oz) |
| | | Ampere Hour Capacity | Volts | Terminal Grounded | Lock Test | | | No-Load Test | | | |
					Amps	Volts	Torque (ft lbs)	Amps	Volts	RPM	
'65	6-170	38	12	Neg.	380	4	20.0	90	11	2,950	32–48
	6-225	48	12	Neg.	380	4	24.0	85	11	1,950	32–48
	8-273	48	12	Neg.	450	4	20.0	90	11	2,400	32–48
'66–'67	6-170	38	12	Neg.	380	4	—	90	11	2,950	32–48
	6-225	48	12	Neg.	380	4	—	85	11	1,950	32–48
	8-273①	48	12	Neg.	450	4	—	90	11	2,400	32–48
'68–'69	6-170	38	12	Neg.	380	4	—	90	11	2,950	32–36
	6-225, 273, 318, 340	48	12	Neg.	425	4	—	90	11	2,300	32–36
	8-383	59	12	Neg.	425	4	—	90	11	2,300	32–36
'70	6 & 8-198, 225, 318, 340	46	12	Neg.	400–450	4	—	90	11	1,925–2,600	32–36
	8-383	59	12	Neg.	400–450	4	—	90	11	1,925–2,600	32–36
	8-426, 440	70	12	Neg.	400–450	4	—	90	11	1,925–2,600	32–36
'71	6 & 8-198, 225, 318	46	12	Neg.	400–450	4	—	90	11	1,925–2,600	32–36
	8-340, 383	59	12	Neg.	400–450	4	—	90	11	1,925–2,600	32–36
	8-426, 440	70	12	Neg.	400–450	4	—	90	11	1,925–2,600	32–36
'72	6 & 8-198, 225, 318	46	12	Neg.	400–450	4	—	90	11	1,925–2,600	32–36
	8-340	46	12	Neg.	400–450	4	—	90	11	1,925–2,600	32–36

① 1967 383 engine, refer to 1968 specifications

Engine Mechanical

DESIGN

6 CYLINDER ENGINES

The 170, 198, and 225 cu in. engines are known as "slant sixes" because each engine is inclined thirty degrees toward the right when it is installed. This design permits a lower hood line and allows space in the engine compartment for the long intake manifold branches. All of these engines have inline overhead valves, wedge-shaped combustion chambers, a one-barrel carburetor, and a single exhaust.

V8 ENGINES

All of the V8 engines used in Barracuda and Challenger models are the valve-in-head type and, except for the 1965–67 273 cu in. engine, they all have hydraulic tappets. Engines vary in compression ratio, piston displacement, camshafts, valve springs, carburetors, intake manifolds, and exhaust systems.

The 426 cu in. Hemi engine is so named because of its hemispherically shaped combustion chambers. As fitted in 1970 and 1971 Barracudas and Challengers, the Hemi has twin four-barrel carburetors, nonsilenced low-restriction air cleaners exhaust headers, and hydraulic tappets.

General Engine Specifications

Year	Engine Displacement (cu in.)	Carburetor Type	Advertised Horsepower @ rpm ∎	Advertised Torque @ rpm (ft lbs)∎	Bore And Stroke (in.)	Advertised Compression Ratio	Oil Pressure @ 2000 rpm
'65	6-170	1–bbl	101 @ 4400	155 @ 2400	3.406 x 3.125	8.2 : 1	45–65
	6-225	1–bbl	145 @ 4000	215 @ 2800	3.406 x 4.125	8.2 : 1	45–65
	8-273	2–bbl	180 @ 4200	260 @ 1600	3.625 x 3.310	8.8 : 1	45–65
	8-273	4–bbl	235 @ 5200	280 @ 4000	3.625 x 3.310	10.5 : 1	45–65
'66	6-170	1–bbl	101 @ 4400	155 @ 2400	3.406 x 3.125	8.5 : 1	55
	6-225	1–bbl	145 @ 4000	215 @ 2400	3.406 x 4.125	8.4 : 1	55
	8-273	2–bbl	180 @ 4200	260 @ 1600	3.625 x 3.310	8.8 : 1	50
	8-273	4–bbl	235 @ 5200	280 @ 4000	3.625 x 3.310	10.5 : 1	50
	8-273	4–bbl	275 @ 6000	295 @ 4400	3.625 x 3.310	10.5 : 1	50
'67	6-170	1–bbl	115 @ 4400	155 @ 2400	3.406 x 3.125	8.5 : 1	55
	6-225	1–bbl	145 @ 4000	215 @ 2400	3.406 x 4.125	8.4 : 1	55
	8-273	2–bbl	180 @ 4200	260 @ 1600	3.625 x 3.310	8.8 : 1	55
	8-273	4–bbl	235 @ 5200	280 @ 4000	3.625 x 3.310	10.5 : 1	55
	8-383	4–bbl	280 @ 4200	400 @ 2400	4.250 x 3.375	10.0 : 1	55
'68	6-170	1–bbl	115 @ 4400	155 @ 2400	3.406 x 3.125	8.5 : 1	55
	6-225	1–bbl	145 @ 4000	215 @ 2400	3.406 x 4.125	8.4 : 1	55
	8-273	2–bbl	190 @ 4400	260 @ 2000	3.625 x 3.310	9.0 : 1	55
	8-318	2–bbl	230 @ 4400	340 @ 2400	3.910 x 3.310	9.2 : 1	55
	8-340	4–bbl	275 @ 5000	340 @ 3200	4.040 x 3.310	10.5 : 1	55
	8-383	4–bbl	300 @ 4400	400 @ 2400	4.250 x 3.375	10.0 : 1	55
'69	6-170	1–bbl	115 @ 4400	155 @ 2400	3.406 x 3.125	8.5 : 1	55

General Engine Specifications

Year	Engine Displacement (cu in.)	Carburetor Type	Advertised Horsepower @ rpm ■	Advertised Torque @ rpm (ft lbs)■	Bore And Stroke (in.)	Advertised Compression Ratio	Oil Pressure @ 2000 rpm
'69	6-225	1–bbl	145 @ 4000	215 @ 2400	3.406 x 4.125	8.4 : 1	55
	8-273	2–bbl	190 @ 4400	260 @ 2000	3.625 x 3.310	9.0 : 1	55
	8-318	2–bbl	230 @ 4400	340 @ 2400	3.910 x 3.310	9.2 : 1	55
	8-340	4–bbl	275 @ 5000	340 @ 3200	4.040 x 3.310	10.5 : 1	55
	8-383	4–bbl	330 @ 5200	410 @ 3600	4.250 x 3.375	10.0 : 1	55
'70	6-198	1–bbl	125 @ 4400	180 @ 2000	3.406 x 3.640	8.4 : 1	'55
	6-225	1–bbl	145 @ 4000	215 @ 2400	3.406 x 4.125	8.4 : 1	55
	8-318	2–bbl	230 @ 4400	320 @ 2000	3.910 x 3.310	8.8 : 1	55
	8-340	4–bbl	275 @ 5000	340 @ 3200	4.040 x 3.310	10.5 : 1	55
	8-383	2–bbl	290 @ 4400	390 @ 2800	4.250 x 3.375	8.7 : 1	55
	8-383	4–bbl	330 @ 5000	425 @ 3200	4.250 x 3.375	9.5 : 1	55
	8-383 HP	4–bbl	335 @ 5200	425 @ 3400	4.250 x 3.375	10.5 : 1	55
	8-426 Hemi	2 x 4–bbl	425 @ 5000	490 @ 4000	4.250 x 3.750	10.2 : 1	55
	8-440 HP	4–bbl	375 @ 4600	480 @ 3200	4.320 x 3.750	9.7 : 1	55
	8-440 Six Pack	3 x 2–bbl	390 @ 4700	490 @ 3200	4.320 x 3.750	10.5 : 1	55
'71	6-198	1–bbl	125 @ 4400	180 @ 2000	3.406 x 3.640	8.4 : 1	55
	6-225	1–bbl	145 @ 4000	215 @ 2400	3.406 x 4.125	8.4 : 1	55
	8-318	2–bbl	230 @ 4400	320 @ 2000	3.910 x 3.310	8.6 : 1	55
	8-340	4–bbl	275 @ 5000	340 @ 3200	4.040 x 3.310	10.3 : 1	55
	8-340	3 x 2–bbl	290 @ 5000	340 @ 3200	4.040 x 3.310	10.3 : 1	55
	8-383	2–bbl	275 @ 4400	375 @ 2800	4.250 x 3.375	8.5 : 1	55
	8-383 HP	4–bbl	300 @ 4800	410 @ 3400	4.250 x 3.375	8.5 : 1	55
	8-426 Hemi	4–bbl	425 @ 5000	490 @ 4000	4.250 x 3.750	10.2 : 1	55
	8-440 Six Pack	2 x 4–bbl	385 @ 4700	490 @ 3200	4.320 x 3.750	10.3 : 1	55
'72	6-198	1–bbl	100 @ 4400①	160 @ 2400②	3.406 x 3.640	8.4 : 1	55
	6-225	1–bbl	110 @ 4000③	185 @ 2000④	3.406 x 4.125	8.4 : 1	55
	8-318	2–bbl	150 @ 4000	260 @ 1600	3.910 x 3.310	8.6 : 1	55
	8-340	4–bbl	240 @ 4800	290 @ 3600	4.040 x 3.310	8.5 : 1	55

■ 1972 horsepower and torque are SAE net figures. They are measured at the rear of the transmission with all accessories installed and operating. Since the figures vary when a given engine is installed in different models, some figures are representative rather than exact.

① For California vehicles, advertised horsepower is 94 @ 4400 rpm

② For California vehicles, advertised torque is 158 @ 2400 rpm

③ For California vehicles, advertised horsepower is 97 @ 4000 rpm

④ For California vehicles, advertised torque is 180 @ 2000 rpm

HP High Performance

Cylinder Bore, Piston and Ring Specifications

| Year | Engine Displacement (cu in.) | Cylinders (in.) | | Pistons (in.) | Rings (in.) | | | |
| | | Standard bore diameter | Maximum bore oversize | Oversizes available | Side clearance | | End-gap | |
					Compression	Oil	Compression	Oil
1965–72	170, 198, 225	3.4000	0.040	0.005, 0.020, 0.040	0.0015–0.0040	0.0002–0.0050	0.010–0.020	0.015–0.055
	273	3.6250–3.6270	0.040	0.005, 0.020, 0.040	0.0015–0.0030	0.0002–0.0050	0.010–0.020	0.015–0.055
	318	3.9100–3.9120	0.040	0.005, 0.020, 0.040	0.0015–0.0030	0.0002–0.0050	0.010–0.020	0.015–0.055
	340	4.0400–4.0420	0.040	0.005, 0.020, 0.040	0.0015–0.0030	0.0002–0.0050	0.010–0.020	0.015–0.055
	383	4.2495–4.2515	0.040	0.005, 0.020, 0.040	0.0015–0.0030	0.0000–0.0050	0.013–0.023	0.015–0.055
	440	4.3200–4.3220	0.040	0.005, 0.020, 0.040	0.0015–0.0040	0.0000–0.0050	0.013–0.023	0.015–0.055
	426	4.2497 (A) 4.2502 (B) 4.2507 (C) 4.2512 (D) 4.2517 (E)	0.040	0.005, 0.020, 0.040	0.0010–0.0030	0.0002–0.0050	0.013–0.023	0.015–0.055

Crankshaft and Connecting Rod Specifications

Year	Engine Displacement (cu in.)	Main Bearing Journals (in.)					Connecting Rod Bearing Journals (in.)		
		Journal Diameter	No. of Main Bearings	Oil Clearance	Shaft End-Play	Thrust On No.	Journal Diameter	Oil Clearance	End-Play
1965–72	170, 198, 225	2.750	4	0.0005–0.0015	0.002–0.007	3	2.187	0.0005–0.0025	0.006–0.012
	273, 318, 340	2.500	5	0.0005–0.0015	0.002–0.007	3	2.125	0.0005–0.0025	0.006–0.012
	383	2.625	5	0.0005–0.0015	0.002–0.007	3	2.375	0.0007–0.0032	0.009–0.017
	440	2.750	5	0.0005–0.0015	0.002–0.007	3	2.375	0.0007–0.0032	0.009–0.017
	426 Hemi	2.750	5	0.0015–0.0025	0.002–0.007	3	2.375	0.0010–0.0035	0.009–0.017

Valve Specifications

Year and Model		Seat Angle (Deg)	Face Angle (Deg)	Valve Lift Intake (in.)	Valve Lift Exhaust (in.)	Valve Spring Pressure (Valve Open) Lbs @ In.	Valve Spring Installed Height (in.)	Stem to Guide Clearance (in.)		Stem Diameter (in.)	
								Intake	Exhaust	Intake	Exhaust
1965–66	170	45	①	0.371	0.364	145 @ 15/16	1 11/16	0.001–0.003	0.002–0.004	0.372–0.373	0.371–0.372
	225	45	①	0.394	0.390	145 @ 15/16	1 11/16	0.001–0.003	0.002–0.004	0.372–0.373	0.371–0.372
	273, 2-BBL	45	45	0.395	0.405	145 @ 15/16	1 11/16	0.001–0.003	0.002–0.004	0.372–0.373	0.371–0.372
	273, 4-BBL	45	45	0.415	0.425	177 @ 15/16	1 11/16	0.001–0.003	0.002–0.004	0.372–0.373	0.371–0.372
1967	225	45	②	0.395	0.395	145 @ 15/16	1 11/16	0.001–0.003	0.002–0.004	0.372–0.373	0.371–0.372
	273, 2 BBL	45	45	0.395	0.405	145 @ 15/16	1 11/16	0.001–0.003	0.002–0.004	0.372–0.373	0.371–0.372
	273, 4-BBL	45	45	0.415	0.425	177 @ 15/16	1 11/16	0.001–0.003	0.002–0.004	0.372–0.373	0.371–0.372
	383, 4-BBL	45	45	0.425	0.435	230 @ 1 13/32	1 5/64	0.001–0.003	0.002–0.004	0.372–0.373	0.371–0.372
1968	225	45	①	0.395	0.395	145 @ 15/16	1 11/16	0.001–0.003	0.002–0.004	0.372–0.373	0.371–0.372
	318	45	①	0.373	0.399	177 @ 15/16	1 11/16	0.001–0.003	0.002–0.004	0.372–0.373	0.371–0.372
	340	45	①	③	④	242 @ 1 7/32	1 11/16	0.001–0.003	0.002–0.004	0.372–0.373	0.371–0.372
	383, 4-BBL	45	45	0.425	0.435	230 @ 1 13/32	1 5/64	0.001–0.003	0.002–0.004	0.372–0.373	0.371–0.372
1969	225	45	①	0.395	0.395	145 @ 15/16	1 11/16	0.001–0.003	0.002–0.004	0.372–0.373	0.371–0.372
	273, 318	45	①	0.373	0.399	177 @ 15/16	1 11/16	0.001–0.003	0.002–0.004	0.372–0.373	0.371–0.372
	340	45	①	0.429	0.444	242 @ 1 7/32	1 11/16	0.001–0.003	0.002–0.004	0.372–0.373	0.371–0.372
	383, 4-BBL	45	45	0.450	0.458	246 @ 1 13/64	1 5/64	0.001–0.003	0.002–0.004	0.372–0.373	0.371–0.372
1970	225	44.5–45.0	45.0–45.5	0.397	0.393	156 @ 1.26	1.65	0.001–0.003	0.002–0.004	0.372–0.373	0.371–0.372
	318	44.5–45.0	45.0–45.5	0.372	0.400	189 @ 1.28	1.65	0.001–0.003	0.002–0.004	0.372–0.373	0.371–0.372

Valve Specifications

Year and Model		Seat Angle (Deg)	Face Angle (Deg)	Valve Lift Intake (in.)	Valve Lift Exhaust (in.)	Valve Spring Pressure (Valve Open) Lbs @ In.	Valve Spring Installed Height (in.)	Stem to Guide Clearance (in.)		Stem Diameter (in.)	
								Intake	Exhaust	Intake	Exhaust
1970	340	44.5–45.0	45.0–45.5	0.430	0.445	242 @ 1.21	1.65	0.001–0.003	0.002–0.004	0.372–0.373	0.371–0.372
	383, 2-BBL	44.5–45.0	45.0–45.5	0.425	0.437	200 @ 1 7/16	1 55/64	0.0010–0.0027	0.0020–0.0037●	0.372–0.373	0.371–0.372
	383, 4-BBL	44.5–45.0	45.0–45.5	0.425	0.437	234 @ 1 7/16	1 55/64	0.0010–0.0027	0.0020–0.0037●	0.372–0.373	0.371–0.372
	383, Hi Perf	44.5–45.0	45.0–45.5	0.450	0.465	234 @ 1 7/10	1 55/64	0.0010–0.0027	0.0020–0.0037●	0.372–0.373	0.371–0.372
	426	44.5–45.0	45.0–45.5	0.490	0.480	310 @ 1 3/8	1 55/64	0.002–0.004	0.003–0.005	0.3085–0.3095	0.3075–0.3085●
	440, Hi Perf	44.5–45.0	45.0–45.5	0.450	0.465	234 @ 1 7/10	1 55/64	0.0010–0.0027	0.0020–0.0037	0.372–0.373	0.371–0.372
	440, 3-2-BBL	44.5–45.0	45.0–45.5	0.450	0.465	310 @ 1 3/8	1 55/64	0.0010–0.0027	0.0020–0.0037	0.372–0.373	0.371–0.372
1971	198, 225	44.5–45.0	45.0–45.5	0.406	0.414	156 @ 1.26	1 11/16	0.001–0.003	0.002–0.004	0.372–0.373	0.371–0.372
	318	44.5–45.0	45.0–45.5	0.372	0.400	189 @ 1.28	1 11/16	0.001–0.003	0.002–0.004	0.372–0.373	0.371–0.372
	340, 4-BBL/6-BBL	44.5–45.0	45.0–45.5	0.430	0.445	242 @ 1.21	1 11/16	0.0015–0.0035	0.0025–0.0045	0.3715–0.3725	0.3705–0.3715
	383, 2-BBL	44.5–45.0	45.0–45.5	0.425	0.437	200 @ 1 7/16	1 55/64	0.0010–0.0027	0.0020–0.0037●	0.3715–0.3725	0.3713–0.3720●
	383	44.5–45.0	45.0–45.5	0.450	0.465	234 @ 1.40	1 55/64	0.0015–0.0032	0.0020–0.0037●	0.3718–0.3725	0.3708–0.3715●
	426 Hemi	44.5–45.0	45.0–45.5	0.490	0.480	310 @ 1 3/8	1 55/64	0.002–0.004	0.003–0.005	0.3085–0.3095	0.3075–0.3085
	440, 3-2-BBL	44.5–45.0	45.0–45.5	0.450	0.465	310 @ 1 3/8	1 55/64	0.0015–0.0032	0.0025–0.0042●	0.3718–0.3725	0.3708–0.3715●
1972	6 Cyl	44.5–45.0	45.0–45.5	0.397	0.393	156 @ 1.26	1.65	0.001–0.003	0.002–0.004	0.372–0.373	0.371–0.372
	318	44.5–45.0	45.0–45.5	0.372	0.400	189 @ 1.28	1.65	0.001–0.003	0.002–0.004	0.372–0.373	0.371–0.372
	340	44.5–45.0	45.0–45.5	0.430	0.445	242 @ 1.21	1.65	0.001–0.003	0.002–0.004	0.372–0.373	0.371–0.372

① —Intake 45; Exhaust 43.
② —Intake 45; Exhaust 47.
③ —Manual trans. 0.444; Auto trans. 0.429.
④ —Manual trans. 0.453; Auto trans. 0.444.
●—Hot Eng.

Torque Specifications

(All readings in ft lbs)

Year	Engine Displacement (cu in.)	Cylinder Head Bolts	Rod Bearing Bolts	Main Bearing Bolts	Crankshaft Pulley Bolt	Flywheel to Crankshaft Bolts	Manifold	
							Intake	Exhaust
1965–67	170	65	45	85	Press Fit	55	10	10
	225	65	45	85	Press Fit	55	10	10
	273	85	45	85	135	55	35	30
	383	70	45	85	135	55	35	30
1968–70	225	65	45	85	Press Fit	55	10	10
	318, 340	95①	45	85	135	55	35	30
	383, 440	70	45	85	135	55	35	30
	426	70–75②	75	100③	135	70	④	24
1971–72	198, 225	65	45	85	Press Fit	55	10	10
	318, 340	95	45	85	100	55	35	30
	383, 440	70	45	85	135	55	40	30
	426	70–75②	75	100③	135	70	④	24

①—1968–70 318 cu in., 85 ft lbs.
②—Bolts and studs same torque.
③—Side bolts, 45 ft lbs.
④—See text.

ENGINE REMOVAL AND INSTALLATION

1. Scribe hood hinge outlines on the hood and remove the hood.

2. Drain the cooling system and remove the battery.

3. Remove all hoses, fan shroud (if so equipped), oil cooler lines, and radiator.

4. Disconnect the fuel lines, and the linkage and wires connected to the engine. Remove the air cleaner and carburetor.

5. Remove the closed ventilation system and evaporative control system (if so equipped).

6. On all engines, except the 426 Hemi, attach the engine lifting fixture to the carburetor flange studs on the intake manifold. *Do not use the intake manifold studs to remove the 426 engine assembly.* On this engine, attach the front lifting strap to the front of the left cylinder head and the rear strap to the rear of the right cylinder head.

7. Raise the car on a hoist and install a suitable device on the chassis to support the rear of the engine (factory tool C–3487A).

8. Drain the crankcase and the transmission.

9. Disconnect the exhaust pipes at the manifolds. Disconnect the drive shaft, wires, linkage, speedometer cable, and oil cooler lines at the transmission.

10. Remove the rear engine support crossmember and remove the transmission.

11. Lower the car and attach a suitable engine lifting tool to the engine lifting fixture attached to the engine.

12. Remove the front engine mounts and use the lifting tool to remove the engine from the car.

13. Installation is the reverse of the above.

CYLINDER HEAD

Removal and Installation

The procedures described in this section are for servicing the cylinder heads while the engine is in the car but they can be adapted to other situations. Refer to the individual component sections for their removal and installation procedures.

6 CYLINDER ENGINES

The chrome alloy, cast-iron cylinder head is held in place by fourteen bolts. The spark plugs are located at the wide edge of the combustion chambers and aluminum spark plug tubes serve as spark plug gaskets. To remove the cylinder head:

1. Drain the cooling system and disconnect the battery.

2. Remove the air cleaner and the fuel line from the carburetor.

3. Disconnect the accelerator linkage.

4. Remove the vacuum advance line from between the carburetor and the distributor.

5. Disconnect the cables from the spark plugs.

6. Disconnect the heater hose and the clamp which secures the by-pass hose.

7. Disconnect the water temperature sending unit.

8. Disconnect the exhaust pipe at the exhaust manifold flange.

9. Remove the intake and exhaust manifolds, and the carburetor, as an assembly.

10. Remove the closed ventilation system, the evaporative control system (if so equipped), and the valve cover.

11. Remove the rocker arm and shaft assembly.

12. Remove the pushrods and keep them in order to ensure installation in their original locations.

13. Remove the fourteen head bolts and remove the cylinder head.

To install the cylinder head, proceed as follows.

1. Clean all the gasket surfaces of the engine block and the cylinder head, and install the spark plugs.

2. Inspect all surfaces with a straight-edge. If out-of-flatness is indicated, measure the amount. This amount must not exceed 0.00075 times the span length in any direction. For example, if a 12 in. span is 0.004 in. out of flat, the maximum allowable is 12 in. × 0.00075 = 0.009 in. In this case, the head is within limits. If the out-of-flatness exceeds the specified limits, either replace the head or lightly machine the head gasket surface.

3. Coat a new cylinder head gasket with sealer, install the gasket and refit the cylinder head.

4. Install the cylinder head bolts. Torque the cylinder head bolts to 50 ft lbs in the sequence indicated in the illustration. Repeat this sequence to retorque all the head bolts to 65 ft lbs.

5. Reverse the removal procedure steps 1 through 12 to complete the installation. When installing the intake and exhaust manifold assembly, loosen the three bolts which secure the intake manifold to the exhaust manifold to maintain proper alignment. After installation, torque the three bolts to 15 ft lbs in this sequence: inner bolt first, then the outer two bolts.

273, 318, 340, 383, AND 440
CU IN. ENGINES

The chrome alloy, cast-iron cylinder heads are held in place by ten bolts on the 273, 318, and 340 cu in. engines or by seventeen bolts on the 383 and 440 cu in. engines. The spark plugs are located between the valves. To remove the cylinder heads:

1. Drain the cooling system and disconnect the battery ground cable.

2. Remove the alternator, air cleaner, and fuel line.

3. Disconnect the accelerator linkage.

4. Remove the vacuum advance line from between the carburetor and the distributor.

5. Remove the distributor cap and wires as an assembly.

6. Disconnect the coil wires, water temperature sending unit, heater hoses, and by-pass hose.

7. Remove the closed ventilation system, the evaporative control system (if so equipped), and the valve covers.

8. Remove the intake manifold, ignition coil, and carburetor as an assembly.

9. Remove the exhaust manifolds.

10. Remove the rocker and shaft assemblies.

11. Remove the pushrods and keep them in order to ensure installation in their original locations.

12. Remove the head bolts from each cylinder head and remove the cylinder heads.

To install the cylinder heads, proceed as follows.

1. Clean all the gasket surfaces of the engine block and the cylinder heads. Install the spark plugs.

2. Inspect all surfaces with a straight-edge. If out-of-flatness is indicated, measure the amount. This amount must not exceed 0.00075 times the span length in any direction. For example, if a 12 in. span is 0.004 in. out of flat, the maximum allowable is 12 in. × .00075 = 0.009 in. In this case, the head is within limits. If the out-of-flatness exceeds the specified limits, either replace the head or lightly machine the head gasket surface.

3. Coat new cylinder head gaskets with sealer, install the gaskets, and refit the cylinder heads.

4. Install the cylinder head bolts. For 273, 318, and 340 cu in. engines, torque the cylinder head bolts to 50 ft lbs in the sequence indicated in the illustration. Repeat this sequence to retorque all the cylinder head bolts to 85 ft lbs for the 273 and 318 cu in. engines or to 95 ft lbs for the 340 cu in. engine. For 383 and 440 cu in. engines, torque the cylinder head bolts to 40 ft lbs in the sequence indicated. Repeat this sequence to retorque all the cylinder head bolts to 70 ft lbs for both engines.

5. Reverse the removal procedure steps 1 through 12 to complete the installation.

426 HEMI ENGINE

Each chrome alloy, cast-iron cylinder head is held in place by thirteen bolts and five studs, nuts, and washers. The stud nuts are tightened from inside the tappet chamber. Aluminum spark plug tubes serve as spark plug gaskets. These tubes project through the valve covers and are sealed against oil leaks. To remove the cylinder heads:

1. Disconnect the battery ground cable and drain the cooling system.

2. Remove the air cleaner, the distributor cap and the cable assembly.

Removing or Installing cylinder head stud nuts—426 Hemi

3. Remove the cables from the spark plugs and remove the spark plugs.

4. Disconnect the brake lines at the master cylinder and remove the cotter pin and the clevis pin from the linkage at the rear of the power brake unit.

5. Remove the four nuts securing the brake booster to its mounting bracket and remove the power brake and master cylinder assembly.

6. Remove the valve covers and gaskets.

7. Remove the rocker and shaft assemblies.

8. Remove the pushrods and keep them in order to ensure installation in their original locations.

9. Remove the alternator and disconnect the accelerator cable and transmission throttle rod from the upper bellcrank.

10. Disconnect the fuel line at the tee fitting.

11. Disconnect the intake manifold heat tubes located at the rear of the manifold. Remove the air tube between the automatic choke and the exhaust manifold.

12. Remove the intake manifold securing bolts. (There are three locating dowels at each end of the manifold.)

13. Remove the intake manifold with the ignition coil, both carburetors, fuel lines, fuel filters, throttle linkage, and the upper bellcrank as an assembly.

14. Disconnect the exhaust headers from the cylinder heads and tie them out of the way.

15. Remove the *lower* eight cylinder head bolts.

16. Remove the four stud nuts from the cylinder head studs inside the tappet chamber.

17. Remove the cylinder heads and place them on suitable supports. *To pro-*

Cylinder Head Torque Sequences

170, 198, and 225 cu in. engines

273, 318, and 340 cu in. engines

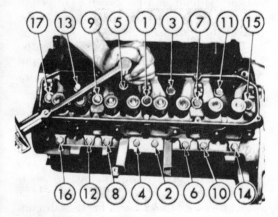

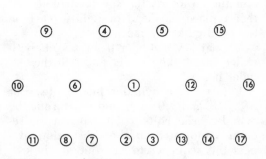

383 and 440 cu in. engines

426 cu in. engine

tect the studs, do not set the cylinder head down on the studs at any time.

To install the cylinder heads, proceed as follows.

1. Clean all the gasket surfaces of the engine block and the cylinder heads.

2. Inspect all surfaces with a straight-edge. If out-of-flatness is indicated, measure the amount. This amount must not exceed 0.00075 times the span length in any direction. For example, if a 12 in. span is 0.004 in. out of flat, the maximum allowable is 12 in. × 0.00075 = 0.009 in. In this case, the head is within limits. If the out-of-flatness exceeds the specified limits, either replace the head or lightly machine the head gasket surface.

3. Coat new cylinder head gaskets with sealer and install the gaskets with their raised beads toward the engine block. If the cylinder head studs were removed or

worked loose, the studs will have to be coated with sealer and torqued to 20 ft lbs. Replace the cylinder heads on the engine block.

4. Install the cylinder head stud nuts inside the tappet chamber and the eight short, lower cylinder head bolts. *Do not tighten at this time.*

5. Install the rocker arm and shaft assemblies and, after refitting the five *long* cylinder head bolts, torque all the head bolts and stud nuts to 50 ft lbs in the sequence indicated in the illustration. Repeat this sequence to retorque all the bolts and stud nuts to 75 ft lbs.

6. Reverse the removal procedure steps 1 through 14 to complete the installation.

Cylinder Head Overhaul

Refer to the engine rebuilding section.

ROCKER SHAFTS

Removal and Installation

6 Cylinder Engines

The rocker arm shaft has twelve straight steel rocker arms arranged on it with hardened steel spacers fitted between each pair of rocker arms. The shaft is secured by bolts and steel retainers which are attached to the seven cylinder head brackets. To remove the rocker arm and shaft assembly:

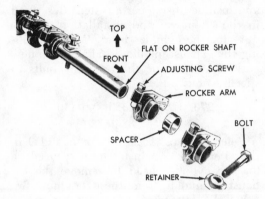

Rocker shaft assembly—six-cylinder engines

1. Remove the closed ventilation system.
2. Remove the evaporative control system (if so equipped).
3. Remove the valve cover and its gasket.
4. Remove the rocker shaft bolts and retainers.
5. Remove the rocker arm and shaft assembly.
6. Reverse the above for installation. The flat on the end of the shaft must be on top and point toward the front of the engine to provide proper lubrication to the rocker arms.
7. Torque all bolts to 25 ft lbs. Before replacing the valve cover, adjust the valves.

273, 318, 340, 383, and 440 Cu In. Engines

The stamped steel rocker arms are arranged on one rocker arm shaft per cylinder head. Because the angle of the push-rods tends to force the rocker arm pairs toward each other, oilite spacers are fitted to absorb the side thrust at each rocker arm. The shaft is secured by bolts and steel retainers attached to the five brackets on the cylinder head. To remove the arm and shaft from each cylinder head:

1. Disconnect the spark plug wires.
2. Disconnect the closed ventilation system and evaporative control system (if so equipped) from the valve cover.
3. Remove each valve cover and gasket.
4. Remove the rocker shaft bolts and retainer.
5. Remove each rocker arm and shaft assembly.
6. Reverse the above for installation. The notch on the end of both rocker shafts should point to the engine centerline and toward the front of the engine on the left cylinder head and toward the rear on the right side.
7. Torque all bolts to the following specifications:

273 cu in. engine, 30 ft lbs;
318 and 340 cu in., 210 in. lbs;
383 and 440 cu in., 25 ft lbs.

426 Hemi Engine

1. Disconnect the battery ground cable.
2. Remove the air cleaner and the distributor cap and cable assembly.
3. Disconnect the spark plug cable and remove the plugs.
4. Disconnect the brake liner at the master cylinder and remove the cotter pin and the clevis pin from the linkage at the rear of the power brake unit.
5. Remove the four nuts securing the brake booster to its mounting bracket and remove the power brake and master cylinder assembly.
6. Remove the valve covers and their gaskets.
7. Remove the five bolts that retain the rocker arm support brackets to the cylinder head and engine block.
8. Remove each rocker arm assembly.
9. Reverse the above for installation. If the rocker arm has been disassembled for cleaning, inspection, or replacement, refer to the illustration for proper reassembly. Note the position of the oil holes in number two and four brackets.

INTAKE MANIFOLD

Removal and Installation

The intake manifold can be removed and installed using certain steps described in the "Removal and Installation" procedures of the cylinder head. When installing the intake manifold, always use new gaskets and seals, and the bolt tightening sequence indicated in the illustration for that particular engine.

273, 318, 340, 383, AND 440 CU IN. ENGINES

Refer to steps 1 through 8 in the "Removal and Installation" procedure in the "Cylinder Head" section to remove the intake manifold from these engines. Reverse the procedure to install the manifold.

When installing the intake manifold on 273, 318, and 340 cu in. engines, use new intake manifold gaskets and side seals. Coat the gaskets and seals with a good commercial sealer. Install the intake manifold gaskets with the bead down and the end seals locked in the tongs of the cylinder head gasket. Add a drop of sealer in the vee notches of the side seals after installation.

Torque the intake manifold bolts on 273, 318, and 340 cu in. engines, in the sequence illustrated, to 25 ft lbs. Using the same sequence, retorque all the bolts to 35 ft lbs. On 383 and 440 cu in. engines, torque the intake manifold bolts in sequence to 25 ft lbs.

426 HEMI ENGINE

Refer to steps 1 through 6 and 9 through 13 in the Hemi "Removal and Installation" procedure of the "Cylinder Head" section. It is not necessary to remove the rocker shaft assemblies and pushrods to remove only the intake manifold.

When installing the intake manifold on the Hemi, use new gaskets and be sure that the gaskets are positioned over the locating dowels marked "A" in the illustration for the intake manifold tightening sequence. Tighten the screws marked "B" to 72 in. lbs and the screws marked "C" to 48 in. lbs in the sequence shown until all the screws maintain their specified torque.

EXHAUST MANIFOLD

Removal and Installation

The exhaust manifolds can be removed and installed using certain steps described in the "Removal and Installation" procedure for the cylinder head. When installing the exhaust manifolds, always use new gaskets and torque the retaining bolts to specifications.

273, 318, 340, 383 AND 440 CU IN. ENGINES

Refer to steps, 1, 2, 3, 5, 6, 7, and 9 in the "Removal and Installation" procedure for the cylinder head to remove the exhaust manifolds from these engines. Reverse the procedure to install the manifolds. Torque the exhaust manifold bolts to 30 ft lbs on all engines.

426 HEMI ENGINES

Refer to steps 1 through 6 in the Hemi "Cylinder Head" removal procedure and proceed as follows:

1. Remove the alternator.

2. Disconnect the intake manifold heat tubes that are located at the rear of the manifold. Remove the air tube which is

Intake Manifold Torque Sequences

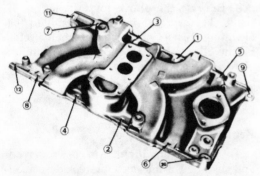

273, 318, and 340 cu in. engines (318 cu in. shown)

426 cu in. engine

found between the automatic choke and the exhaust manifold.

3. Disconnect the exhaust pipes from the exhaust manifolds.

4. Remove the exhaust manifolds.

Reverse the above to install the exhaust manifolds and torque manifold bolts to 35 ft lbs.

COMBINATION MANIFOLD
Removal and Installation
6 CYLINDER ENGINES

The combination intake/exhaust manifold is removed and installed as an assembly on these engines. To remove the manifold assembly, refer to steps 1 through 9 of the "Cylinder Head" removal and installation procedure for these engines.

When installing the manifold assembly, use new gaskets and loosen the three bolts which secure the intake manifold to the exhaust manifold to maintain proper alignment. Torque the three bolts to 15 ft lbs in the sequence: inner bolt first, then the outer two bolts. Torque the manifold assembly-to-cylinder head bolts to 10 ft lbs.

TIMING GEAR COVER
Removal and Installation
6 CYLINDER ENGINES

To remove the timing gear cover:

1. Drain the cooling system.

2. Remove the radiator and the fan.

3. Using a suitable puller, remove the vibration damper from the end of the crankshaft.

4. Loosen the oil pan bolts to allow clearance and remove the timing gear cover and its gasket.

To install the timing gear cover:

1. Be sure that the mating surfaces of the cover and the engine block are clean and free from burrs.

2. Using a new gasket, slide the cover over its locating dowels and torque the securing bolts to 15 ft lbs.

3. Be sure that all of the oil pan gaskets are in place; tighten the pan bolts to 17 ft lbs.

4. Place the damper pulley assembly hub key in the slot in the crankshaft, lubricate the lip of the oil seal with white grease, and slide the hub on the crankshaft.

5. Press the damper pulley assembly onto the crankshaft.

6. Install the fan and radiator. Fill the cooling system.

273, 318, AND 340 CU IN. ENGINES

To remove the timing gear cover:

1. Drain the cooling system and remove the radiator, fan belt, and water pump assembly.

2. Remove the pulley from the vibration damper. Remove the bolt and washer securing the vibration damper on the crankshaft.

3. Using a suitable puller, remove the vibration damper from the end of the crankshaft.

4. Remove the fuel lines and the fuel pump.

5. Loosen the oil pan bolts and remove the front bolt from each side.

6. Remove the timing gear cover while being extremely careful not to damage the oil pan gasket. It is normal to find neoprene particles collected between the crankshaft seal retainer and the crankshaft oil slinger.

To install the timing gear cover:

1. Be sure that the mating surfaces of the cover and the engine block are clean and free from burrs.

2. Using a new gasket, carefully install the cover to avoid damaging the oil pan gasket.

3. Torque the timing gear cover capscrews to 30 ft lbs. Be sure that all of the oil pan gaskets are in place and then torque the pan capscrews to 15 ft lbs.

4. Lubricate the oil seal lip with white grease, position the damper hub slot on the key in the crankshaft, and slide the hub on the crankshaft.

5. Press the damper hub onto the crankshaft.

6. Slide the pulley over the shaft and secure it with the bolts and lockwashers. Torque the bolts to 15 ft lbs.

7. Install the damper hub retainer washer and bolt.

8. Install the fuel pump and fuel lines.

9. Using new gaskets, install the water pump and housing assembly. Torque the securing bolts to 30 ft lbs.

10. Install the radiator, fan and belt, and the hoses. Fill the cooling system.

383 and 440 Cu. In. Engines

To remove the timing gear cover:

1. Drain the cooling system and remove the radiator and the water pump assembly.

2. Remove the crankshaft damper retaining bolt.

3. Remove two of the pulley bolts. Using a suitable puller, remove the vibration damper from the end of the crankshaft.

4. Remove the timing gear cover and its gasket. *It is normal to find neoprene particles collected between the crankshaft seal retainer and the crankshaft oil slinger.*

To install the timing gear cover,

1. Be sure that the mating surfaces of the cover and the engine block are clean and free from burrs.

2. Using a new gasket, slide the cover over its locating dowels and torque the securing bolts to 15 ft lbs.

3. Lubricate the oil seal lip with Lubriplate, position the damper hub slot on the key in the crankshaft, and slide the hub on the crankshaft.

4. Press the damper onto the crankshaft.

5. Install the damper retainer washer and bolt. Torque the retainer bolt to 135 ft lbs.

6. Slide the belt pulley over the shaft and secure it with the bolts and lockwashers. Torque the bolts to 200 in. lbs.

426 Hemi Engine

To remove the timing gear cover:

1. Drain the cooling system and remove the radiator, fan belt and water pump assembly housing. If the car is equipped with power steering, remove the pump and tie it out of the way.

2. Remove the pulley from the vibration damper. Remove the bolt and washer that secure the vibration damper on the crankshaft.

3. Using a suitable puller, remove the damper assembly from the end of the crankshaft.

4. Remove the two front oil pan bolts.

5. Remove the timing gear cover while being extremely careful not to damage the oil pan gasket. *It is normal to find neoprene particles collected between the crankshaft seal retainer and the crankshaft oil slinger.*

To install the timing gear cover:

1. Be sure that the mating surfaces of

the cover and the engine block are clean and free from burrs.

2. Using a new gasket, slide the cover over its locating dowels and torque the securing bolts to 15 ft lbs.

3. Lubricate the oil seal lip with white grease, position the damper hub slot on the key in the crankshaft, and slide the damper on the crankshaft.

4. Press the damper onto the crankshaft.

5. Install the damper retainer washer and bolt. Torque the retainer bolt to 135 ft lbs.

6. Slide the belt pulley over the shaft and secure it with the bolts and lockwashers. Torque the bolts to 200 in. lbs.

Timing Gear Cover Oil Seal Replacement

All Engines

The timing gear cover oil seal can be removed and replaced easily by using the special factory tool (Chrysler Tool no. C —3506). Therefore, it is recommended that the tool be used in this procedure.

1. Remove the timing gear cover.

2. Position the remover screw of the special tool through the timing gear cover with the inside of the cover up.

3. Position the remover blocks directly opposite each other and force the angular lip between the neoprene and the flange of the seal retainer.

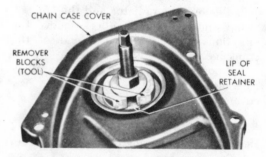

Oil seal remover blocks in position

4. Place the washer and nut on the remover screw. Tighten the nut, forcing the blocks into the gap until the seal retainer lip is distorted. This will position the remover.

5. Place the sleeve over the retainer. Then place the removing and installing plate into the sleeve.

6. Fit the flat washer and nut on the remover screw. Hold the center screw and

tighten the locknut to remove the seal.

7. Insert the remover screw through the removing and installing plate so that the thin shoulder will be facing up.

8. Position the remover screw and plate through the seal opening with the inside of the cover up.

9. Place the new oil seal in the cover opening with the neoprene down. Place the seal installing plate into the new seal with the protective recess toward the seal retainer lip.

10. Fit the flat washer and nut on the remover screw. Hold the center screw and tighten the locknut to install the new seal.

11. The seal is correctly installed when the neoprene is tight against the face of the cover. Try to insert a 0.0015 in. feeler gauge between the neoprene and the cover. If the seal is installed properly, the feeler gauge cannot be inserted. *Do not overcompress the neoprene.*

12. Install the timing gear cover.

TIMING CHAIN

Because there is no timing chain tensioner on these engines, the timing chain should be replaced if it is stretched to the point where camshaft sprocket axial motion, with the crankshaft stationary, exceeds $3/16$ in. To check the timing chain stretch, proceed as follows.

1. Remove the timing gear cover.

2. Slide the crankshaft oil slinger off the crankshaft end.

3. Place a straightedge that is calibrated in inches next to the timing chain at the camshaft sprocket. Any chain movement can be measured here.

4. To take up the timing chain slack, use a torque wrench to rotate the camshaft sprocket lockbolt in the direction of crankshaft rotation. Apply a torque of 30 ft lbs with the cylinder heads installed or 15 ft lbs with the heads removed.

NOTE: *When applying the torque to the camshaft sprocket bolt, the crankshaft should not be allowed to move. If necessary, block the crankshaft to prevent rotation.*

5. Now apply the specified torque to the camshaft sprocket in the reverse direction of crankshaft rotation and note the amount of chain movement. Hold the straightedge so that its dimensional rule is even with the edge of a chain link. If chain move-

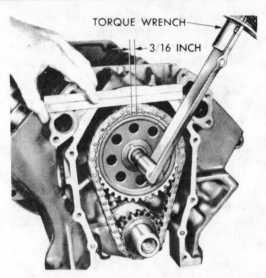

Measuring timing chain stretch

ment exceeds $3/16$ in., install a new timing chain.

6. If the chain is satisfactory, slide the crankshaft oil slinger over the shaft and up against the sprocket with the flange away from the sprocket.

7. Install the timing gear cover.

Removal and Installation

170, 198, AND 225 Cu In. ENGINES

1. Remove the timing gear cover and the crankshaft oil slinger.

2. Remove the camshaft sprocket lockbolt and remove the timing chain with the camshaft sprocket.

3. Turn the crankshaft to line up the timing mark on the crankshaft sprocket.

4. Install the camshaft sprocket and the timing chain.

5. Line up the timing marks on the sprockets with the centerline of the crankshaft and camshaft.

6. Torque the camshaft sprocket lockbolt to 35 ft lbs.

7. Slide the crankshaft oil slinger over the shaft and up against the sprocket with the flange away from the sprocket.

8. Install the timing gear cover.

273, 318, 340, 383, 440, AND 426 Cu In. ENGINES

CAUTION: *When installing a timing chain on a V8 engine, have an assistant support the camshaft with a screwdriver to prevent the camshaft from contacting the freeze plug in the rear of the engine block. Remove the distributor and the oil pump/distributor drive gear. Position the screwdriver against the rear side of the cam gear and be careful not to damage the cam lobes.*

1. Remove the timing gear cover and the crankshaft oil slinger.

2. On 273, 318, and 340 cu in. engines, remove the camshaft sprocket lockbolt, securing cup washer, and fuel pump eccentric. Remove the timing chain with the camshaft and crankshaft sprockets. On 383, 440, and 426 cu in. engines, remove the camshaft sprocket lockbolt and remove the timing chain with the camshaft and crankshaft sprockets.

3. Place the camshaft and crankshaft sprockets on a flat surface with their timing marker on an imaginary centerline through both sprocket bores.

4. Position the timing chain around both sprockets.

5. Turn the crankshaft and camshafts to line up with the keyway location in the crankshaft sprocket and the dowel hole in the camshaft sprocket.

6. Lift the sprockets and timing chains while keeping the sprockets tight against the chain in the correct position, and slide both sprockets evenly onto their respective shafts.

7. Use a straightedge to measure the alignment of the sprocket timing marks.

8. On 273, 318, and 340 cu in. engines, install the fuel pump eccentric, cup washer, and camshaft sprocket lockbolt. Torque the lockbolt to 35 ft lbs. On 383 and 440 cu in. engines, install the washer and camshaft sprocket lockbolt. Torque the lockbolt to 35 ft lbs. Check to make sure that the rear face of the camshaft sprocket is flush with the camshaft end. On the 426 Hemi, install the washers and camshaft lockbolt. Torque the lockbolt to 40 ft lbs.

CAMSHAFT

The camshafts used on all engines have an integral oil pump and distributor drive gear. The fuel pump eccentric is also integral with the camshaft on all engines except the 273, 318, and 340 cu in. engines, which have a bolt-on fuel pump eccentric. These three engines have a plate on the camshaft to absorb the rearward thrust of the camshaft. The other engines absorb the camshaft thrust on the rear face of the aluminum camshaft sprocket hub, which bears directly on the front of the engine block.

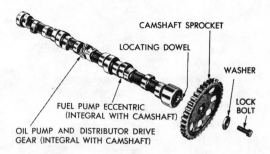

Camshaft and sprocket assembly—170, 198, and 225 cu in. engines

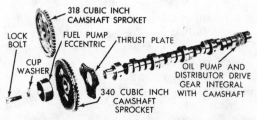

Camshaft and sprocket assembly—318 and 340 cu in. engines. The assembly for the 273 cu in. engine is similar.

Alignment of timing marks

Removal and Installation

When servicing the camshaft, refer to the "Cylinder Head" removal and installation procedures because the cylinder head(s) must be removed before the camshaft can be removed.

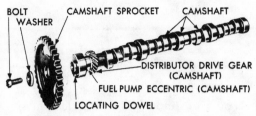

Camshaft and sprocket assembly—383 and 440 cu in. engines

NOTE: *Whenever a new camshaft and/or new tappets are installed, the manufacturer recommends that one quart of their engine oil supplement (Chrysler part no. 1879406), or equivalent, should be added to the engine oil to aid break-in. This oil mixture should be left in the engine for a minimum of 500 miles.*

6 Cylinder Engines

1. Remove the cylinder head. Remove the timing gear cover, camshaft sprocket, and timing chain.
2. Remove the valve tappets, keeping them in order to ensure installation in their original location.
3. Remove the crankshaft sprocket.
4. Remove the distributor and the oil pump.
5. Remove the fuel pump.
6. Fit a long bolt into the front of the camshaft to facilitate camshaft removal.
7. Remove the camshaft, being careful not to damage the cam bearings with the cam lobes.
8. Lubricate the camshaft lobes and bearing journals with camshaft lubricant. Insert the camshaft into the engine block.
9. Install the fuel pump and oil pump.
10. Install the distributor (refer to the "Distributor Installation" procedure).
11. Inspect the crowns of all the tappet faces with a straightedge. Replace any tappets that have dished or worn surfaces. Install the tappets.
12. Replace the timing gear, timing gear cover, and the cylinder head.

V8 Engines

1. Remove the cylinder heads. Remove the timing gear cover, camshaft and crankshaft sprocket, and the timing chain.
2. Remove the valve tappets, keeping them in order to ensure installation in their original location.
3. Remove the distributor and lift out the oil pump and distributor driveshaft.
4. Remove the camshaft thrust plate (if so equipped).
5. Fit a long bolt into the front of the camshaft and remove the camshaft, being careful not to damage the cam bearings with the cam lobes.
6. Lubricate the camshaft lobes and bearing journals with camshaft lubricant. Insert the camshaft into the engine block within two inches of its final position in the block.
7. Have an assistant support the camshaft with a screwdriver to prevent the camshaft from contacting the freeze plug in the rear of the engine block. Remove the distributor and the oil pump distributor drive gear. Position the screwdriver against the rear side of the cam gear and be careful not to damage the cam lobes.
8. Refit the camshaft thrust plate (if so equipped).
9. Install the oil pump and distributor driveshaft. Install the distributor (refer to the "Distributor Installation" procedure).
10. Inspect the crown of all the tappet faces with a straightedge. Replace any tappets that have dished or worn surfaces. Install the tappets.
11. Install the timing gear, gear cover, and the cylinder heads.

PISTONS AND CONNECTING RODS

Removal and Installation

All Engines

1. Use a ridge reamer to remove the top ridge of the cylinder bores. Keep the piston tops covered during the reaming operation.
2. Inspect the connecting rods and rod caps for cylinder identification. If necessary, make identification marks.
3. Rotate the crankshaft so that the piston and connecting rod to be removed are at bottom dead center.
4. Remove the connecting rod cap bolts and remove the cap. Cover the rod bolt threads with masking tape or small pieces

INDENT—ASSEMBLE TOWARDS FRONT OF ENGINE

OIL HOLE—ASSEMBLE TOWARDS RIGHT SIDE OF ENGINE

Correct positioning of piston and connecting rod —all six-cylinder engines

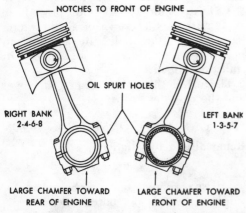

NOTCHES TO FRONT OF ENGINE

OIL SPURT HOLES

RIGHT BANK 2-4-6-8

LEFT BANK 1-3-5-7

LARGE CHAMFER TOWARD REAR OF ENGINE

LARGE CHAMFER TOWARD FRONT OF ENGINE

Correct positioning of piston and connecting rod —all eight-cylinder engines

of rubber tubing. This will protect the bolts and the camshaft journals.

5. Push each piston out of the top of its cylinder bore. Install its corresponding rod bearing cap.

6. Reverse the above to reassemble. Be sure that the rod bolt threads are pro-

tected and that the respective connecting rod crankshaft journal is at bottom dead center. Refer to the illustration for the correct positioning of the piston and connecting rod. Torque the rod bearing cap bolts to specifications.

Engine Lubrication

6 Cylinder Engines

The six-cylinder engine lubrication system has a rotor-type oil pump which is mounted externally on the lower right side of the engine block. A full-flow replaceable-element type of oil filter is located at the rear of the oil pump body. The pump forces the engine oil to a series of passages in the engine as depicted in the illustration.

V8 Engines

The V8 engine lubrication system is shown in the illustration. The 273, 318, and 340 cu in. engines have their oil pumps mounted internally, while the 383, 440, and 426 cu in. engines have externally mounted pumps. The pump forces oil through a full-flow replaceable-element type of filter to a series of oil passages in the engine.

OIL PAN

Removal and Installation

6 Cylinder Engines

1. Raise the car on a hoist. Drain the oil pan.

2. Remove the center link from the steering and idler arm ball joints. (See chapter 8.)

3. Remove the motor mount stud nuts.

4. Lower the car. Disconnect the battery ground cable. Remove the oil level dipstick, air cleaner, and fan shroud (if so equipped).

5. Attach an engine lift plate and raise the engine from one and one-half to two inches.

6. Raise the car again. Remove the oil pan bolts. Rotate the crankshaft so that the oil pan will clear the counterweight and remove the pan.

7. Installation is the reverse of the

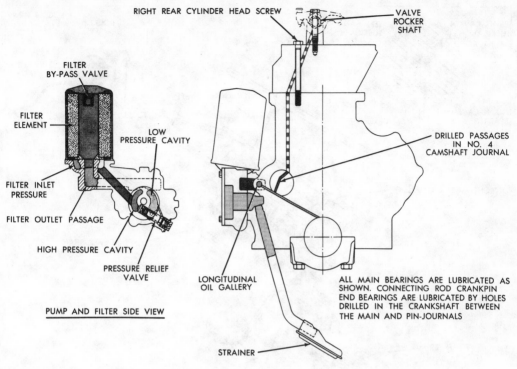

RIGHT REAR CYLINDER HEAD SCREW

VALVE
ROCKER
SHAFT

FILTER
BY-PASS VALVE

FILTER
ELEMENT

LOW
PRESSURE CAVITY

DRILLED PASSAGES
IN NO. 4
CAMSHAFT JOURNAL

FILTER INLET
PRESSURE

FILTER OUTLET PASSAGE

HIGH PRESSURE CAVITY

PRESSURE RELIEF
VALVE

LONGITUDINAL
OIL GALLERY

ALL MAIN BEARINGS ARE LUBRICATED AS
SHOWN. CONNECTING ROD CRANKPIN
END BEARINGS ARE LUBRICATED BY HOLES
DRILLED IN THE CRANKSHAFT BETWEEN
THE MAIN AND PIN-JOURNALS

PUMP AND FILTER SIDE VIEW

STRAINER

Engine lubrication system—170, 198, and 225 cu in. engines

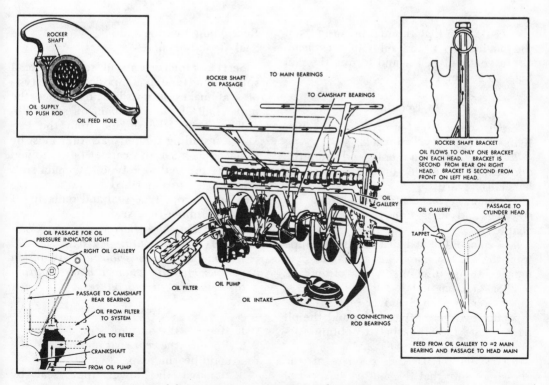

ROCKER
SHAFT

ROCKER SHAFT
OIL PASSAGE

TO MAIN BEARINGS

TO CAMSHAFT BEARINGS

OIL SUPPLY
TO PUSH ROD

OIL FEED HOLE

ROCKER SHAFT BRACKET

OIL FLOWS TO ONLY ONE BRACKET
ON EACH HEAD. BRACKET IS
SECOND FROM REAR ON RIGHT
HEAD. BRACKET IS SECOND FROM
FRONT ON LEFT HEAD.

OIL
GALLERY

OIL PASSAGE FOR OIL
PRESSURE INDICATOR LIGHT

RIGHT OIL GALLERY

PASSAGE TO
CYLINDER HEAD

OIL GALLERY

TAPPET

PASSAGE TO CAMSHAFT
REAR BEARING

OIL FROM FILTER
TO SYSTEM

OIL TO FILTER

CRANKSHAFT

FROM OIL PUMP

OIL FILTER

OIL PUMP

OIL INTAKE

TO CONNECTING
ROD BEARINGS

FEED FROM OIL GALLERY TO =2 MAIN
BEARING AND PASSAGE TO HEAD MAIN

Engine lubrication system—273, 318, and 340 cu in. engines

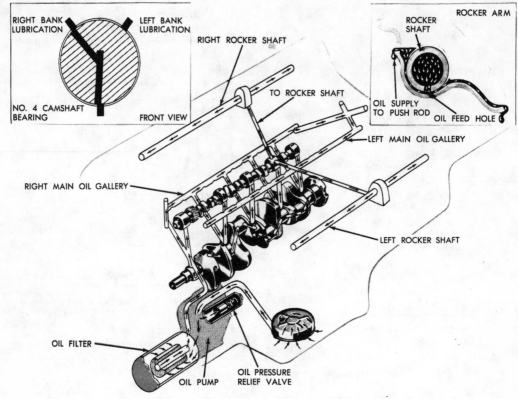

Engine lubrication system—383, 440, and 426 cu in. engines

above. Be sure that the mating surfaces of the engine block and oil pan are clean. Use a new pan gasket and torque the pan bolts to 200 in. lbs.

V8 ENGINES

1. Disconnect the battery ground cable. Remove the oil level dipstick.

2. Raise the car on a hoist and drain the oil. Remove the engine-to-torque converter left housing strut.

3. Remove the center link from the steering and idler arm ball joints. (See chapter 8.)

4. Remove the exhaust crossover pipe from the exhaust manifolds and allow it to hang without disconnecting it from the muffler. On some models it will be necessary to remove the crossover pipe.

5. Remove the oil pan bolts and the oil pan. Rotate the crankshaft to obtain adequate clearance.

6. Installation is the reverse of the above. Be sure that the mating surfaces of the engine block and oil pan are clean. Use a new pan gasket.

Rear Main Bearing Oil Seal Replacement

Service replacement oil seals are of a split-rubber type of composition. This type of seal makes it possible to replace the upper half of the rear main oil seal without removing the engine from the car. When installing rubber seals, they must be replaced as a set and cannot be combined with the original rope-type rear main seal. The procedure described below is for removing the rope-type seal and replacing it with the rubber-type seal.

NOTE: *On those Barracudas and Challengers that are equipped with the 426 Hemi, the transmission and vibration damper must be removed before starting the replacement procedure.*

REMOVAL

1. Remove the oil pan.

2. Remove the rear seal retainer and the rear main bearing cap.

3. Remove the lower rope seal by prying from the side with a small screwdriver.

4. To remove the upper rope seal, use a six-inch piece of ³⁄₁₆ in. brazing rod to drive up on either exposed end of the seal. When the opposite end of the seal starts to protrude from the engine block, have an assistant grasp it with pliers and gently pull it from the block while the opposite end is being driven.

INSTALLATION

1. Wipe the crankshaft clean and lightly oil the crankshaft and the new seal.

2. Loosen all the main bearing caps slightly to lower the crankshaft. This will ease installation.

CAUTION: *Do not allow the crankshaft to drop far enough to permit the main bearings to become displaced on the crankshaft.*

3. Use a thumb to hold the seal tightly against the crankshaft (with its paint stripe to the rear) and install the seal in the engine block groove. If necessary, rotate the crankshaft while installing the seal in the groove. *Make sure that the sharp edges on the block groove do not cut or nick the rear of the seal.*

4. Install the lower seal half (with its paint stripe to the rear) into the lower seal retainer.

5. Install the rear main bearing cap.

6. Be sure that all of the main bearings are located in their proper positions before tightening the main bearing caps. Torque the cap bolts to specification.

OIL PUMP

Removal and Installation

6 CYLINDER ENGINES

1. Drain the radiator and the oil pan. Disconnect the upper and lower radiator hoses. Remove the fan shroud (if so equipped).

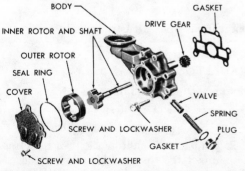

Exploded view of oil pump—170, 198, and 225 cu in. engines

2. Raise the car. Support the front of the engine with a jack stand placed under the right front corner of the oil pan. *Do not support the engine at the crankshaft pulley or vibration damper.*

3. Remove the front engine mount bolts and raise the engine approximately one and one-half to two inches.

4. Remove the oil filter. Withdraw the oil pump mounting bolts and remove the pump assembly.

5. Installation is the reverse of the above. Use new oil seal rings and torque the oil pump mounting bolts to 200 in. lbs.

273, 318, AND 340 CU IN. ENGINES

To service the oil pump on these engines, remove the oil pan and then remove the oil pump from the rear main bearing cap.

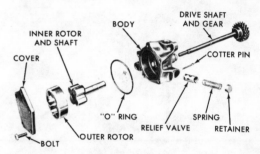

Exploded view of oil pump—273, 318, and 340 cu in. engines

383, 440, AND 426 CU IN. ENGINES

On these engines, the oil pump is removed by first draining the crankcase, and then withdrawing the oil pump mounting bolts. Remove the pump and filter assem-

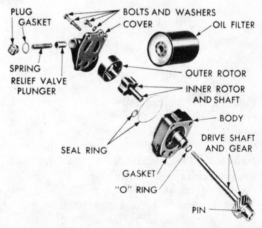

Exploded view of oil pump and filter assembly—383, 440, and 426 cu in. engines

bly. Depending on the particular engine installation, some components of the engine compartment may have to be removed to gain access to the pump and the filter assembly.

Engine Cooling

The Barracuda and Challenger cooling system is of conventional design consisting of a radiator, water pump, and thermostat. On those models that are equipped with automatic transmissions there is a cooler located in the bottom of the radiator tank for the transmission fluid.

top speed of the fan to a predetermined level at higher engine speeds. The other unit is only used on air-conditioned models and is called Thermal Control Drive. This device is essentially the same as the Torque Control Drive unit except for a thermostatic spring. The thermostat senses the radiator temperature and, if the tem-

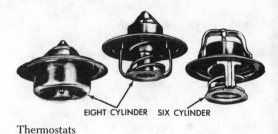

EIGHT CYLINDER   SIX CYLINDER

Thermostats

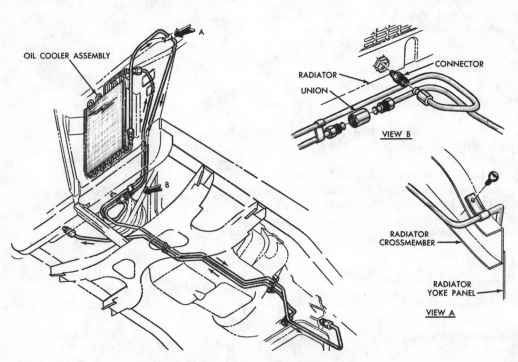

Fluid flow in transmission oil cooler (Hemi automatic shown)

On most engines, a conventional engine-driven cooling fan forces air over the engine. However, some Barracuda and Challenger models are fitted with special cooling fan units which use a silicone fluid coupling device to disengage the fan under certain conditions.

One of these fluid coupling units is called Torque Control Drive. It allows the fan to be driven in the normal manner at low engine speeds while limiting the

perature is above a certain point, will engage the fan drive for a higher fan speed.

RADIATOR

Removal and Installation

ALL MODELS

1. Drain the cooling system.

2. On cars with automatic transmissions, disconnect the fluid cooler lines at the radiator bottom tank. To avoid fluid loss or

dirt contamination, plug the cooler lines.

3. Remove the upper and lower radiator hoses.

4. Remove the fan shroud securing screws and separate the shroud from the radiator. Move the shroud toward the engine as far as possible to obtain maximum clearance for removing the radiator.

5. Remove the radiator mounting screws.

6. Lift the radiator out of the engine compartment.

CAUTION: *Extreme care should be taken not to damage the radiator cooling fins or water tubes during removal.*

7. Reverse the above to install the radiator. Fill the cooling system to one and one-fourth inches below the filler neck with the correct water and antifreeze mixture. Warm up the engine and check the coolant level. On cars with automatic transmissions, check the fluid level after warm-up and add fluid as required.

WATER PUMP

Removal and Installation

ALL MODELS

NOTE: *The water pump is serviced only as an assembly. When replacing the water pump, do not install a standard water pump on an air-conditioned car or vice versa.*

1. Drain the cooling system.

2. Remove the fan shroud securing screws and move the shroud out of the way.

3. It may be necessary to remove the radiator on some models to obtain the working clearance necessary to remove the water pump.

4. Loosen the alternator mounting bolts. Loosen the mounting bolts for the power steering pump, idler pulley, air conditioning compressor, and air pump (if so equipped). Remove all the accessory belts.

5. Remove the fan, spacer or fluid drive, and the pulley.

CAUTION: *For fluid-coupled fan drives, do not position the drive unit with its shaft pointing downward. This will prevent the silicone fluid from draining into the fan-drive bearing and thereby contaminating the grease.*

6. On some models, it may be necessary to remove the alternator or compressor mounting bracket bolts from the water pump to swing the alternator or compressor out of the way.

7. Withdraw the bolts which secure the water pump body to its engine block housing. Remove the water pump and discard the gasket.

8. Install the water pump with a new gasket on its housing. Torque its securing bolts to 30 ft lbs.

9. Rotate the pump shaft by hand to be sure that it rotates freely. Refit the alternator or compressor mounting bracket to the pump if either was removed. Install the pulley, spacer or fluid drive, and the fan. Torque their retaining nuts to 15 ft lbs.

10. Refit all the accessory drive belts and tighten them using the procedure described for the "Alternator Belt Tension Adjustment."

11. Install the radiator if it was removed.

12. Install the fan shroud. Fill the cooling system to one and one-fourth inches below the filler neck with correct water and antifreeze mixture. Warm up the engine and inspect the water pump for any leaks. Check the coolant level and add as required.

THERMOSTAT

The thermostat is located in a housing (to which the upper radiator hose is connected) on the engine. The thermostat is actuated by a copper-impregnated wax pellet which expands and opens the valve as the coolant temperature increases. The thermostat is identified by its opening temperature as listed in the chart below.

Year	Engine Displacement (cu in.)	Standard Thermostat (Opening Temperature, °F)
1965–68	All	180
1969	All	190
1970	225, 340, 383 4-BBL, 426, and 440	190
	318 and 383 2-BBL	195
1971–72	All	185

Removal, Testing, and Installation

ALL MODELS

1. Drain the cooling system to below the level of the thermostat.

2. Remove the upper radiator hose from the thermostat housing.

3. Withdraw the housing bolts and remove the housing and the thermostat.

4. Check to make sure the thermostat valve closes tightly. If the valve does not close completely due to foreign material, carefully clean the sealing edge of the valve while being careful not to damage the sealing edge. If the valve does not close tightly after it has been cleaned, a new thermostat must be installed.

5. Immerse the thermostat in a container of warm water so that its pellet is completely covered and does not touch the bottom or sides of the container.

6. Heat the water and, while stirring the water continuously (to ensure uniform temperature), check the water temperature with a thermometer at the point when a 0.001 in. feeler gauge can be inserted in the valve opening. The water temperature should be within plus or minus five degrees of the standard thermostat opening temperature. If the thermostat does not open within the temperature range, replace it with a new thermostat.

7. Continue heating the water to a temperature of approximately twenty degrees higher than the standard thermostat opening temperature. At this point, the thermostat should be fully open. If it is not, install a new thermostat.

8. To install, use a new gasket and position the thermostat so that its pellet end is toward the engine block. Refit the thermostat housing and tighten its securing bolts.

9. Refit the upper radiator hose.

10. Fill the cooling system to one and one-quarter inches below the filler neck with the correct water and antifreeze mixture. Warm up the engine and inspect the upper radiator hose and the thermostat housing for leaks.

Engine Rebuilding

This section describes, in detail, the procedures involved in rebuilding a typical engine. The procedures specifically refer to an inline engine, however, they are basically identical to those used in rebuilding engines of nearly all design and configurations. Procedures for servicing atypical engines (i.e., horizontally opposed) are described in the appropriate section, although in most cases, cylinder head reconditioning procedures described in this chapter will apply.

The section is divided into two sections. The first, Cylinder Head Reconditioning, assumes that the cylinder head is removed from the engine, all manifolds are removed, and the cylinder head is on a workbench. The camshaft should be removed from overhead cam cylinder heads. The second section, Cylinder Block Reconditioning, covers the block, pistons, connecting rods and crankshaft. It is assumed that the engine is mounted on a work stand, and the cylinder head and all accessories are removed.

Procedures are identified as follows:

Unmarked—Basic procedures that must be performed in order to successfully complete the rebuilding process.

Starred (*)—Procedures that should be performed to ensure maximum performance and engine life.

Double starred (**)—Procedures that may be performed to increase engine performance and reliability. These procedures are usually reserved for extremely heavy-duty or competition usage.

In many cases, a choice of methods is also provided. Methods are identified in the same manner as procedures. The choice of method for a procedure is at the discretion of the user.

The tools required for the basic rebuilding procedure should, with minor exceptions, be those

TORQUE (ft. lbs.)*

U.S.

Bolt Diameter (inches)	Bolt Grade (SAE)				Wrench Size (inches)	
	1 and 2	5	6	8	Bolt	Nut
1/4	5	7	10	10.5	3/8	7/16
5/16	9	14	19	22	1/2	9/16
3/8	15	25	34	37	9/16	5/8
7/16	24	40	55	60	5/8	3/4
1/2	37	60	85	92	3/4	13/16
9/16	53	88	120	132	7/8	7/8
5/8	74	120	167	180	15/16	1
3/4	120	200	280	296	1-1/8	1-1/8
7/8	190	302	440	473	1-5/16	1-5/16
1	282	466	660	714	1-1/2	1-1/2

Metric

Bolt Diameter (mm)	Bolt Grade				Wrench Size (mm)
	5D	8G	10K	12K	Bolt and Nut
6	5	6	8	10	10
8	10	16	22	27	14
10	19	31	40	49	17
12	34	54	70	86	19
14	55	89	117	137	22
16	83	132	175	208	24
18	111	182	236	283	27
22	182	284	394	464	32
24	261	419	570	689	36

*—Torque values are for lightly oiled bolts. CAUTION: Bolts threaded into aluminum require much less torque.

General Torque Specifications

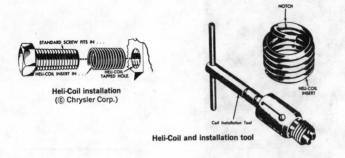

Heli-Coil installation
(© Chrysler Corp.)

Heli-Coil and installation tool

Heli-Coil Insert		Insert Length (In.)	Drill	Tap	Insert. Tool	Extracting Tool
Thread Size	Part No.		Size	Part No.	Part No.	Part No.
1/2 -20	1185-4	3/8	17/64 (.266)	4 CPB	528-4N	1227-6
5/16-18	1185-5	15/32	Q (.332)	5 CPB	528-5N	1227-6
3/8 -16	1185-6	9/16	X (.397)	6 CPB	528-6N	1227-6
7/16-14	1185-7	21/32	29/64 (.453)	7 CPB	528-7N	1227-16
1/2 -13	1185-8	3/4	33/64 (.516)	8 CPB	528-8N	1227-16

Heli-Coil Specifications

included in a mechanic's tool kit. An accurate torque wrench, and a dial indicator (reading in thousandths) mounted on a universal base should be available. Bolts and nuts with no torque specification should be tightened according to size (see chart). Special tools, where required, all are readily available from the major tool suppliers (i.e., Craftsman, Snap-On, K-D). The services of a competent automotive machine shop must also be readily available.

When assembling the engine, any parts that will be in frictional contact must be pre-lubricated, to provide protection on initial start-up. Vortex Pre-Lube, STP, or any product specifically formulated for this purpose may be used. NOTE: *Do not use engine oil.* Where semi-permanent (locked but removable) installation of bolts or nuts is desired, threads should be cleaned and coated with Loctite. Studs may be permanently installed using Loctite Stud and Bearing Mount.

Aluminum has become increasingly popular for use in engines, due to its low weight and excellent heat transfer characteristics. The following precautions must be observed when handling aluminum engine parts:
—Never hot-tank aluminum parts.
—Remove all aluminum parts (identification tags, etc.) from engine parts before hot-tanking (otherwise they will be removed during the process).
—Always coat threads lightly with engine oil or anti-seize compounds before installation, to prevent seizure.
—Never over-torque bolts or spark plugs in aluminum threads. Should stripping occur, threads can be restored according to the following procedure, using Heli-Coil thread inserts:

Tap drill the hole with the stripped threads to the specified size (see chart). Using the specified tap (NOTE: *Heli-Coil tap sizes refer to the size thread being replaced, rather than the actual tap size*), tap the hole for the Heli-Coil. Place the insert on the proper installation tool (see chart). Apply pressure on the insert while winding it clockwise into the hole, until the top of the insert is one turn below the surface. Remove the installation tool, and break the installation tang from the bottom of the in-

sert by moving it up and down. If the Heli-Coil must be removed, tap the removal tool firmly into the hole, so that it engages the top thread, and turn the tool counter-clockwise to extract the insert.

Snapped bolts or studs may be removed, using a stud extractor (unthreaded) or Vise-Grip pliers (threaded). Penetrating oil (e.g., Liquid Wrench) will often aid in breaking frozen threads. In cases where the stud or bolt is flush with, or below the surface, proceed as follows:

Drill a hole in the broken stud or bolt, approximately 1/2 its diameter. Select a screw extractor (e.g., Easy-Out) of the proper size, and tap it into the stud or bolt. Turn the extractor counterclockwise to remove the stud or bolt.

Magnaflux and Zyglo are inspection techniques used to locate material flaws, such as stress cracks. Magnafluxing coats the part with fine magnetic particles, and subjects the part to a magnetic field. Cracks cause breaks

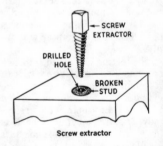

Screw extractor

in the magnetic field, which are outlined by the particles. Since Magnaflux is a magnetic process, it is applicable only to ferrous materials. The Zyglo process coats the material with a fluorescent dye penetrant, and then subjects it to blacklight inspection, under which cracks glow bright-

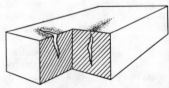

Magnaflux indication of cracks

ly. Parts made of any material may be tested using Zyglo. While Magnaflux and Zyglo are excellent for general inspection, and locating hidden defects, specific checks of suspected cracks may be made at lower cost and more readily using spot check dye. The dye is sprayed onto the suspected area, wiped off, and the area is then sprayed with a developer. Cracks then will show up bright-ly. Spot check dyes will only indicate surface cracks; therefore, structural cracks below the surface may escape detection. When questionable, the part should be tested using Magnaflux or Zyglo.

CYLINDER HEAD RECONDITIONING

Procedure	Method
Identify the valves:  **Valve identification** (© SAAB)	Invert the cylinder head, and number the valve faces front to rear, using a permanent felt-tip marker.
Remove the rocker arms:	Remove the rocker arms with shaft(s) or balls and nuts. Wire the sets of rockers, balls and nuts together, and identify according to the corresponding valve.
Remove the valves and springs:	Using an appropriate valve spring compressor (depending on the configuration of the cylinder head), compress the valve springs. Lift out the keepers with needlenose pliers, release the compressor, and remove the valve, spring, and spring retainer.
Check the valve stem-to-guide clearance:  **Checking the valve stem-to-guide clearance** (© American Motors Corp.)	Clean the valve stem with lacquer thinner or a similar solvent to remove all gum and varnish. Clean the valve guides using solvent and an expanding wire-type valve guide cleaner. Mount a dial indicator so that the stem is at 90° to the valve stem, as close to the valve guide as possible. Move the valve off its seat, and measure the valve guide-to-stem clearance by moving the stem back and forth to actuate the dial indicator. Measure the valve stems using a micrometer, and compare to specifications, to determine whether stem or guide wear is responsible for excessive clearance.
De-carbon the cylinder head and valves:  **Removing carbon from the cylinder head** (© Chevrolet Div. G.M. Corp.)	Chip carbon away from the valve heads, combustion chambers, and ports, using a chisel made of hardwood. Remove the remaining deposits with a stiff wire brush. NOTE: *Ensure that the deposits are actually removed, rather than burnished.*

Procedure	Method
Hot-tank the cylinder head:	Have the cylinder head hot-tanked to remove grease, corrosion, and scale from the water passages. NOTE: *In the case of overhead cam cylinder heads, consult the operator to determine whether the camshaft bearings will be damaged by the caustic solution.*
Degrease the remaining cylinder head parts:	Using solvent (i.e., Gunk), clean the rockers, rocker shaft(s) (where applicable), rocker balls and nuts, springs, spring retainers, and keepers. Do not remove the protective coating from the springs.
Check the cylinder head for warpage:  Checking the cylinder head for warpage (© Ford Motor Co.)	Place a straight-edge across the gasket surface of the cylinder head. Using feeler gauges, determine the clearance at the center of the straight-edge. Measure across both diagonals, along the longitudinal centerline, and across the cylinder head at several points. If warpage exceeds .003″ in a 6″ span, or .006″ over the total length, the cylinder head must be resurfaced. NOTE: *If warpage exceeds the manufacturers maximum tolerance for material removal, the cylinder head must be replaced.* When milling the cylinder heads of V-type engines, the intake manifold mounting position is altered, and must be corrected by milling the manifold flange a proportionate amount.
** Porting and gasket matching:  Marking the cylinder head for gasket matching (© Petersen Publishing Co.)  Port configuration before and after gasket matching (© Petersen Publishing Co.)	** Coat the manifold flanges of the cylinder head with Prussian blue dye. Glue intake and exhaust gaskets to the cylinder head in their installed position using rubber cement and scribe the outline of the ports on the manifold flanges. Remove the gaskets. Using a small cutter in a hand-held power tool (i.e., Dremel Moto-Tool), gradually taper the walls of the port out to the scribed outline of the gasket. Further enlargement of the ports should include the removal of sharp edges and radiusing of sharp corners. Do not alter the valve guides. NOTE: *The most efficient port configuration is determined only by extensive testing. Therefore, it is best to consult someone experienced with the head in question to determine the optimum alterations.*

Procedure	Method
** Polish the ports:  Relieved and polished ports (© Petersen Publishing Co.)  Polished combustion chamber (© Petersen Publishing Co.)	** Using a grinding stone with the above mentioned tool, polish the walls of the intake and exhaust ports, and combustion chamber. Use progressively finer stones until all surface imperfections are removed. NOTE: *Through testing, it has been determined that a smooth surface is more effective than a mirror polished surface in intake ports, and vice-versa in exhaust ports.*
* Knurling the valve guides:  Cut-away view of a knurled valve guide (© Petersen Publishing Co.)	* Valve guides which are not excessively worn or distorted may, in some cases, be knurled rather than replaced. Knurling is a process in which metal is displaced and raised, thereby reducing clearance. Knurling also provides excellent oil control. The possibility of knurling rather than replacing valve guides should be discussed with a machinist.
Replacing the valve guides: NOTE: *Valve guides should only be replaced if damaged or if an oversize valve stem is not available.* 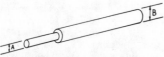 A-VALVE GUIDE I.D. B-SLIGHTLY SMALLER THAN VALVE GUIDE O.D. Valve guide removal tool 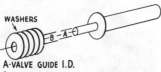 A-VALVE GUIDE I.D. B-LARGER THAN THE VALVE GUIDE O.D. Valve guide installation tool (with washers used during installation)	Depending on the type of cylinder head, valve guides may be pressed, hammered, or shrunk in. In cases where the guides are shrunk into the head, replacement should be left to an equipped machine shop. In other cases, the guides are replaced as follows: Press or tap the valve guides out of the head using a stepped drift (see illustration). Determine the height above the boss that the guide must extend, and obtain a stack of washers, their I.D. similar to the guide's O.D., of that height. Place the stack of washers on the guide, and insert the guide into the boss. NOTE: *Valve guides are often tapered or beveled for installation.* Using the stepped installation tool (see illustration), press or tap the guides into position. Ream the guides according to the size of the valve stem.

Procedure	Method
Replacing valve seat inserts:	Replacement of valve seat inserts which are worn beyond resurfacing or broken, if feasible, must be done by a machine shop.
Resurfacing (grinding) the valve face:  Grinding a valve (© Subaru) 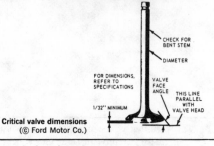 Critical valve dimensions (© Ford Motor Co.)	Using a valve grinder, resurface the valves according to specifications. CAUTION: *Valve face angle is not always identical to valve seat angle.* A minimum margin of 1/32″ should remain after grinding the valve. The valve stem tip should also be squared and resurfaced, by placing the stem in the V-block of the grinder, and turning it while pressing lightly against the grinding wheel.
Resurfacing the valve seats using reamers:  Reaming the valve seat (© S.p.A. Fiat) Valve seat width and centering (© Ford Motor Co.)	Select a reamer of the correct seat angle, slightly larger than the diameter of the valve seat, and assemble it with a pilot of the correct size. Install the pilot into the valve guide, and using steady pressure, turn the reamer clockwise. CAUTION: *Do not turn the reamer counter-clockwise.* Remove only as much material as necessary to clean the seat. Check the concentricity of the seat (see below). If the dye method is not used, coat the valve face with Prussian blue dye, install and rotate it on the valve seat. Using the dye marked area as a centering guide, center and narrow the valve seat to specifications with correction cutters. NOTE: *When no specifications are available, minimum seat width for exhaust valves should be 5/64″, intake valves 1/16″.* After making correction cuts, check the position of the valve seat on the valve face using Prussian blue dye.
* Resurfacing the valve seats using a grinder:  Grinding a valve seat (© Subaru)	Select a pilot of the correct size, and a coarse stone of the correct seat angle. Lubricate the pilot if necessary, and install the tool in the valve guide. Move the stone on and off the seat at approximately two cycles per second, until all flaws are removed from the seat. Install a fine stone, and finish the seat. Center and narrow the seat using correction stones, as described above.

Procedure	Method
Checking the valve seat concentricity: 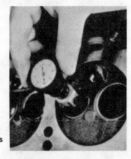 Checking the valve seat concentricity using a dial gauge (© American Motors Corp.)	Coat the valve face with Prussian blue dye, install the valve, and rotate it on the valve seat. If the entire seat becomes coated, and the valve is known to be concentric, the seat is concentric.
	* Install the dial gauge pilot into the guide, and rest the arm on the valve seat. Zero the gauge, and rotate the arm around the seat. Run-out should not exceed .002″.
* Lapping the valves: NOTE: *Valve lapping is done to ensure efficient sealing of resurfaced valves and seats. Valve lapping alone is not recommended for use as a resurfacing procedure.*  Hand lapping the valves  HAND DRILL · ROD · SUCTION CUP Home made mechanical valve lapping tool	* Invert the cylinder head, lightly lubricate the valve stems, and install the valves in the head as numbered. Coat valve seats with fine grinding compound, and attach the lapping tool suction cup to a valve head (NOTE: *Moisten the suction cup*). Rotate the tool between the palms, changing position and lifting the tool often to prevent grooving. Lap the valve until a smooth, polished seat is evident. Remove the valve and tool, and rinse away all traces of grinding compound.
	** Fasten a suction cup to a piece of drill rod, and mount the rod in a hand drill. Proceed as above, using the hand drill as a lapping tool. CAUTION: *Due to the higher speeds involved when using the hand drill, care must be exercised to avoid grooving the seat.* Lift the tool and change direction of rotation often.
Check the valve springs: 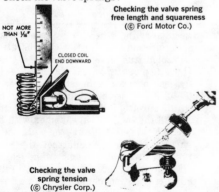 NOT MORE THAN 1/16″ CLOSED COIL END DOWNWARD Checking the valve spring free length and squareness (© Ford Motor Co.) Checking the valve spring tension (© Chrysler Corp.)	Place the spring on a flat surface next to a square. Measure the height of the spring, and rotate it against the edge of the square to measure distortion. If spring height varies (by comparison) by more than 1/16″ or if distortion exceeds 1/16″, replace the spring.
	** In addition to evaluating the spring as above, test the spring pressure at the installed and compressed (installed height minus valve lift) height using a valve spring tester. Springs used on small displacement engines (up to 3 liters) should be ± 1 lb. of all other springs in either position. A tolerance of ± 5 lbs. is permissible on larger engines.

Procedure	*Method*
* Install valve stem seals:  **Valve stem seal installation** (© Ford Motor Co.) SEAL	* Due to the pressure differential that exists at the ends of the intake valve guides (atmospheric pressure above, manifold vacuum below), oil is drawn through the valve guides into the intake port. This has been alleviated somewhat since the addition of positive crankcase ventilation, which lowers the pressure above the guides. Several types of valve stem seals are available to reduce blow-by. Certain seals simply slip over the stem and guide boss, while others require that the boss be machined. Recently, Teflon guide seals have become popular. Consult a parts supplier or machinist concerning availability and suggested usages. NOTE: *When installing seals, ensure that a small amount of oil is able to pass the seal to lubricate the valve guides; otherwise, excessive wear may result.*
Install the valves:	Lubricate the valve stems, and install the valves in the cylinder head as numbered. Lubricate and position the seals (if used, see above) and the valve springs. Install the spring retainers, compress the springs, and insert the keys using needlenose pliers or a tool designed for this purpose. NOTE: *Retain the keys with wheel bearing grease during installation.*
Checking valve spring installed height: 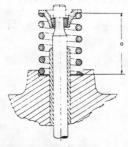  **Valve spring installed** **height dimension** (© Porsche) **Measuring valve spring** **installed height** (© Petersen Publishing Co.)	Measure the distance between the spring pad and the lower edge of the spring retainer, and compare to specifications. If the installed height is incorrect, add shim washers between the spring pad and the spring. CAUTION: *Use only washers designed for this purpose.*
** CC'ing the combustion chambers:	** Invert the cylinder head and place a bead of sealer around a combustion chamber. Install an apparatus designed for this purpose (burette mounted on a clear plate; see illustration) over the combustion chamber, and fill with the specified fluid to an even mark on the burette. Record the burette reading, and fill the combustion chamber with fluid. (NOTE: *A hole drilled in the plate will permit air to escape*). Subtract the burette reading, with the combustion chamber filled, from the previous reading, to determine combustion chamber volume in cc's. Duplicate this procedure in all combustion

Procedure	Method

CC'ing the combustion chamber (© Petersen Publishing Co.)

chambers on the cylinder head, and compare the readings. The volume of all combustion chambers should be made equal to that of the largest. Combustion chamber volume may be increased in two ways. When only a small change is required (usually), a small cutter or coarse stone may be used to remove material from the combustion chamber. NOTE: *Check volume frequently.* Remove material over a wide area, so as not to change the configuration of the combustion chamber. When a larger change is required, the valve seat may be sunk (lowered into the head). NOTE: *When altering valve seat, remember to compensate for the change in spring installed height.*

Inspect the rocker arms, balls, studs, and nuts (where applicable):

Stress cracks in rocker nuts (© Ford Motor Co.)

SMALL FRACTURES

Visually inspect the rocker arms, balls, studs, and nuts for cracks, galling, burning, scoring, or wear. If all parts are intact, liberally lubricate the rocker arms and balls, and install them on the cylinder head. If wear is noted on a rocker arm at the point of valve contact, grind it smooth and square, removing as little material as possible. Replace the rocker arm if excessively worn. If a rocker stud shows signs of wear, it must be replaced (see below). If a rocker nut shows stress cracks, replace it. If an exhaust ball is galled or burned, substitute the intake ball from the same cylinder (if it is intact), and install a new intake ball. NOTE: *Avoid using new rocker balls on exhaust valves.*

Replacing rocker studs:

Reaming the stud bore for oversize rocker studs (© Buick Div. G.M. Corp.)

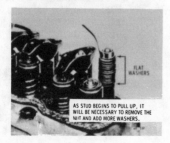

Extracting a pressed in rocker stud (© Buick Div. G.M. Corp.)

FLAT WASHERS

AS STUD BEGINS TO PULL UP, IT WILL BE NECESSARY TO REMOVE THE NUT AND ADD MORE WASHERS.

In order to remove a threaded stud, lock two nuts on the stud, and unscrew the stud using the lower nut. Coat the lower threads of the new stud with Loctite, and install.

Two alternative methods are available for replacing pressed in studs. Remove the damaged stud using a stack of washers and a nut (see illustration). In the first, the boss is reamed .005-.006″ oversize, and an oversize stud pressed in. Control the stud extension over the boss using washers, in the same manner as valve guides. Before installing the stud, coat it with white lead and grease. To retain the stud more positively, drill a hole through the stud and boss, and install a roll pin. In the second method, the boss is tapped, and a threaded stud installed. Retain the stud using Loctite Stud and Bearing Mount.

Procedure	*Method*
Inspect the rocker shaft(s) and rocker arms (where applicable):  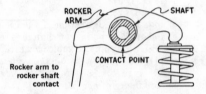 **Disassembled rocker shaft parts arranged for inspection** (© American Motors Corp.) ROCKER ARM — SHAFT — CONTACT POINT — Rocker arm to rocker shaft contact	Remove rocker arms, springs and washers from rocker shaft. NOTE: *Lay out parts in the order they are removed.* Inspect rocker arms for pitting or wear on the valve contact point, or excessive bushing wear. Bushings need only be replaced if wear is excessive, because the rocker arm normally contacts the shaft at one point only. Grind the valve contact point of rocker arm smooth if necessary, removing as little material as possible. If excessive material must be removed to smooth and square the arm, it should be replaced. Clean out all oil holes and passages in rocker shaft. If shaft is grooved or worn, replace it. Lubricate and assemble the rocker shaft.
Inspect the camshaft bushings and the camshaft (overhead cam engines):	See next section.
Inspect the pushrods:	Remove the pushrods, and, if hollow, clean out the oil passages using fine wire. Roll each pushrod over a piece of clean glass. If a distinct clicking sound is heard as the pushrod rolls, the rod is bent, and must be replaced.
	* The length of all pushrods must be equal. Measure the length of the pushrods, compare to specifications, and replace as necessary.
Inspect the valve lifters:  Check for Concave Wear on Face of Tappet Using Tappet for Straight Edge **Checking the lifter face** (© American Motors Corp.)	Remove lifters from their bores, and remove gum and varnish, using solvent. Clean walls of lifter bores. Check lifters for concave wear as illustrated. If face is worn concave, replace lifter, and carefully inspect the camshaft. Lightly lubricate lifter and insert it into its bore. If play is excessive, an oversize lifter must be installed (where possible). Consult a machinist concerning feasibility. If play is satisfactory, remove, lubricate, and reinstall the lifter.
* Testing hydraulic lifter leak down: 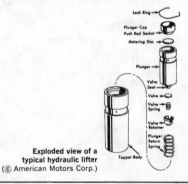 Lock Ring — Plunger Cap — Push Rod Socket — Metering Disc — Plunger — Valve Seat — Valve — Valve Spring — Valve Retainer — Plunger Return Spring — Tappet Body **Exploded view of a typical hydraulic lifter** (© American Motors Corp.)	Submerge lifter in a container of kerosene. Chuck a used pushrod or its equivalent into a drill press. Position container of kerosene so pushrod acts on the lifter plunger. Pump lifter with the drill press, until resistance increases. Pump several more times to bleed any air out of lifter. Apply very firm, constant pressure to the lifter, and observe rate at which fluid bleeds out of lifter. If the fluid bleeds very quickly (less than 15 seconds), lifter is defective. If the time exceeds 60 seconds, lifter is sticking. In either case, recondition or replace lifter. If lifter is operating properly (leak down time 15-60 seconds), lubricate and install it.

CYLINDER BLOCK RECONDITIONING

Procedure	*Method*
Checking the main bearing clearance:	Invert engine, and remove cap from the bearing to be checked. Using a clean, dry rag, thoroughly clean all oil from crankshaft journal and bearing insert. NOTE: *Plastigage is soluble in oil; therefore, oil on the journal or bearing could result in erroneous readings.* Place a piece of Plastigage along the full length of journal, reinstall cap, and torque to specifications. Remove bearing cap, and determine bearing clearance by comparing width of Plastigage to the scale on Plastigage envelope. Journal taper is determined by comparing width of the Plastigage strip near its ends. Rotate crankshaft 90° and retest, to determine journal eccentricity. NOTE: *Do not rotate crankshaft with Plastigage installed.* If bearing insert and journal appear intact, and are within tolerances, no further main bearing service is required. If bearing or journal appear defective, cause of failure should be determined before replacement.

Plastigage installed on main bearing journal
(© Chevrolet Div. G.M. Corp.)

Measuring Plastigage to determine
main bearing clearance
(© Chevrolet Div. G.M. Corp.)

Causes of bearing failure
(© Ford Motor Co.)

* Remove crankshaft from block (see below). Measure the main bearing journals at each end twice (90° apart) using a micrometer, to determine diameter, journal taper and eccentricity. If journals are within tolerances, reinstall bearing caps at their specified torque. Using a telescope gauge and micrometer, measure bearing I.D. parallel to piston axis and at 30° on each side of piston axis. Subtract journal O.D. from bearing I.D. to determine oil clearance. If crankshaft journals appear defective, or do not meet tolerances, there is no need to measure bearings; for the crankshaft will require grinding and/or undersize bearings will be required. If bearing appears defective, cause for failure should be determined prior to replacement.

Checking the connecting rod bearing clearance:

Connecting rod bearing clearance is checked in the same manner as main bearing clearance, using Plastigage. Before removing the crankshaft, connecting rod side clearance also should be measured and recorded.

Plastigage installed on connecting rod
bearing journal
(© Chevrolet Div. G.M. Corp.)

* Checking connecting rod bearing clearance, using a micrometer, is identical to checking main bearing clearance. If no other service

Procedure	Method

Measuring Plastigage to determine connecting rod bearing clearance
(© Chevrolet Div. G.M. Corp.)

is required, the piston and rod assemblies need not be removed.

Removing the crankshaft:

Connecting rod matching marks
(© Ford Motor Co.)

Using a punch, mark the corresponding main bearing caps and saddles according to position (i.e., one punch on the front main cap and saddle, two on the second, three on the third, etc.). Using number stamps, identify the corresponding connecting rods and caps, according to cylinder (if no numbers are present). Remove the main and connecting rod caps, and place sleeves of plastic tubing over the connecting rod bolts, to protect the journals as the crankshaft is removed. Lift the crankshaft out of the block.

Remove the ridge from the top of the cylinder:

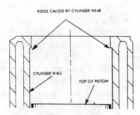

Cylinder bore ridge
(© Pontiac Div. G.M. Corp.)

In order to facilitate removal of the piston and connecting rod, the ridge at the top of the cylinder (unworn area; see illustration) must be removed. Place the piston at the bottom of the bore, and cover it with a rag. Cut the ridge away using a ridge reamer, exercising extreme care to avoid cutting too deeply. Remove the rag, and remove cuttings that remain on the piston. CAUTION: *If the ridge is not removed, and new rings are installed, damage to rings will result.*

Removing the piston and connecting rod:

Removing the piston
(© SAAB)

Invert the engine, and push the pistons and connecting rods out of the cylinders. If necessary, tap the connecting rod boss with a wooden hammer handle, to force the piston out. CAUTION: *Do not attempt to force the piston past the cylinder ridge* (see above).

Procedure	Method
Service the crankshaft:	Ensure that all oil holes and passages in the crankshaft are open and free of sludge. If necessary, have the crankshaft ground to the largest possible undersize.
	** Have the crankshaft Magnafluxed, to locate stress cracks. Consult a machinist concerning additional service procedures, such as surface hardening (e.g., nitriding, Tuftriding) to improve wear characteristics, cross drilling and chamfering the oil holes to improve lubrication, and balancing.
Removing freeze plugs:	Drill a hole in the center of the freeze plugs, and pry them out using a screwdriver or drift.
Remove the oil gallery plugs:	Threaded plugs should be removed using an appropriate (usually square) wrench. To remove soft, pressed in plugs, drill a hole in the plug, and thread in a sheet metal screw. Pull the plug out by the screw using pliers.
Hot-tank the block:	Have the block hot-tanked to remove grease, corrosion, and scale from the water jackets. NOTE: *Consult the operator to determine whether the camshaft bearings will be damaged during the hot-tank process.*
Check the block for cracks:	Visually inspect the block for cracks or chips. The most common locations are as follows: Adjacent to freeze plugs. Between the cylinders and water jackets. Adjacent to the main bearing saddles. At the extreme bottom of the cylinders. Check only suspected cracks using spot check dye (see introduction). If a crack is located, consult a machinist concerning possible repairs.
	** Magnaflux the block to locate hidden cracks. If cracks are located, consult a machinist about feasibility of repair.
Install the oil gallery plugs and freeze plugs:	Coat freeze plugs with sealer and tap into position using a piece of pipe, slightly smaller than the plug, as a driver. To ensure retention, stake the edges of the plugs. Coat threaded oil gallery plugs with sealer and install. Drive replacement soft plugs into block using a large drift as a driver.
	* Rather than reinstalling lead plugs, drill and tap the holes, and install threaded plugs.

Procedure	*Method*

Check the bore diameter and surface:

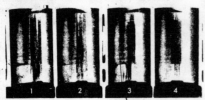

1, 2, 3 Piston skirt seizure resulted in this pattern. Engine must be rebored

4. Piston skirt and oil ring seizure caused this damage. Engine must be rebored

5, 6 Score marks caused by a split piston skirt. Damage is not serious enough to warrant reboring

7. Ring seized longitudinally, causing a score mark 1 3/16" wide, on the land side of the piston groove. The honing pattern is destroyed and the cylinder must be rebored

8. Result of oil ring seizure. Engine must be rebored

9. Oil ring seizure here was not serious enough to warrant reboring. The honing marks are still visible

Cylinder wall damage
(© Daimler-Benz A.G.)

Visually inspect the cylinder bores for roughness, scoring, or scuffing. If evident, the cylinder bore must be bored or honed oversize to eliminate imperfections, and the smallest possible oversize piston used. The new pistons should be given to the machinist with the block, so that the cylinders can be bored or honed exactly to the piston size (plus clearance). If no flaws are evident, measure the bore diameter using a telescope gauge and micrometer, or dial gauge, parallel and perpendicular to the engine centerline, at the top (below the ridge) and bottom of the bore. Subtract the bottom measurements from the top to determine taper, and the parallel to the centerline measurements from the perpendicular measurements to determine eccentricity. If the measurements are not within specifications, the cylinder must be bored or honed, and an oversize piston installed. If the measurements are within specifications the cylinder may be used as is, with only finish honing (see below). NOTE: *Prior to submitting the block for boring, perform the following operation(s).*

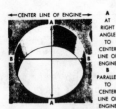   

Cylinder bore measuring positions (© Ford Motor Co.)

Measuring the cylinder bore with a telescope gauge (© Buick Div. G.M. Corp.)

Determining the cylinder bore by measuring the telescope gauge with a micrometer (© Buick Div. G.M. Corp.)

Measuring the cylinder bore with a dial gauge (© Chevrolet Div. G.M. Corp.)

Procedure	Method
Check the block deck for warpage:	Using a straightedge and feeler gauges, check the block deck for warpage in the same manner that the cylinder head is checked (see Cylinder Head Reconditioning). If warpage exceeds specifications, have the deck resurfaced. NOTE: *In certain cases a specification for total material removal (Cylinder head and block deck) is provided. This specification must not be exceeded.*
* Check the deck height:	The deck height is the distance from the crankshaft centerline to the block deck. To measure, invert the engine, and install the crankshaft, retaining it with the center main cap. Measure the distance from the crankshaft journal to the block deck, parallel to the cylinder centerline. Measure the diameter of the end (front and rear) main journals, parallel to the centerline of the cylinders, divide the diameter in half, and subtract it from the previous measurement. The results of the front and rear measurements should be identical. If the difference exceeds .005″, the deck height should be corrected. NOTE: *Block deck height and warpage should be corrected concurrently.*
Check the cylinder block bearing alignment:  **Checking main bearing saddle alignment** (© Petersen Publishing Co.)	Remove the upper bearing inserts. Place a straightedge in the bearing saddles along the centerline of the crankshaft. If clearance exists between the straightedge and the center saddle, the block must be align-bored.
Clean and inspect the pistons and connecting rods:  Piston ring expander **Removing the piston rings** (© Subaru)	Using a ring expander, remove the rings from the piston. Remove the retaining rings (if so equipped) and remove piston pin. NOTE: *If the piston pin must be pressed out, determine the proper method and use the proper tools; otherwise the piston will distort.* Clean the ring grooves using an appropriate tool, exercising care to avoid cutting too deeply. Thoroughly clean all carbon and varnish from the piston with solvent. CAUTION: *Do not use a wire brush or caustic solvent on pistons.* Inspect the pistons for scuffing, scoring, cracks, pitting, or excessive ring groove wear. If wear is evident, the piston must be replaced. Check the connecting rod length by measuring the rod from the inside of the large end to the inside of the small end using calipers (see

Procedure	*Method*

Ring Groove Cleaner

A1404-C

Cleaning the piston ring grooves
(© Ford Motor Co.)

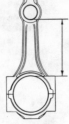

Connecting rod
length checking
dimension

illustration). All connecting rods should be equal length. Replace any rod that differs from the others in the engine.

* Have the connecting rod alignment checked in an alignment fixture by a machinist. Replace any twisted or bent rods.

* Magnaflux the connecting rods to locate stress cracks. If cracks are found, replace the connecting rod.

Fit the pistons to the cylinders:

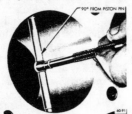

90° FROM PISTON PIN

Measuring the cylinder
with a telescope gauge
for piston fitting
(© Buick Div.
G.M. Corp.)

60-91

Measuring the piston
for fitting
(© Buick Div.
G.M. Corp.)

90°   60-90

Using a telescope gauge and micrometer, or a dial gauge, measure the cylinder bore diameter perpendicular to the piston pin, 2½" below the deck. Measure the piston perpendicular to its pin on the skirt. The difference between the two measurements is the piston clearance. If the clearance is within specifications or slightly below (after boring or honing), finish honing is all that is required. If the clearance is excessive, try to obtain a slightly larger piston to bring clearance within specifications. Where this is not possible, obtain the first oversize piston, and hone (or if necessary, bore) the cylinder to size.

Assemble the pistons and connecting rods:

Installing piston pin lock rings
(© Nissan Motor Co., Ltd.)

Inspect piston pin, connecting rod small end bushing, and piston bore for galling, scoring, or excessive wear. If evident, replace defective part(s). Measure the I.D. of the piston boss and connecting rod small end, and the O.D. of the piston pin. If within specifications, assemble piston pin and rod. CAUTION: *If piston pin must be pressed in, determine the proper method and use the proper tools; otherwise the piston will distort.* Install the lock rings; ensure that they seat properly. If the parts are not within specifications, determine the service method for the type of engine. In some cases, piston and pin are serviced as an assembly when either is defective. Others specify reaming the piston and connecting rods for an oversize pin. If the connecting rod bushing is worn, it may in many cases be replaced. Reaming the piston and replacing the rod bushing are machine shop operations.

Procedure	Method
Clean and inspect the camshaft: 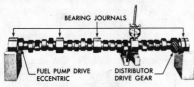 **Checking the camshaft for straightness** (© Chevrolet Motor Div. G.M. Corp.) **Camshaft lobe measurement** (© Ford Motor Co.)	Degrease the camshaft, using solvent, and clean out all oil holes. Visually inspect cam lobes and bearing journals for excessive wear. If a lobe is questionable, check all lobes as indicated below. If a journal or lobe is worn, the camshaft must be reground or replaced. NOTE: *If a journal is worn, there is a good chance that the bushings are worn.* If lobes and journals appear intact, place the front and rear journals in V-blocks, and rest a dial indicator on the center journal. Rotate the camshaft to check straightness. If deviation exceeds .001″, replace the camshaft. * Check the camshaft lobes with a micrometer, by measuring the lobes from the nose to base and again at 90° (see illustration). The lift is determined by subtracting the second measurement from the first. If all exhaust lobes and all intake lobes are not identical, the camshaft must be reground or replaced.
Replace the camshaft bearings: 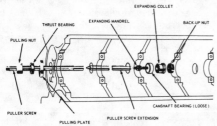 **Camshaft removal and installation tool (typical)** (© Ford Motor Co.)	If excessive wear is indicated, or if the engine is being completely rebuilt, camshaft bearings should be replaced as follows: Drive the camshaft rear plug from the block. Assemble the removal puller with its shoulder on the bearing to be removed. Gradually tighten the puller nut until bearing is removed. Remove remaining bearings, leaving the front and rear for last. To remove front and rear bearings, reverse position of the tool, so as to pull the bearings in toward the center of the block. Leave the tool in this position, pilot the new front and rear bearings on the installer, and pull them into position. Return the tool to its original position and pull remaining bearings into position. NOTE: *Ensure that oil holes align when installing bearings.* Replace camshaft rear plug, and stake it into position to aid retention.
Finish hone the cylinders: 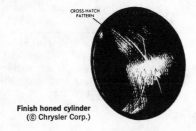 **Finish honed cylinder** (© Chrysler Corp.)	Chuck a flexible drive hone into a power drill, and insert it into the cylinder. Start the hone, and move it up and down in the cylinder at a rate which will produce approximately a 60° cross-hatch pattern (see illustration). NOTE: *Do not extend the hone below the cylinder bore.* After developing the pattern, remove the hone and recheck piston fit. Wash the cylinders with a detergent and water solution to remove abrasive dust, dry, and wipe several times with a rag soaked in engine oil.

Procedure	Method
Check piston ring end-gap:  Checking ring end-gap (© Chevrolet Motor Div. G.M. Corp.)	Compress the piston rings to be used in a cylinder, one at a time, into that cylinder, and press them approximately 1″ below the deck with an inverted piston. Using feeler gauges, measure the ring end-gap, and compare to specifications. Pull the ring out of the cylinder and file the ends with a fine file to obtain proper clearance. CAUTION: *If inadequate ring end-gap is utilized, ring breakage will result.*
Install the piston rings: 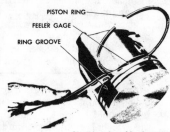 Checking ring side clearance (© Chrysler Corp.) 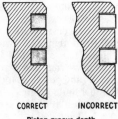 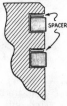 CORRECT INCORRECT Correct ring Piston groove depth spacer installation	Inspect the ring grooves in the piston for excessive wear or taper. If necessary, recut the groove(s) for use with an overwidth ring or a standard ring and spacer. If the groove is worn uniformly, overwidth rings, or standard rings and spacers may be installed without recutting. Roll the outside of the ring around the groove to check for burrs or deposits. If any are found, remove with a fine file. Hold the ring in the groove, and measure side clearance. If necessary, correct as indicated above. NOTE: *Always install any additional spacers above the piston ring.* The ring groove must be deep enough to allow the ring to seat below the lands (see illustration). In many cases, a "go-no-go" depth gauge will be provided with the piston rings. Shallow grooves may be corrected by recutting, while deep grooves require some type of filler or expander behind the piston. Consult the piston ring supplier concerning the suggested method. Install the rings on the piston, lowest ring first, using a ring expander. NOTE: *Position the ring markings as specified by the manufacturer (see car section).*
Install the camshaft:	Liberally lubricate the camshaft lobes and journals, and slide the camshaft into the block. CAUTION: *Exercise extreme care to avoid damaging the bearings when inserting the camshaft.* Install and tighten the camshaft thrust plate retaining bolts.
Check camshaft end-play: 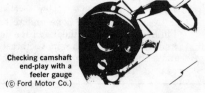 Checking camshaft end-play with a feeler gauge (© Ford Motor Co.)	Using feeler gauges, determine whether the clearance between the camshaft boss (or gear) and backing plate is within specifications. Install shims behind the thrust plate, or reposition the camshaft gear and retest end-play.

Procedure	Method

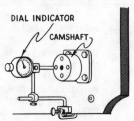

Checking camshaft end-play with a dial indicator

* Mount a dial indicator stand so that the stem of the dial indicator rests on the nose of the camshaft, parallel to the camshaft axis. Push the camshaft as far in as possible and zero the gauge. Move the camshaft outward to determine the amount of camshaft end-play. If the end-play is not within tolerance, install shims behind the thrust plate, or re-position the camshaft gear and retest.

Install the rear main seal (where applicable):

Seating the rear main seal
(© Buick Div. G.M. Corp.)

Position the block with the bearing saddles facing upward. Lay the rear main seal in its groove and press it lightly into its seat. Place a piece of pipe the same diameter as the crankshaft journal into the saddle, and firmly seat the seal. Hold the pipe in position, and trim the ends of the seal flush if required.

Install the crankshaft:

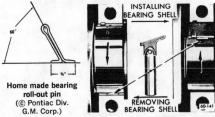

Home made bearing roll-out pin
(© Pontiac Div. G.M. Corp.)

Removal and installation of upper bearing insert using a roll-out pin
(© Buick Div. G.M. Corp.)

Thoroughly clean the main bearing saddles and caps. Place the upper halves of the bearing inserts on the saddles and press into position. NOTE: *Ensure that the oil holes align.* Press the corresponding bearing inserts into the main bearing caps. Lubricate the upper main bearings, and lay the crankshaft in position. Place a strip of Plastigage on each of the crankshaft journals, install the main caps, and torque to specifications. Remove the main caps, and compare the Plastigage to the scale on the Plastigage envelope. If clearances are within tolerances, remove the Plastigage, turn the crankshaft 90°, wipe off all oil and retest. If all clearances are correct, remove all Plastigage, thoroughly

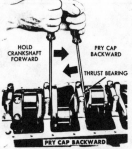
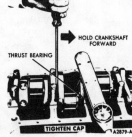

Aligning the thrust bearing
(© Ford Motor Co.)

Procedure	*Method*
	lubricate the main caps and bearing journals, and install the main caps. If clearances are not within tolerance, the upper bearing inserts may be removed, without removing the crankshaft, using a bearing roll out pin (see illustration). Roll in a bearing that will provide proper clearance, and retest. Torque all main caps, excluding the thrust bearing cap, to specifications. Tighten the thrust bearing cap finger tight. To properly align the thrust bearing, pry the crankshaft the extent of its axial travel several times, the last movement held toward the front of the engine, and torque the thrust bearing cap to specifications. Determine the crankshaft end-play (see below), and bring within tolerance with thrust washers.
Measure crankshaft end-play:  Checking crankshaft end-play with a dial indicator (© Ford Motor Co.)  A 2908-A  Checking crankshaft end-play with a feeler gauge (© Chevrolet Div. (G.M. Corp.)	Mount a dial indicator stand on the front of the block, with the dial indicator stem resting on the nose of the crankshaft, parallel to the crankshaft axis. Pry the crankshaft the extent of its travel rearward, and zero the indicator. Pry the crankshaft forward and record crankshaft end-play. NOTE: *Crankshaft end-play also may be measured at the thrust bearing, using feeler gauges* (see illustration).
Install the pistons:	Press the upper connecting rod bearing halves into the connecting rods, and the lower halves into the connecting rod caps. Position the piston ring gaps according to specifications (see car section), and lubricate the pistons. Install a ring compresser on a piston, and press two long (8″) pieces of plastic tubing over the rod bolts. Using the plastic tubes as a guide, press the pistons into the bores and onto the crankshaft with a wooden hammer handle. After seating the rod on the crankshaft journal, remove the tubes and install the cap finger tight. Install the remaining pistons in the same man-

Procedure	*Method*

Tubing used as guide when installing
a piston
(© Oldsmobile Div. G.M. Corp.)

ner. Invert the engine and check the bearing clearance at two points (90° apart) on each journal with Plastigage. NOTE: *Do not turn the crankshaft with Plastigage installed.* If clearance is within tolerances, remove *all* Plastigage, thoroughly lubricate the journals, and torque the rod caps to specifications. If clearance is not within specifications, install different thickness bearing inserts and recheck. CAUTION: *Never shim or file the connecting rods or caps.* Always install plastic tube sleeves over the rod bolts when the caps are not installed, to protect the crankshaft journals.

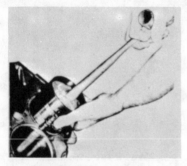

Installing a piston
(© Chevrolet Div. G.M. Corp.)

Check connecting rod side clearance:

Determine the clearance between the sides of the connecting rods and the crankshaft, using feeler gauges. If clearance is below the minimum tolerance, the rod may be machined to provide adequate clearance. If clearance is excessive, substitute an unworn rod, and recheck. If clearance is still outside specifications, the crankshaft must be welded and reground, or replaced.

Checking connecting rod side clearance
(© Chevrolet Div. G.M. Corp.)

Inspect the timing chain:

Visually inspect the timing chain for broken or loose links, and replace the chain if any are found. If the chain will flex sideways, it must be replaced. Install the timing chain as specified. NOTE: *If the original timing chain is to be reused, install it in its original position.*

Procedure	Method
Check timing gear backlash and runout:  **Checking camshaft gear backlash** (© Chevrolet Div. G.M. Corp.)  **Checking camshaft gear runout** (© Chevrolet Div. G.M. Corp.)	Mount a dial indicator with its stem resting on a tooth of the camshaft gear (as illustrated). Rotate the gear until all slack is removed, and zero the indicator. Rotate the gear in the opposite direction until slack is removed, and record gear backlash. Mount the indicator with its stem resting on the edge of the camshaft gear, parallel to the axis of the camshaft. Zero the indicator, and turn the camshaft gear one full turn, recording the runout. If either backlash or runout exceed specifications, replace the worn gear(s).

Completing the Rebuilding Process

Following the above procedures, complete the rebuilding process as follows:

Fill the oil pump with oil, to prevent cavitating (sucking air) on initial engine start up. Install the oil pump and the pickup tube on the engine. Coat the oil pan gasket as necessary, and install the gasket and the oil pan. Mount the flywheel and the crankshaft vibrational damper or pulley on the crankshaft. NOTE: *Always use new bolts when installing the flywheel.* Inspect the clutch shaft pilot bushing in the crankshaft. If the bushing is excessively worn, remove it with an expanding puller and a slide hammer, and tap a new bushing into place.

Position the engine, cylinder head side up. Lubricate the lifters, and install them into their bores. Install the cylinder head, and torque it as specified in the car section. Insert the pushrods (where applicable), and install the rocker shaft(s) (if so equipped) or position the rocker arms on the pushrods. If solid lifters are utilized, adjust the valves to the "cold" specifications.

Mount the intake and exhaust manifolds, the carburetor(s), the distributor and spark plugs. Adjust the point gap and the static ignition timing. Mount all accessories and install the engine in the car. Fill the radiator with coolant, and the crankcase with high quality engine oil.

Break-in Procedure

Start the engine, and allow it to run at low speed for a few minutes, while checking for leaks. Stop the engine, check the oil level, and fill as necessary. Restart the engine, and fill the cooling system to capacity. Check the point dwell angle and adjust the ignition timing and the valves. Run the engine at low to medium speed (800-2500 rpm) for approximately ½ hour, and retorque the cylinder head bolts. Road test the car, and check again for leaks.

Follow the manufacturer's recommended engine break-in procedure and maintenance schedule for new engines.

4 · Emission Controls and Fuel System

Emission Controls

PCV VALVE

Operation and Service

The Positive Crankcase Ventilation (PCV) valve has been included on all Barracuda and Challenger models since 1965. Because the PCV valve is part of the CAP/CAS emission control systems, its de-

scription and the service used for it, can be found in the section below.

CAP AND CAS

Operation

1966–69 BARRACUDA

The Cleaner Air Package (CAP) system is designed to constantly maintain carburetion and ignition timing at the best settings for performance and combustion

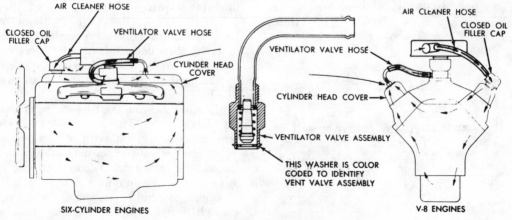

PCV system

under all driving requirements and conditions. These adjustments, if maintained, will keep the engine at a good performance level and within the exhaust requirements of federal law.

In the past, normal engines have had comparatively low exhaust emissions at cruise and acceleration attitudes. Excessive emissions occur during deceleration and low-speed operation. Therefore, the CAP system concentrates on reduction of emissions in the idle and deceleration ranges.

The CAP system uses a carburetor and distributor which have been redesigned, and a vacuum advance control valve on cars with manual transmissions.

The carburetor is calibrated to provide leaner mixtures at idle and at low speeds. The distributor is designed to give retarded timing at idle. The vacuum advance control valve, in conjunction with the distributor, provides advanced timing during deceleration.

A number of changes have been made that reshape the intake manifold and combustion chamber for more even mixture distribution and better combustion.

CAP idle timing, for all engines, is retarded. Exhaust emission is reduced at idle by using leaner air/fuel mixtures, increased engine speed, and retarded ignition timing. The increased air flow at this idle condition is similar to the distribution and combustion conditions of cruise.

The system operates with late timing during idle and with conventional spark advance during acceleration and cruise.

The vacuum advance control valve provides additional spark advance during deceleration.

Engine applications involving manual shift transmissions require slightly different handling. They need earlier ignition of the fuel mixture to accomplish efficient combustion and to more completely consume residual fuels.

The vacuum advance control valve is connected by hoses to the carburetor, the intake manifold, and to the distributor vacuum chamber. Carburetor vacuum and manifold vacuum act on the vacuum advance control valve. From these two signals, the vacuum advance control valve senses engine speed and load conditions, and relays a vacuum command to the distributor to modify spark timing when necessary.

Initial, or basic, timing may be retarded as much as fifteen degrees from conventional timing. The vacuum advance control valve does not affect timing at idle because the distributor vacuum chamber receives the same vacuum signal as in the conventional system, namely, carburetor vacuum.

This is not strong enough to overcome the distributor vacuum diaphragm spring.

Manifold vacuum acts on the vacuum control valve diaphragm. However, it is not strong enough to overcome the vacuum control spring. The spring holds the vacuum control valve closed to manifold vacuum and open to low carburetor vacuum.

Under acceleration and during normal cruise, the throttle is opened and the increased air flow through the carburetor throat creates carburetor vacuum much greater than under closed throttle conditions.

Manifold vacuum is not enough to overcome the vacuum advance control valve spring. However, the stronger carburetor vacuum overcomes the distributor vacuum diaphragm spring, advancing spark timing.

The conventional system (without exhaust emission control) permits greatest objectionable emissions during deceleration. Carburetor vacuum is too weak to overcome the distributor vacuum advance diaphragm spring.

Manifold vacuum is at its strongest during deceleration. Therefore, the CAP system, when equipped with a vacuum advance control valve, uses manifold vacuum instead of carburetor vacuum to control spark timing. To summarize: during deceleration, manifold vacuum is strong enough to overcome the vacuum advance control valve spring and the distributor

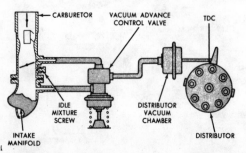

Carburetor/control valve/distributor relationship

vacuum diaphragm spring, moving the spark timing to maximum advance.

1970–72 BARRACUDA AND CHALLENGER

The CAP system has been improved to become, CAS, the Cleaner Air System. This system utilizes:

1. Heated air intake system;
2. Modified carburetor;

Carburetors have leaner mixtures and external idle mixture limiting devices. The automatic choke has been redesigned to release more quickly on engine warmup. An electrical solenoid throttle stop is used on 340, 440, 440 Six Pack, and 426 Hemi engines. These engines use high idle speeds to achieve acceptable emission levels. The solenoid throttle stop de-energizes

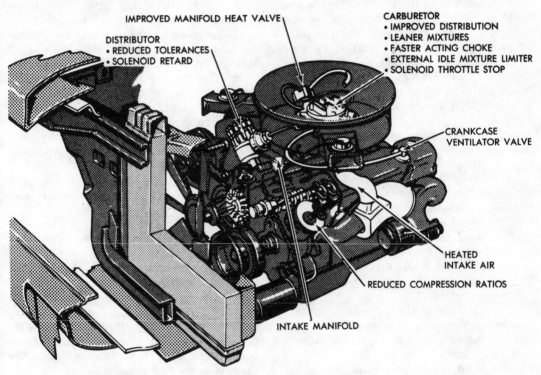

IMPROVED MANIFOLD HEAT VALVE

DISTRIBUTOR
• REDUCED TOLERANCES
• SOLENOID RETARD

CARBURETOR
• IMPROVED DISTRIBUTION
• LEANER MIXTURES
• FASTER ACTING CHOKE
• EXTERNAL IDLE MIXTURE LIMITER
• SOLENOID THROTTLE STOP

CRANKCASE VENTILATOR VALVE

HEATED INTAKE AIR

REDUCED COMPRESSION RATIOS

INTAKE MANIFOLD

Cleaner Air System

3. Lower compression ratio;
4. Solenoid retarded distributor.

The heated air system is used on all engines except 340, 426 Hemi, 440 Six Pack, and those with the fresh-air scoop option. When air temperature is below 10° F, intake air flows through a manifold heat stove into the air cleaner. When air temperature is between 10° F and 100° F, intake air is a mixture of heated and unheated air. The volume of heated and unheated air is regulated by a thermostat, a vacuum diaphragm, and an air control valve in the air cleaner housing. The thermostat regulates the air control valve opening. Under conditions of greatly reduced vacuum, such as a sudden burst of acceleration, the vacuum diaphragm overrides the thermostat to open the air control valve fully to unheated air.

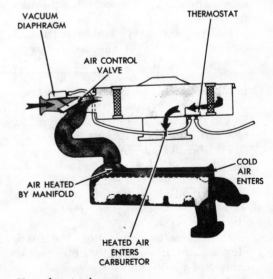

VACUUM DIAPHRAGM

THERMOSTAT

AIR CONTROL VALVE

COLD AIR ENTERS

AIR HEATED BY MANIFOLD

HEATED AIR ENTERS CARBURETOR

Heated air intake system

when the ignition is switched off, allowing the throttle blades to close more completely. This prevents running on.

318, 383, and 440 (except 440 Six Pack) engines have lower compression ratios to reduce hydrocarbon emissions.

Service

To ensure that exhaust emissions are maintained within the limits of legislation, without objectionable effects on performance, engine inspection is recommended at intervals not to exceed twelve months.

The following engine checks should be made at these periods:

1. Check spark plugs.
    A. Clean/renew and gap as necessary.
    B. Be sure they are of the proper heat range.
    C. Torque to 30 ft lbs.
2. Check distributor breaker points.
    A. Replace if necessary and adjust to recommended dwell or gap.
    B. Clean and lubricate cam and wick.
    C. Apply five to ten drops of light engine oil to the oil cup.
3. Check ignition system operation.
    A. Connect one end of a test probe to a good ground.
    B. Disconnect the secondary ignition cable at the spark plug end.
    C. Insulate the secondary cable end from ground.
    D. With the engine idling, move the test probe along the entire length of the cable. If cable insulation is breaking down, there will be a spark jump to the probe.
    E. The secondary (coil-to-distributor cap) cable should be checked the same way.
    F. Be sure that one spark plug cable is disconnected (to create greater resistance). Then, run the probe along the length of the coil secondary cable. Cracked or otherwise poor insulation should be obvious by a spark jump at the point of the probe. Bad cables should be replaced.
4. Resistance of secondary cables should also be checked. Use an ohmmeter for this purpose.
    A. Remove the cable from the spark plug and install an adaptor between the cable and spark plug.
    B. Remove the cap from the distributor (secondary cables attached).

C. Connect an ohmmeter between the plug adaptor and the corresponding electrode inside the cap.
    D. Read the ohmmeter. If resistance is more than 30,000 ohms, remove the cable from the cap and check cable resistance only.
    E. If resistance is still more than 30,000 ohms, replace the cable. If resistance is much less than 30,000 ohms, clean the cap wire towers or renew the cap.
5. Inspect the ignition coil for indications of oil leakage. Any indication of oil leakage justifies replacing the coil.
6. Test the battery with a hydrometer. Specific gravity should be 1.220 or more, with temperature corrections. Add mineral free water, if required, to bring fluid up to the correct level.
    A. Clean the battery posts and cable terminals.
    B. After tightening the cable post clamps, coat the battery posts and clamps with light grease.
    C. Reseal any breaks around the posts with rubber cement to retard corrosion.
7. The carburetor choke shaft should be serviced with carburetor cleaner to prevent sticking from gum deposits. Be sure that the choke operates freely.
8. Under normal driving conditions, the carburetor air cleaner should be inspected and cleaned every six months. Replace it every two years.

If equipped with an oil bath cleaner, the oil level should be checked every six months and should be thoroughly cleaned and refilled once a year.
9. Inspect and, if necessary, free the manifold heat control valve with manifold heat control valve solvent. Apply the solvent and work the shaft only when the unit is cold.
10. A very critical, and much neglected, item of engine performance is the crankcase emission control (PCV) valve. The crankcase emission control valve depends entirely upon the fine balance of spring pressure opposed to manifold vacuum. This balance can very easily be upset by small deposits of varnish or sludge. A closed valve induces crankcase pressure and engine sludge. A poorly seated (open) valve upsets engine idle and results in poor low-speed operation.

Inspect and service the closed crankcase ventilating system every six months and replace the control valve every twelve months.

A. A tentative check of PCV valve operation is to idle the engine.

B. Disconnect the ventilator valve assembly from the rocker cover. You should be able to hear the valve plunger, when shaking the valve.

C. If the valve is open, a hissing sound will be heard from the valve opening and vacuum can be felt with the finger.

D. If the valve is closed, or the line is obstructed anywhere between the valve and the intake manifold, crankcase pressure will develop. Check for plugging of the hose, freedom of the connection at the carburetor base or a valve stuck closed. Free vacuum passages. Replace the PCV valve if necessary.

E. Another approach is through the use of a tachometer hook-up while pinching the PCV hose. If pinching the hose has no effect on engine idle rpm, the system is plugged or the PCV valve is not opening. If pinching the hose smooths out the idle, the PCV valve is not seating.

11. Adjust idle rpm to specifications.

12. Check ignition timing.

Set ignition basic timing to specifications.

On 1970–71 models, check the distributor solenoid for proper operation by disconnecting the wire at the carburetor. Timing should advance 5½ degrees and engine speed should increase.

13. Adjust the air/fuel ratio.

14. To check the setting and operation of the distributor control valve, refer to the "Distributor Vacuum Control Valve Adjustment" procedure in this chapter.

15. Road-test the car, noting performance in all driving ranges. All adjustments should be in the interest of better performance and economy. However, any changes must comply with specifications and legislation.

CAUTION: *If contrary or confusing tune-up data is encountered, refer to the decal containing information pertinent to the specific engine/vehicle application. This decal is posted in a conspicuous location in the engine compartment of each vehicle, beginning with 1968 production.*

Carburetor Dashpot Adjustment

MANUAL TRANSMISSION MODELS WITH CAP OR CAS

The carburetor dashpot is a device which is used to slow down the closing of the throttle when the accelerator pedal is suddenly released. The purpose of the dashpot is to prevent engine stalling. The dashpot is adjusted as follows:

1. With the engine idling at its specified curb idle rpm and the air/fuel mixture properly set, connect a tachometer to the engine.

2. Position the throttle lever so that the actuating tab on the lever contacts the stem of the dashpot but does not depress it.

3. The tachometer reading should now be 2,000 rpm. If an adjustment is necessary, loosen the locknut which secures the dashpot to the bracket and rotate (screw) the dashpot in or out until the correct setting is obtained.

4. Tighten the locknut and check the distributor vacuum control valve adjustment if applicable.

Distributor Vacuum Control Valve Adjustment

1966–69 BARRACUDA

Certain Barracuda engines from 1966 to 1969 have a vacuum control valve which regulates the amount of manifold vacuum to the carburetor and distributor. Before adjusting this valve, be sure that the ignition timing and curb idle speed are correct. Adjust the control valve as follows.

1. Connect a tachometer to the engine and warm up the engine to its normal operating temperature.

2. Use a tee fitting to connect a vacuum gauge between the control valve and the distributor vacuum tube. The vacuum gauge should have a scale which reads 0–30 in. mercury (Hg) and the tee fitting

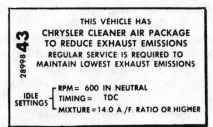

THIS VEHICLE HAS
CHRYSLER CLEANER AIR PACKAGE
TO REDUCE EXHAUST EMISSIONS
REGULAR SERVICE IS REQUIRED TO
MAINTAIN LOWEST EXHAUST EMISSIONS

28998 **43**

IDLE SETTINGS
RPM = 600 IN NEUTRAL
TIMING = TDC
MIXTURE = 14.0 A./F. RATIO OR HIGHER

Tune-up data plate

should have the same inside diameter as the distributor vacuum tube.

3. If the carburetor is fitted with a dashpot, adjust it so that it does not contact the throttle lever at curb idle.

4. Using a suitable clamp, close the tube which connects the control valve to the manifold vacuum.

5. Disconnect the distributor vacuum tube at the distributor and clamp the tube closed.

6. Adjust the carburetor to obtain the specified engine speed and exhaust emission level. Refer to the "Tune-Up Procedures." The distributor vacuum must be below 6 inches Hg at curb idle.

7. Remove the clamps from the vacuum tubes and connect the vacuum tube to the distributor. Keep the vacuum gauge connected.

8. Remove the control valve cover. Increase the engine speed to 2,000 rpm and hold this speed for approximately five seconds. Release the throttle and observe the reading on the vacuum gauge. When the throttle is released, the distributor vacuum should increase to above 16 inches Hg and remain there for a minimum of one second. After the throttle is released, the distributor vacuum must fall below 6 inches Hg within three seconds.

9. If necessary, adjust the valve by turning the adjusting screw counterclockwise to increase the time that the distributor vacuum remains above 6 inches Hg (after the throttle is released), or vice versa. One turn of the adjusting screw will change the valve setting by approximately ½ inch Hg. If the valve cannot be adjusted to the correct specifications, replace the valve with a new unit.

10. Replace the control valve cover. Reset the carburetor dashpot (if so equipped) and check the control valve performance as described in step 8. If the distributor vacuum does not fall below 6 inches Hg within four seconds after the throttle is released, readjust or replace the dashpot.

11. After the adjustment is completed, stop the engine and remove the vacuum gauge. Reconnect the distributor tube to the control valve. Disconnect the tachometer.

Ignition Retard Solenoid

An ignition retard solenoid mounted on the side of the distributor is used on 1971, and some earlier, Barracuda and Challenger models. Its function is to retard the ignition timing when the throttle is closed. The solenoid must be operating when the ignition timing is adjusted.

To be sure that the solenoid is working, first check and adjust the ignition timing. Disconnect the ground lead from the solenoid. If the engine idle speed increases noticeably, the solenoid is functioning properly. If the solenoid is defective, it must be replaced with a new unit.

Ignition Advance Solenoid

The ignition retard solenoid was replaced by an ignition advance solenoid in 1972. This solenoid, located on the side of the distributor, is connected to the starter relay and it is designed to advance the ignition timing only while the engine is cranked. When the engine starts, the solenoid ceases to operate, as it is only used as an aid in starting. If the solenoid is not working, starting the engine will be difficult. A defective solenoid may cause the carburetor to "pop" while the engine is cranked.

To check the operation of the solenoid, run the engine at idle speed and connect a jumper wire from the battery to the solenoid lead. If the solenoid is functioning properly, the engine speed will increase noticeably. *Disconnect the jumper wire immediately after checking the operation of the solenoid.* If the solenoid is defective, it must be replaced with a new unit.

ECS

Operation

All 1970 vehicles sold in California and all 1971 and later vehicles have an evaporation control system to reduce evaporation losses from the fuel system. The system has an expansion tank in the main fuel tank. This prevents spillage due to expansion of warm fuel. A special filler cap with a two-way relief valve is used. An internal pressure differential, caused by thermal expansion, opens the valve, as does an external pressure differential, caused by fuel usage. Fuel vapors from the carburetor and fuel tank are routed to the crankcase ventilation system. A separator is installed to prevent liquid fuel from entering the crankcase ventilation system.

Evaporation control systems used on

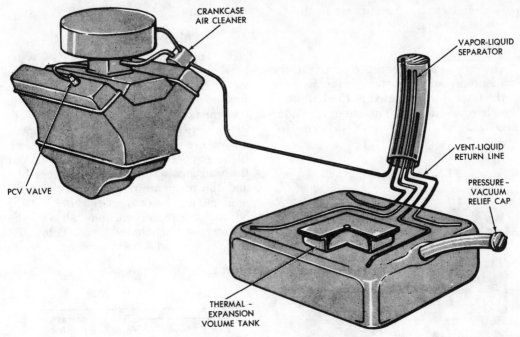

Evaporation control system—1970–71 models

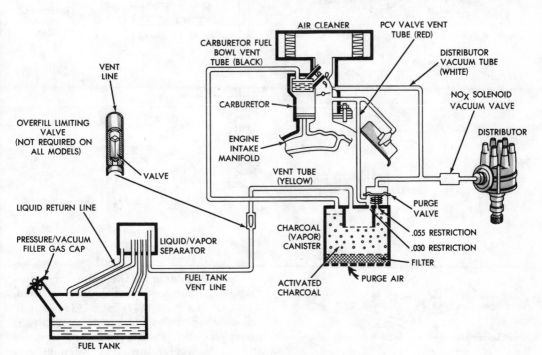

Evaporation control system—1972 models

1972 vehicles also include a charcoal canister and an overflow limiting valve.

The limiting valve prevents the fuel tank from being overfilled by trapping air in the filler when the tank is full. When pressure in the tank becomes greater than the valve operating pressure, the valve opens and allows the gasoline vapors to flow into the charcoal canister.

The charcoal canister is mounted in the engine compartment. It absorbs vapors and retains them until clean air is drawn through a line from it that runs to the PCV valve. Absorption occurs while the car is parked and cleaning occurs when the car engine is running.

Service

The only routine service required to the evaporation control system, is replacement of the filter that is located in the bottom of the charcoal canister. This should be done every 12 mos/12,000 miles, or more frequently in dusty areas.

Closed vapor canister filter replacement

If any of the hoses in the system should require replacement, use only fuel-resistant hoses.

NO_x CONTROL SYSTEM

All 1971 and later vehicles sold in California have a NO_x system to control the emission of oxides of nitrogen. Engines with this system all have a special camshaft and a 185° F thermostat.

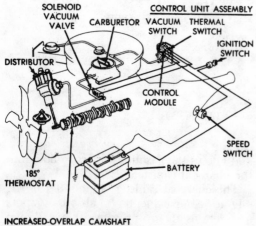

NO_x system—automatic transmission

Operation

MANUAL TRANSMISSION

The manual transmission NO_x system uses a transmission switch, a thermal switch, and a solenoid vacuum valve. The transmission switch is screwed into the transmission housing and is closed, except in high gear. The thermal switch, mounted on the firewall, is open whenever the ambient temperature is above 70° F. With the transmission in any gear, except high, and the temperature above 70°, the solenoid vacuum valve is energized. This shuts off the distributor vacuum advance line, preventing vacuum advance. Below 70°, the vacuum advance functions normally.

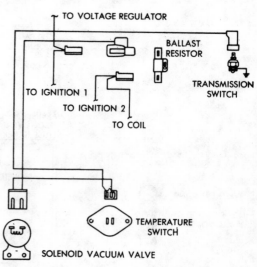

NO_x system schematic—manual transmission

AUTOMATIC TRANSMISSION

The NO_x system for the automatic transmission is more complex than the manual transmission system. It prevents vacuum advance when the ambient temperature is above 70° F, speed is below 30 mph, or the car is accelerating. The solenoid vacuum valve is interchangeable with that used in the manual transmission system. The speed switch senses the vehicle speed and is driven by the speedometer cable. The control unit is mounted on the firewall. It contains a control module, thermal switch, and a vacuum switch. The control unit senses ambient temperature and manifold vacuum.

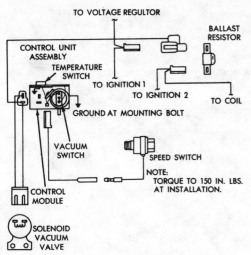

NOx system schematic—automatic transmission

Testing

MANUAL TRANSMISSION

1. Be sure that ambient temperature is well above 70° F.

2. Switch ignition on. Shift into Neutral.

3. Disconnect wire from B+ connector of ballast resistor while holding solenoid vacuum valve. The valve solenoid should be felt to de-energize.

4. Reconnect the wire. The valve solenoid should be felt to energize.

5. Shift into high gear. Repeat steps 3 and 4. The system should be inoperative.

6. To test the solenoid vacuum valve, remove the connector on the valve. Connect the piggyback connector on the ballast resistor to one of the solenoid vacuum valve terminals. Ground the other terminal. The solenoid should energize with the ignition turned on.

7. To test the thermal switch, disconnect and replace it with a length of wire. The solenoid should energize.

8. To test the transmission switch, turn on the ignition switch and shift into Neutral. Remove and ground the wire from the transmission switch. The solenoid should energize. Switch installation torque must be 180 in. lbs.

AUTOMATIC TRANSMISSION

1. Warm the engine to normal operating temperature. Be sure that the ambient temperature is well above 70° F.

2. T-connect a vacuum gauge between the distributor and the solenoid vacuum valve.

3. Raise the car on a lift, with the wheels hanging free.

4. Disconnect the vacuum line at the vacuum switch on the control unit.

5. Start the engine and run at a speed above 850 rpm. The vacuum gauge should read zero.

6. Disconnect the wire from the control unit. The vacuum gauge should read normal advance. Reconnect the wire. The gauge should drop to zero.

7. Unplug and reconnect the vacuum line to the vacuum switch. Disconnect the wire from the control unit to the speed switch. The gauge should read normal advance.

8. Place the transmission in Drive. Sharp acceleration should cause the gauge reading to drop sharply to zero. Do not exceed 40 mph.

9. Accelerate above 30 mph. The gauge should read normal vacuum advance. If the solenoid valve did not operate during the tests, replace the control unit.

AIR INJECTION SYSTEM

Operation

In addition to the CAS, ECS, and NO_x emission controls systems, an exhaust port air injection system is used on all 1972 six-cylinder models sold in California. This system adds a controlled amount of air, through special passages in the cylinder head, to exhaust gases in the exhaust ports, causing oxidation of the gases and thereby reducing carbon monoxide and hydrocarbon emissions to the required levels.

The air injection system consists of a belt-driven air pump, rubber hose, a check valve to protect the hoses and pump from hot gases, injection tubes, and a combination diverter/pressure relief valve assembly.

Service

For correct emission control and engine durability, it is important that the air pump be operating at all times (except when performing tests). Check the condition of the air pump drive belt and adjust the belt tension, as described in the "Belt Tension Adjustment" procedure in chapter 3, at minimum intervals of 12,000 miles or 12 months. If any hoses are in need of re-

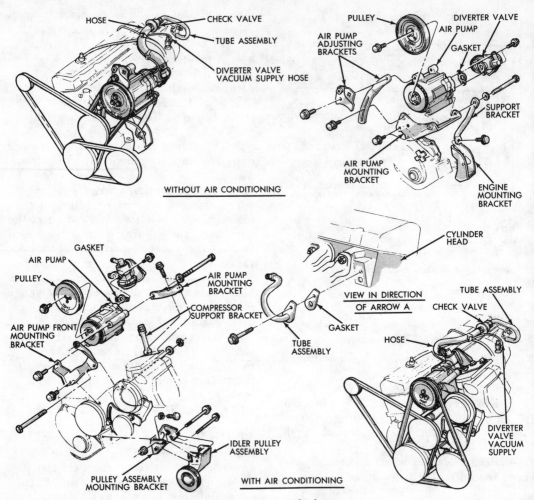

Air injection system—six-cylinder engines

placement, be sure to use the correct replacement hose as the hoses used in emission control systems are made of a special material to resist the corrosive effect of the exhaust gases and gasoline vapor.

AIR PUMP

The only service that may be performed on the air pump is removing and replacing the centrifugal fan filter, or the entire pump. Do not disassemble the pump for any reason. If the pump squeaks when it is turned by hand, do not assume that the pump is defective. Do not attempt to lubricate the pump in any way.

NOTE: *If the engine compartment is to be cleaned with steam or high-pressure detergent, the centrifugal fan filter should be masked off to prevent any liquid from entering the pump.*

The centrifugal fan filter should not be

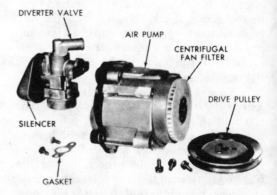

Centrifugal fan filter and air pump assembly

cleaned with compressed air or solvents. The removal procedure will destroy the filter so do not remove it unless a new filter is required.

1. Disconnect the air and vacuum hoses from the diverter valve.

2. Loosen the pump pivot and adjusting bolts and remove the drive belt.

3. Withdraw the pivot and adjusting bolts from the pump. Remove the pump and the diverter valve as an assembly.

CAUTION: *Do not clamp the pump in a vise or use a hammer or pry bar on the pump housing.*

4. To change the filter, remove the three pulley securing screws and lift off the pulley.

5. Remove the remaining portion of the fan filter from the pump hub. Be careful to make sure that filter fragments do not enter the air intake hole.

6. Position the new centrifugal fan filter on the pump hub. Place the pump pulley against the fan filter and install the securing screws. Torque the screws alternately to 95 in. lbs and the fan filter will be pressed onto the pump hub.

7. Install the pump on the engine and adjust its drive belt as described in the "Belt Tension Adjustment" procedure in chapter 3.

NOTE: *A slight amount of interference between the fan filter and the pump housing bore is normal. After a new fan filter has been installed, it may squeal upon initial operation or until its outside diameter sealing lip is worn in. This may require a short period of pump operation at various engine speeds.*

DIVERTER VALVE

Service to the diverter valve is limited to the replacement of the entire valve, if it is found to be defective. Failure of the diverter valve will cause excessive pump noise, chirping, rumbling, or knocking in the air injection system. If air escapes from the silencer at engine idle speed, either the relief valve or the diverter valve has failed and the entire valve assembly should be replaced.

1. Disconnect the air and vacuum hoses from the diverter valve.

2. Withdraw the two screws which secure the diverter valve assembly to the air pump and remove the valve assembly.

3. Remove the gasket material from the diverter valve and pump flanges.

4. To install a new valve, position a new gasket on the pump flange. Fit the new valve assembly on the pump flange and install the securing screws. Torque the screws to 95 in. lbs.

5. Connect the air and vacuum hoses.

CHECK VALVE

The check valve cannot be repaired so, in the event of valve failure, it should be removed and replaced with a new valve. Check valve failure can be determined by removing the air hose from the check valve inlet tube while the engine is running. If exhaust gas escapes from the inlet tube, the valve has failed. If the ignition tube assembly is leaking, remove the tube assembly and replace its gaskets. This assembly must be removed to replace the check valve.

1. Release the clamp and disconnect the air hose from the check valve.

2. Withdraw the screw which secures the injection tube to the cylinder head and remove the injection tube and check valve as an assembly.

3. If a new check valve is needed, remove the old valve from the injection tube and install a new unit.

4. Remove all the old gasket material from the cylinder head and injection tube mating surfaces.

5. Position a new gasket on the cylinder head flange and install the injection tube assembly. Torque the securing screw to 200 in. lbs.

6. Connect the air hose to the check valve inlet and secure it with the clamp.

Fuel System

CARBURETORS

General Overhaul Procedures

Normally, when a carburetor requires major service, a reconditioned unit is purchased on an exchange basis or a rebuild-

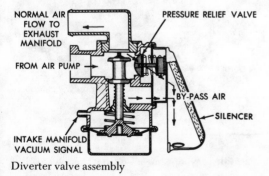
Diverter valve assembly

ing kit is obtained to overhaul the carburetor.

The overhaul kit contains all the necessary replacement parts and some form of instructions for carburetor rebuilding. The instructions may be merely an exploded view of the carburetor or detailed step-by-step overhaul procedures. Unless one is familiar with carburetor overhaul, the latter kit should be obtained.

The following are some basic overhaul procedures which should always be observed:

1. Always dismantle the carburetor completely (except the choke and throttle valve).

2. All parts, except those made of plastic and the choke diaphragm assembly, should be cleaned in carburetor cleaning solvent. If a commercial solvent is used that calls for rinsing with water, hot rinse water must be used.

3. Blow out all traces of water from the carburetor passages with compressed air, after rinsing with hot water. Rerinse all parts in clean kerosine or gasoline.

CAUTION: *Never use a wire or a drill to clean the jets. Using such a mechanical means of cleaning may enlarge the jet orifices which will result in an incorrect fuel mixture when the carburetor is reassembled.*

Fast Idle Cam Adjustment

Although the fast idle engine speed should be adjusted with the carburetor on the engine, the fast idle cam position can be set with the carburetor on or off the engine as follows.

ALL CARBURETORS—EXCEPT CARTER THERMO-QUAD

1. With the fast idle speed adjustment screw touching the second highest step on the fast idle cam, close the choke valve by applying light pressure to it.

2. Insert the proper size drill or gauge (refer to the "Fast Idle Cam Adjustment Specifications") between the top of the choke valve and the wall of the air horn. Withdraw the drill or gauge and a slight interference should be felt. If none is felt, an adjustment is required.

3. To adjust the fast idle cam, bend the fast idle connector rod at its lower angle until the proper setting is obtained.

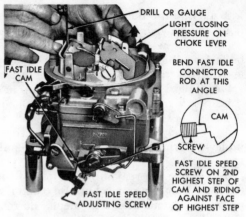

Typical fast idle cam adjustment (Carter AVS shown)

NOTE: *On some carburetors, the choke unloader is automatically adjusted when the fast idle cam is properly set. For those carburetors which require a separate unloader adjustment, refer to the proper procedure in this chapter.*

CARTER THERMO-QUAD

1. Position the fast idle screw on the second step of the cam so that it rests against the shoulder of the first step.

2. Measure the clearance between the air horn wall and the long side of the choke valve nearest the lever. This dimension should be 0.110 in.

3. If necessary, bend the fast idle connector rod to obtain the required clearance.

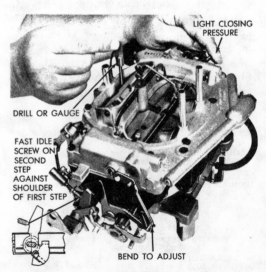

Fast idle cam adjustment—Carter Thermo-Quad

Fast Idle Cam Adjustment Specifications

Carburetor Type	Drill or Gauge Size (in.) Year							
	1965	1966	1967	1968	1969	1970	1971	1972
Ball & Ball								
BBS	0.078	—	—	—	—	—	0.076	—
BBD	0.109	0.095	0.096	0.096	0.096	②	③	0.096
Stromberg WW3	0.141	—	—	—	—	—	—	—
Rochester 2GV	—	—	—	—	—	—	0.052	—
Holley								
1920	0.078	0.063	①	①	0.063	0.063	0.063	0.063
2210	—	—	—	—	—	0.110	—	—
2300	—	—	—	—	—	0.060	0.060	—
4160	—	—	—	—	—	0.060	0.060	—
Carter								
AFB	0.070	0.070	0.070	—	—	0.070	0.070	—
AVS	—	—	—	0.055	0.070	0.070	0.070	—
Thermo-Quad	—	—	—	—	—	—	0.110	0.110

① Manual transmission, 0.096; Automatic transmission, 0.067.
② 318 cu in., 0.096 in.
   383 cu in., 0.141 in.
③ 318 cu in., 0.096 in.
   383 cu in., 0.161 in.

Fast Idle Speed Adjustment

ALL CARBURETORS WITHOUT CAP/CAS—1965–67

1. Allow the engine to warm up to its normal operating temperature. Connect a tachometer to the engine. First set the curb idle speed (refer to "Tune-Up" section), then proceed with the following adjustments:
2. With the engine running and the transmission in Neutral, open the throttle slightly.
3. Close the choke valve twenty degrees. Allow the throttle to close, then open the choke valve.
4. The fast idle screw should now contact the lowest step on the fast idle cam. Turn the fast idle screw in or out, as required to obtain the proper idle speed (see the "Fast Idle Speed Adjustment" Specifications chart).

NOTE: *The cam and throttle must be repositioned after every screw adjustment to maintain normal throttle closing torque.*

ALL CARBURETORS WITH CAP/CAS—1966–72

NOTE: *The 1966–67 CAP carburetors can be identified by a green tag on the air horn.*

1. Warm up the engine by driving the car for at least five miles. Connect a tachometer. Make the curb idle and mixture adjustments first (refer to "Tune-Up" section), then proceed with the following:
2. Switch off the ignition and place the

Fast Idle Speed Adjustment Specifications

Carburetor	Type	Engine Displacement (cu in.)	1965	1966	1967	1968	1969	1970	1971	1972
Ball & Ball	BBS	170, 198 M.T.	700	—	—	—	—	—	1,900	—
		170, 198 A.T.	700	—	—	—	—	—	1,800	—
		225 M.T.	700	—	—	—	—	—	—	—
		225 A.T.	700	—	—	—	—	—	—	—
Holley	1920	170, 198 M.T.	700	—	—	—	—	—	—	—
		170, 198 A.T.	700	—	—	—	—	—	—	—
		225 M.T.	700	700①	700①	1,550	1,600	1,600	1,600	2,000
		225 A.T.	700	700①	700①	1,500	1,800	1,800	1,900	2,000
Stromberg	WW3	273 M.T.	700	—	—	—	—	—	—	—
		273 A.T.	700	—	—	—	—	—	—	—
Ball & Ball	BBD	273 M.T.	700	700②	700②	—	—	—	—	—
		273 A.T.	700	700②	700②	—	—	—	—	—
		318 M.T.	—	—	—	1,300	1,300	1,600	1,600	1,700④
		318 A.T.	—	—	—	1,500	1,700	2,000	1,900	1,900④
		383 M.T.	—	—	—	—	—	1,700	1,900	—
		383 A.T.	—	—	—	—	—	1,700	1,700	—
Rochester	2GV	318 A.T.	—	—	—	—	—	—	1,800	—
Carter	AFB	273 M.T.	625	625③	625③	—	—	—	—	—
		273 A.T.	700	700③	700③	—	—	—	—	—
		383 M.T.	—	—	700	—	—	—	—	—
		383 A.T.	—	—	700	—	—	—	—	—
	AVS	340 M.T.	—	—	—	1,700	1,700	2,000	—	—
		340 A.T.	—	—	—	1,400	1,700	2,000	—	—
		383 M.T.	—	—	—	1,600	1,700	1,700	—	—
		383 A.T.	—	—	—	1,600	1,700	1,700	—	—
		440 M.T.	—	—	—	—	—	2,000	—	—
		440 A.T.	—	—	—	—	—	1,800	—	—
	Thermo-Quad	340 M.T.	—	—	—	—	—	—	1,800	1,900
		340 A.T.	—	—	—	—	—	—	1,800	1,900
Holley	2210	383 A.T.	—	—	—	—	—	1,700	—	—
	2300	340 M.T.	—	—	—	—	—	—	2,600	—
		340 A.T.	—	—	—	—	—	—	2,800	—
		440 M.T.	—	—	—	—	—	2,200	1,800	—
		440 A.T.	—	—	—	—	—	1,800	1,800	—
	4160	383 M.T.	—	—	—	—	—	2,000	1,800	—
		383 A.T.	—	—	—	—	—	1,800	1,700	—
		440 M.T.	—	—	—	—	—	—	—	—
		440 A.T.	—	—	—	—	—	1,600	—	—
Carter	AFB	426 M.T.	—	—	—	—	—	2,000	2,300	—
		426 A.T.	—	—	—	—	—	2,000	2,300	—

M.T.—Manual Transmission.
A.T.—Automatic Transmission.
CAP—Cleaner Air Package.
Calif.—California

① With CAP, 1,550 rpm.
② With CAP, M.T.—1,400; A.T.—1,500.
③ With CAP, M.T.—1,500; A.T.—1,600.
④ Calif., M.T.—2,000; A.T.—1,800.

transmission in Neutral or Park. Open the throttle slightly.

3. Close the choke valve so that the fast idle screw can be placed on the second highest step of the fast idle cam.

4. Start the engine and allow its speed to stabilize. Turn the fast idle screw in or out, as required to obtain the specified fast idle speed (refer to the "Fast Idle Speed Adjustment" Specifications chart).

5. It is unnecessary to stop the engine between adjustments, but always reposition the fast idle screw on the fast idle cam after each adjustment to maintain proper throttle closing torque.

NOTE: *Always check the ignition timing for correct adjustment before adjusting the curb idle and fast idle speeds.*

Float and Fuel Level Adjustment

BALL & BALL BBS AND BBD, STROMBERG WW3, AND ROCHESTER 2GV

1. Remove the carburetor from the engine.

2. Remove the clips and disengage the accelerator pump operating rod.

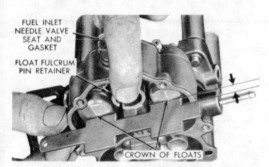

Float setting—Ball & Ball BBS and BBD

3. Remove the clips and disengage the fast idle connector rod from the fast idle cam and choke lever.

4. Remove the vacuum hose from between the carburetor main body and the choke vacuum diaphragm.

5. Remove the clip from the choke operating link and disengage the link from the diaphragm plunger (stem) and choke lever.

6. Remove the choke vacuum diaphragm and bracket assembly.

7. Remove the air horn retaining screws and lift the air horn straight up and away from the main body.

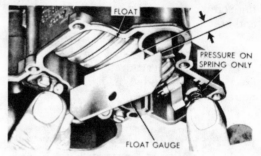

Float setting—Stromberg WW3

8. Invert the main body (catch the pump intake check ball) so that the weight of the floats only is forcing the needle against its seat.

9. Using a suitable depth gauge, measure the distance from the surface of the fuel bowl to the crown of each float. This measurement should be as specified in the "Float Level Specifications" chart.

10. If an adjustment is necessary, hold the floats on the bottom of the bowl and bend the float lip toward or away from the needle. Recheck the setting and then repeat the lip bending operation as required.

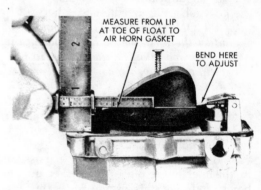

Float setting—Rochester 2GV

CAUTION: *When bending the float lip, do not allow the lip to push against the needle as the synthetic rubber tip can be compressed sufficiently to cause a false setting which will affect the correct level of fuel in the bowl.*

11. After the correct setting has been obtained, reverse steps 1 through 8 to reassemble the carburetor and install the carburetor on the engine.

HOLLEY 1920

1. Remove the carburetor from the engine.

2. Remove the economizer cover retain-

ing screws, then lift the cover, diaphragm, and stem out of the carburetor.

3. Remove the fuel bowl securing screws and remove the fuel bowl and baffle.

4. Invert the carburetor and slide the float gauge (included in carburetor overhaul kit) into position.

Float setting—Holley 1920

5. The float should just contact the TOUCH leg of the gauge. Reverse the gauge and the float should just clear the NO TOUCH leg of the gauge.

6. If an adjustment is necessary, bend the float tab using needle-nose pliers.

CAUTION: *Do not allow the float tab to contact the float needle head during the bending operation as the synthetic rubber tip of the needle can be compressed sufficiently to cause a false setting. Do not touch the contact area of the float tab with the pliers.*

7. When the float adjustment is correct, refit the economizer assembly.

8. Be sure that the baffle is in position in the fuel bowl, place the gasket on the bowl, and refit this assembly to the carburetor.

9. Install the bowl securing screws and washers and tighten the screws gently so that only the washers are compressed and the fuel bowl is not distorted.

Holley 2210

1. Remove the carburetor from the engine.

2. Remove the nut and washer which secure the accelerator pump rocker arm to the accelerator pump shaft. Remove the arm from the flats on the pump shaft, then disengage the accelerator pump rod from the center slot in the arm and from the hole in the throttle lever.

3. Remove the nut and washer which

secure the choke lever to the choke shaft. Disengage the fast idle connector rod from the lever and fast idle cam.

4. Remove the choke vacuum diaphragm hose from the throttle body tube fitting. Remove the screws which attach the choke diaphragm and mounting bracket to the air horn.

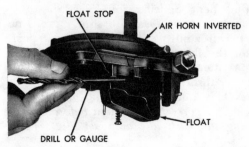

Float setting—Holley 2210

5. Remove the choke diaphragm and, at the same time, disengage the choke operating link from the slot in the choke operating lever.

6. Remove the clip which retains the bowl vent valve operating lever on the stub shaft of the air horn. Slide the lever off the shaft, being careful not to lose the lever spring. Note the position of the spring.

7. Remove the air horn retaining screws and lift the air horn straight up and away from the main body. *Use extreme care when handling the air horn so that the main well tubes will not be bent or damaged.*

8. Invert the air horn so that the weight of the float only is forcing the needle against its seat.

9. Using the proper size gauge (refer to "Float Level Adjustment Specifications"), measure the clearance between the top of the float and the float stop. Be sure that the gauge is perfectly level when measuring.

10. If an adjustment is necessary, bend the float lip toward or away from the needle, using a narrow-blade screwdriver, until the correct clearance is obtained.

11. Check the float drop by holding the air horn in an upright position. The bottom edge of the float should be parallel to the underside surface of the air horn. If an adjustment is necessary, bend the tang on the float arm until parallel surfaces are obtained.

12. After all adjustments are complete, reverse steps 1 through 7 to reassemble the carburetor and install the carburetor on the engine.

HOLLEY 2300

This carburetor has an external float adjusting nut which allows the float level to be set with the carburetor on the engine.

CAUTION: *Place a container under the fuel bowl to catch any fuel that might be liberated due to a high or improper previous setting.*

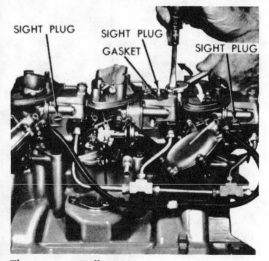

Float setting—Holley 2300

1. Start the engine and remove the sight plug from the fuel bowl.

2. Using a wrench and screwdriver, turn the adjusting nut up or down until fuel just dribbles out of the sight hole.

3. Reinstall the sight plug and gasket and tighten securely. Check the other fuel bowls in the same manner.

HOLLEY 4160

The fuel bowls can be removed from the carburetor without removing the carburetor body from the engine.

CAUTION: *Place a container under each fuel bowl to catch any fuel which might be liberated when the bowl is removed.*

1. Withdraw the securing screws and remove the primary fuel bowl.

2. Invert the primary bowl and using the proper size feeler gauge (refer to "Float Level Specifications"), measure the clearance between the toe of the float and the surface of the fuel bowl. If an adjustment is necessary, bend the float tang until the correct clearance is obtained. Refit the primary fuel bowl.

3. Withdraw the securing screws and remove the secondary fuel bowl.

4. Invert the secondary bowl and, using the proper size feeler gauge (refer to "Float Level Specifications"), measure the

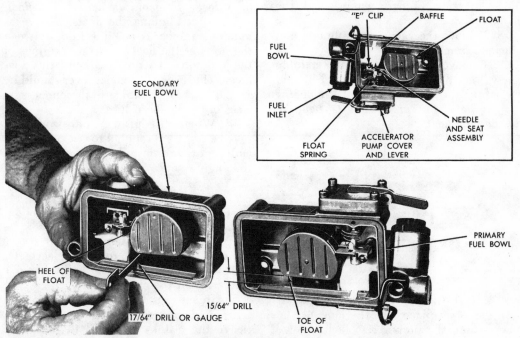

Float setting adjustment (primary and secondary)—Holley 4160

clearance between the heel of the float and the surface of the fuel bowl. If an adjustment is necessary, bend the float tang until the correct clearance is obtained. Refit the secondary fuel bowl.

CARTER AFB AND AVS

1. Remove the carburetor from the engine.

2. Remove the clip which secures the fast idle connector rod to the choke lever. Disengage the rod from the lever and swing the rod in an arc until it can be disengaged from the fast idle cam.

3. Remove the pin and clip which secure the throttle connector rod to the accelerator pump arm and the primary throttle shaft lever. Disengage the rod from the arm and lever and remove it from the carburetor.

4. Withdraw the securing screws from the step-up piston and rod cover plates. *Hold the cover down while removing the screws to keep the piston and rods from flying out.*

5. Lift off the plates and slide the step-up pistons and rods out of the air horn. Remove the step-up piston springs.

6. Remove the vacuum hose from between the carburetor throttle body and the vacuum diaphragm.

7. Remove the clip from the choke operating link and disengage the link from the diaphragm plunger (stem) and the choke lever.

8. Remove the vacuum diaphragm and bracket assembly.

9. Remove the air horn retaining screws and lift the air horn straight up and away from the main body. *When removing the air horn, be careful not to bend or damage the floats.*

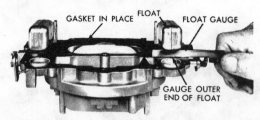

Float setting—Carter AFB and AVS

10. Invert the air horn. With the air horn gasket in place and the float needle seated, slide the proper size feeler gauge (refer to "Float Level Adjustment Specifications") between the top of the float at its outer end and the air horn gasket. The float should just touch the gauge.

11. Check the other float in the same manner. If an adjustment is necessary, bend the float arm until the correct clearance is obtained.

12. After the proper clearance has been obtained, check the float alignment by sighting down the side of each float shell to determine if the side of the float is parallel to the outer cage of the air horn.

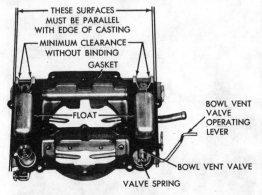

Checking float alignment—Carter AFB and AVS

13. If the sides of the float are not in alignment with the edge of the casting, bend the float lever by applying thumb pressure to the end of the float shell. *Apply only enough pressure to bend the float lever to avoid damaging the float.*

14. After aligning the floats, remove as much clearance as possible from between the arms of the float lever and the lugs of the air horn. To do this, bend the float lever. The arms of the float lever should be as parallel as possible to the inner surfaces of the air horn lugs.

15. When all adjustments are complete, reverse steps 1 through 9 to reassemble the carburetor and install the carburetor on the engine.

CARTER THERMO-QUAD

1. Remove the carburetor from the engine.

2. Remove the retainers which secure the throttle connector rod to the accelerator pump arm and throttle lever. Remove the rod from the carburetor.

3. Remove the accelerator pump arm screw and disengage the pump rod S-link (leave the S-link connected to the pump rod) and then remove the lever.

4. Remove the choke countershaft fast idle lever attaching screw while holding the lever. Disengage the lever from the countershaft and then swing the fast idle connector rod in an arc until it can be disengaged from the fast idle operating lever.

5. Remove the retainers and washer which secure the choke diaphragm connector rod to the choke vacuum diaphragm and air valve lever. Remove the lever.

6. Remove the retainer which secures the choke connector rod to the choke countershaft. Disengage and swing the rod in an arc to remove the choke shaft lever assembly.

7. Remove the step-up piston cover plate securing screw and cover plate. Remove the step-up piston and link assembly with the step-up rods. Remove the step-up piston spring.

8. Remove the pump jet housing screw, housing, and gasket. Invert the carburetor and remove the discharge check needle.

9. Withdraw the bowl cover retaining screws and remove the bowl cover.

10. Invert the bowl cover. With the bowl cover gasket in place and the float needle seated, use a depth gauge to measure the distance from the bowl cover gasket to the bottom side of the float. This dimension should be 1.00 inch.

11. If an adjustment is necessary, bend the float lever until the correct distance is obtained. *Never allow the lip of the float to be pressed against the needle when adjusting the float.*

12. When the float adjustment is complete, reverse steps 1 through 9 to reassemble the carburetor and install the carburetor on the engine.

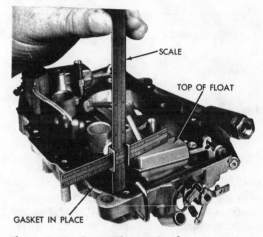

Float setting—Carter Thermo-Quad

Float Level Adjustment Specifications

Carburetor Type	Gauge Size (in.) Year							
	1965	1966	1967	1968	1969	1970	1971	1972
Ball & Ball								
BBS	0.250	—	—	—	—	—	0.250	—
BBD	0.250	0.250	0.250	0.250	0.250	③	③	0.250
Stromberg WW3	0.219	—	—	—	—	—	—	—
Rochester 2GV	—	—	—	—	—	—	0.656	—
Holley								
1920	①	①	①	①	①	①	①	①
2210	—	—	—	—	—	0.200	—	—
2300	—	—	—	—	—	④	④	—
4160	—	—	—	—	—	0.234 (pri) 0.266 (sec)	0.234 (pri) 0.266 (sec)	—

Float Level Adjustment Specifications

	Gauge Size (in.) Year							
Carburetor Type	1965	1966	1967	1968	1969	1970	1971	1972
Carter	0.219	0.219	0.219	——	——	0.219	0.219	——
AFB	0.219	0.219	0.219	——	——	0.219	0.219	——
AVS	——	——	——	0.313	②	⑤	0.219	——
Thermo-Quad	——	——	——	——	——	——	1.00	1.00

① Use gauge; see text.
② 340 cu in., 0.219 in.
   383 cu in., 0.313 in.
③ 318 cu in., 0.250 in.
   383 cu in., 0.313 in.
④ See text.

⑤ 340 cu in., 0.219 in.
   383 cu in., 0.313 in.
   440 cu in. (All except manual transmission with CAS), 0.438 in., 440 cu in. (manual transmission with CAS), 0.219 in.

Unloader Adjustment

ALL CARBURETORS EXCEPT HOLLEY 1920 AND STROMBERG WW3

The choke unloader partially opens the choke valve at full throttle to prevent choke enrichment during engine cranking. Engines that have been stalled or flooded by too much choke enrichment can be started by using the unloader (fully depressing the accelerator pedal).

Unloader adjustment is performed in the following manner.

1. Hold the throttle valve(s) wide open. Insert the proper size drill (see chart below) between the upper edge of the choke valve and the air horn inner wall.

2. Lightly press against the valve and withdraw the drill. A slight drag should be felt. If none is felt, or if there is too much drag, an adjustment is required.

3. To adjust the unloader on all but the Holley 4160, Carter AVS, and Thermo-Quad carburetors, bend the tang on the throttle lever until the proper opening has been reached.

4. On the Holley 4160, Carter AVS, and Thermo-Quad, bend the unloader tang on the fast idle cam until the proper opening has been reached.

HOLLEY 1920

When the fast idle cam is adjusted, the choke unloader is automatically adjusted and requires no further attention.

STROMBERG WW3

1. Hold the choke valve closed with light pressure. Open the throttle valves fully. The choke valve should open enough to allow a 0.312 in. drill to be inserted between it and the air horn wall.

2. If adjustment is required, bend the tang on the throttle lever until proper clearance has been reached.

3. Open the choke valve. Continue holding it open while opening and closing the throttle valves. If the throttle does not open fully, the choke assembly has not been put together properly.

4. Hold the throttle valves open. Slowly open the choke valve to its fullest extent. No binding should be felt throughout the travel of the choke valve.

Unloader Adjustment Specifications

Carburetor Type	Drill or Gauge Size (in.)	Bend to Adjust Unloader
Holley 1920 Ball & Ball	None	None—See text
BBS	0.188	Tang on throttle lever
BBD	0.250	
Stromberg WW3	0.312	
Carter AFB	0.375①	Lip on throttle lever
AVS	0.250	Tang on fast idle cam
Thermo-Quad	0.190	
Rochester 2GV	0.136	Tang on throttle lever
Holley 2210	0.172	Tang on throttle lever
2300	0.156	
4160	0.150	Tang on fast idle cam

① 1967, 0.219 in.; 1970, 0.250 in.

Vacuum Kick Adjustment

This adjustment can be performed with the carburetor on or off the engine. Because the choke diaphragm must be energized to measure the vacuum kick adjustment, an auxiliary vacuum source, such as a distributor test machine or vacuum supplied by another vehicle, must be used when the adjustment is performed off the vehicle.

ALL CARBURETORS—EXCEPT STROMBERG WW3, CARTER AFB, AND THERMO—QUAD

1. If the adjustment is to be made *on* the engine (with the engine running at curb idle), back off the fast idle screw until the choke can be closed to the kick position. Note the number of screw turns required so that the fast idle can be returned to the original adjustment.

2. If the adjustment is to be made *off* the engine, open the throttle valve and move the choke to its closed position. Release the throttle first and then release the choke. Disconnect the vacuum hose from the carburetor body and connect it to the auxiliary vacuum source. Apply a vacuum of at least 10 in. Hg.

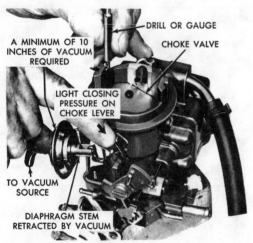

Typical vacuum kick adjustment (Holley 1920 shown)

3. Insert the specified size drill or gauge (refer to the "Vacuum Kick Adjustment Specifications" chart) between the choke valve and the wall of the air horn.

4. Apply sufficient closing pressure to the choke lever to provide a minimum valve opening without distorting the diaphragm link (which connects the choke lever to the vacuum diaphragm). Note that the cylindrical stem of the diaphragm will extend as its internal spring is compressed. This spring must be fully compressed for the proper measurement of the vacuum kick adjustment.

5. Remove the drill or gauge. If a slight drag is not felt as the drill or gauge is removed, an adjustment of the diaphragm link is necessary to obtain the proper clearance. Shorten or lengthen the diaphragm link by carefully closing or opening the U-bend in the link until the correct adjustment is obtained.

CAUTION: *When adjusting the link, be careful not to bend or twist the diaphragm.*

6. Refit the vacuum hose to the carburetor body (if it had been removed) and return the fast idle screw to its original location.

7. With *no* vacuum applied to the diaphragm, the choke valve should move freely between its open and closed positions. If it does not move freely, examine the linkage for misalignment or interference which may have been caused by the bending operation. If necessary, repeat the adjustment to provide the proper link operation.

STROMBERG WW3 AND CARTER AFB

The vacuum kick adjustment for these carburetors is performed in the same manner as described above with one exception. To avoid possible damage to the diaphragm and the choke lever slot, the choke diaphragm link must be removed from the carburetor to adjust its operating length. Remove the retaining clip and disengage the link from the choke lever, then disengage the link from the diaphragm stem.

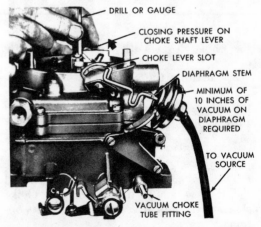

Vacuum kick adjustment—Carter AFB

This procedure is necessary to adjust the WW3 and single AFB installations only (1965–67 Barracuda). The dual AFB system used on 1970–71 Barracudas and Challengers with the Hemi engine has no vacuum kick adjustment.

THERMO-QUAD

Before the vacuum kick adjustment can be performed, the choke control lever and the choke diaphragm connector rod must be correctly set. These settings can be made on or off the vehicle.

1. If the setting is to be made *on* the engine, remove the choke assembly, stainless steel cup, and gasket. If the setting is to be made *off* the vehicle, place the carburetor on a clean, flat surface, such as a table top or workbench, so that the carburetor flange is flush against the work surface.

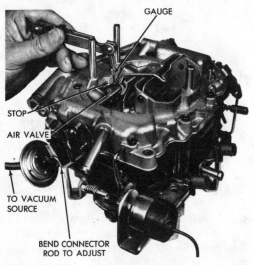

Adjusting choke diaphragm connector rod (secondary air valve control)—Carter Thermo-Quad

2. Close the choke valve by pushing on the choke lever with the throttle partly open.

3. Measure the vertical distance from the top of the rod hole in the choke control lever down to the clean choke pad surface (on engine), or down to the work surface (off engine). This measurement should be $5^{41}/_{64}$ in. on the engine, or $3^{27}/_{64}$ in. off the engine.

4. If an adjustment is necessary, bend the link which connects the two choke shafts until the correct measurement is obtained.

5. Refit the choke assembly (if it had been removed).

After the choke control lever has been properly set, continue this procedure to adjust the choke diaphragm connector rod and the vacuum kick. The choke diaphragm must be energized during both of these adjustments.

1. If the adjustment is to be made *on* the engine (with the engine running at curb idle), measure the clearance between the air valve and its stop (see illustration). The clearance should be 0.040 in. with the air valve closed. If necessary, adjust the connector rod as illustrated until the correct clearance is obtained. Then back off the fast idle screw until the choke can be closed to the kick position. Note the number of screw turns required so that the fast idle can be returned to the original adjustment.

2. If the adjustment is to be made *off* the engine, disconnect the vacuum hose from the carburetor body and connect it to the auxiliary vacuum source. Apply a vacuum of at least 10 in. Hg and measure the clearance between the air valve and its stop. The clearance should be 0.040 in.

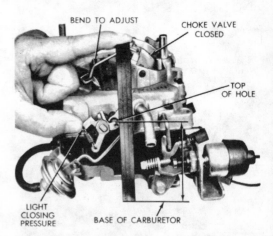

Adjusting choke control lever—Carter Thermo-Quad

with the air valve closed. If necessary, adjust the connector rod as illustrated until the correct clearance is obtained. Disconnect the vacuum line from the auxiliary source, open the throttle valves, and move the choke valve to its closed position with the control lever. Release the throttle before releasing the choke to trap the fast idle cam in the closed choke position. Reconnect the vacuum line to the auxiliary vacuum source and again apply a vacuum of at least 10 in. Hg.

3. Insert the specified size drill or gauge (refer to the "Vacuum Kick Adjustment Specifications" chart) between the long side (lower edge) of the choke valve and the air horn wall.

4. Apply sufficient closing pressure to the choke control lever to provide a minimum choke valve opening without distorting the choke linkage. Note that only this carburetor extends a spring connecting the control lever to an adjustment lever. This

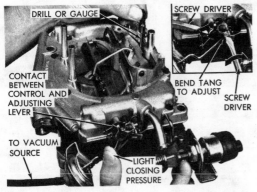

Vacuum kick adjustment—Carter Thermo-Quad

spring must be fully extended for the proper measurement of the vacuum kick adjustment.

5. Remove the drill or gauge. If a slight drag is not felt as the drill or gauge is removed, an adjustment of the adjusting lever is necessary to obtain the proper clearance. While applying a counterforce to the adjusting lever, bend the adjusting lever tang to change the contact with the end of the diaphragm rod.

CAUTION: *Do not adjust the diaphragm rod. Do not load the link which connects the two choke shafts because the choke control lever adjustment will be changed.*

6. Refit the vacuum hose to the carburetor body (if it had been removed) and return the fast idle screw to its original position.

7. With *no* vacuum applied to the diaphragm, the choke valve should move freely between its open and closed positions. If it does not move freely, examine the linkage for misalignment or interference which may have been caused by the bending operation. If necessary, repeat the adjustment to provide the proper linkage operation.

Vacuum Kick Adjustment Specifications

| Carburetor | Type | Engine Displacement (cu in.) | Drill or Gauge Size (in.) | | | | | | | |
| | | | Year | | | | | | | |
			1965	1966	1967	1968	1969	1970	1971	1972
Ball & Ball	BBS	170, 198 M.T.	0.156	——	——	——	——	——	0.110	
		170, 198 A.T.	0.096	——	——	——	——	——	0.110	——
		225 M.T.	0.125	——	——	——	——	——	——	——
		225 A.T.	0.096	——	——	——	——	——	——	——
Holley	1920	170, 198 M.T.	0.116	——	——	——	——	——	——	——
		170, 198 A.T.	0.094	——	——	——	——	——	——	——
		225 M.T.	0.116	0.129①	0.129①	0.141	0.100	0.100	0.100	0.100
		225 A.T.	0.081	0.102	0.089③	0.102	0.070	0.070	0.100	0.100

Vacuum Kick Adjustment Specifications

Carburetor	Type	Engine Displacement (cu in.)	Drill or Gauge Size (in.) Year							
			1965	1966	1967	1968	1969	1970	1971	1972
Stromberg	WW3	273 M.T.	0.266	—	—	—	—	—	—	—
		273 A.T.	0.209	—	—	—	—	—	—	—
Ball & Ball	BBD	273 M.T.	0.177	0.177	0.180	—	—	—	—	—
		273 A.T.	0.129	0.128	0.125	—	—	—	—	—
		318 M.T.	—	—	—	0.209	0.161	0.161	0.161	0.149
		318 A.T.	—	—	—	0.141	0.141	0.161	0.161	0.149
		383 M.T.	—	—	—	—	—	0.161	0.161	—
		383 A.T.	—	—	—	—	—	0.141	0.141	—
Rochester	2GV	318 A.T.	—	—	—	—	—	—	0.096	—
Carter	AFB	273 M.T.	0.125	0.125	0.125	—	—	—	—	—
		273 A.T.	0.094	0.094②	0.094②	—	—	—	—	—
		383 M.T.	—	—	0.125④	—	—	—	—	—
		383 A.T.	—	—	0.094④	—	—	—	—	—
	AVS	340 M.T.	—	—	—	0.191	0.110	0.110	—	—
		340 A.T.	—	—	—	0.070	0.070	0.070	—	—
		383 M.T.	—	—	—	0.191	0.110	0.086	—	—
		383 A.T.	—	—	—	0.102	0.070	0.086	0.086	—
		440 M.T.	—	—	—	—	—	0.161	—	—
		440 A.T.	—	—	—	—	—	0.161	—	—
	Thermo-Quad	340 M.T.	—	—	—	—	—	—	0.110	0.160
		340 A.T.	—	—	—	—	—	—	0.110	0.140
Holley	2210	383 A.T.	—	—	—	—	—	0.200	—	—
	2300	340 M.T.	—	—	—	—	—	—	0.141	—
		340 A.T.	—	—	—	—	—	—	0.100	—

Vacuum Kick Adjustment Specifications

| Carburetor | Type | Engine Displacement (cu in.) | Drill or Gauge Size (in.) | | | | | | | |
| | | | Year | | | | | | | |
			1965	1966	1967	1968	1969	1970	1971	1972
Holley	2300	440 M.T.	——	——	——	——	——	0.141	0.141	——
		440 A.T.	——	——	——	——	——	0.070	0.070	——
	4160	383 M.T.	——	——	——	——	——	0.170	170⑤	——
		383 A.T.	——	——	——	——	——	0.081	0.081⑥	——
		440 A.T.	——	——	——	——	——	0.081	——	——

M.T.—Manual Transmission.
A.T.—Automatic Transmission.
CAP—Cleaner Air Package
① With CAP, 0.141 in.
② With CAP, 0.125 in.

③ With CAP, 0.102 in.
④ With CAP, 0.086 in.
⑤ With Fresh Air Intake System, 0.081 in.
⑥ With Fresh Air Intake System, 0.170 in.

Barracuda and Challenger Carburetor Assemblies

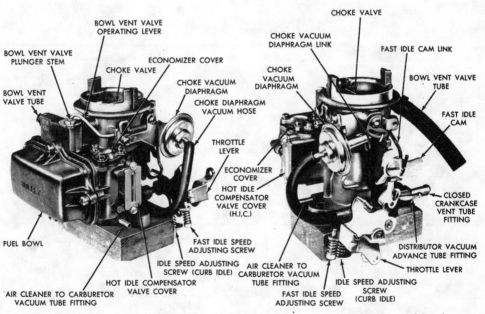

Holley 1920 (with ECS)—other models do not have the hot idle compensator valve and bowl vent valve tube

Barracuda and Challenger Carburetor Assemblies

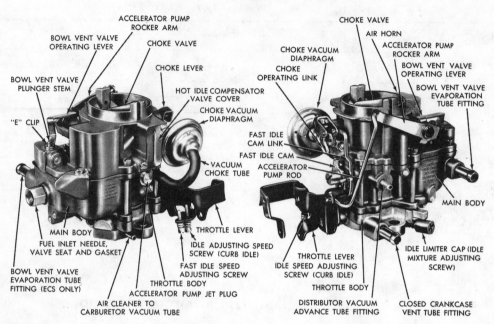

Ball & Ball BBS (with ECS)—earlier model does not have the hot idle compensator valve and bowl vent valve assembly

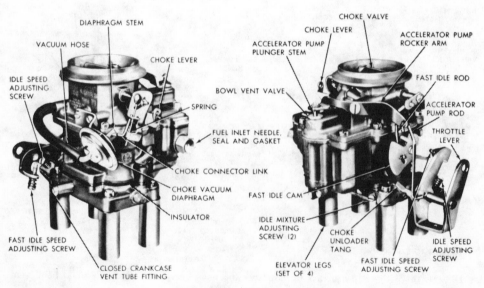

Stromberg WW3

Barracuda and Challenger Carburetor Assemblies

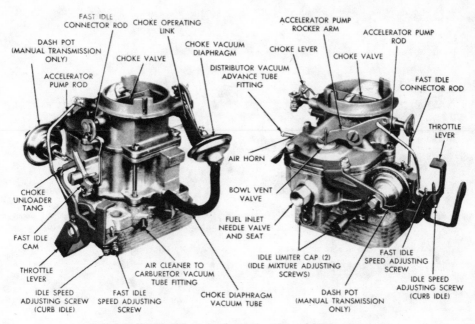

Ball & Ball BBD 1¼ in. (with CAS)—273 and 318 cu in. engines

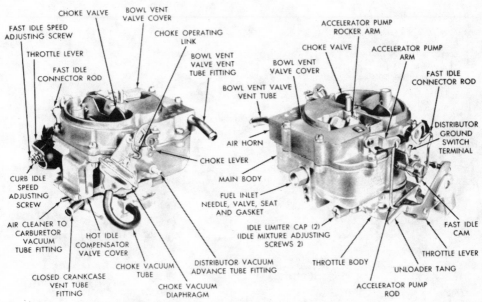

Ball & Ball BBD 1½ in. (with ECS)—383 cu in. engine

Barracuda and Challenger Carburetor Assemblies

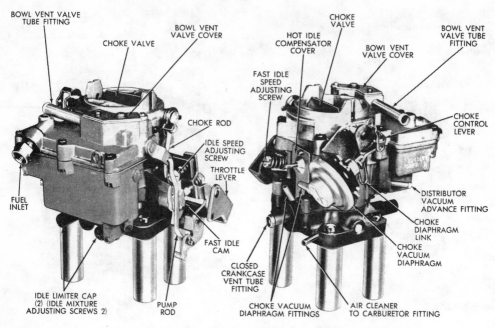

BOWL VENT VALVE TUBE FITTING
CHOKE VALVE
BOWL VENT VALVE COVER
CHOKE ROD
IDLE SPEED ADJUSTING SCREW
THROTTLE LEVER
FUEL INLET
FAST IDLE CAM
IDLE LIMITER CAP (2) (IDLE MIXTURE ADJUSTING SCREWS 2)
PUMP ROD

CHOKE VALVE
HOT IDLE COMPENSATOR COVER
BOWL VENT VALVE COVER
BOWL VENT VALVE TUBE FITTING
FAST IDLE SPEED ADJUSTING SCREW
CHOKE CONTROL LEVER
DISTRIBUTOR VACUUM ADVANCE FITTING
CHOKE DIAPHRAGM LINK
CHOKE VACUUM DIAPHRAGM
CLOSED CRANKCASE VENT TUBE FITTING
CHOKE VACUUM DIAPHRAGM FITTINGS
AIR CLEANER TO CARBURETOR FITTING

Rochester 2GV

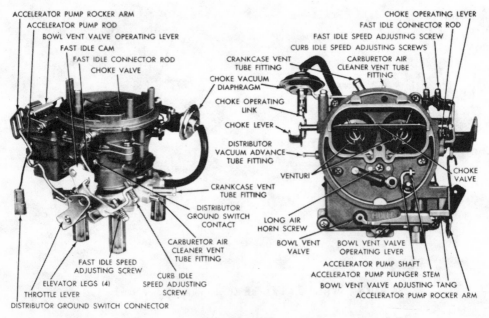

ACCELERATOR PUMP ROCKER ARM
ACCELERATOR PUMP ROD
BOWL VENT VALVE OPERATING LEVER
FAST IDLE CAM
FAST IDLE CONNECTOR ROD
CHOKE VALVE
CRANKCASE VENT TUBE FITTING
CHOKE VACUUM DIAPHRAGM
CHOKE OPERATING LINK
CHOKE LEVER
DISTRIBUTOR VACUUM ADVANCE TUBE FITTING
CRANKCASE VENT TUBE FITTING
DISTRIBUTOR GROUND SWITCH CONTACT
CARBURETOR AIR CLEANER VENT TUBE FITTING
FAST IDLE SPEED ADJUSTING SCREW
ELEVATOR LEGS (4)
THROTTLE LEVER
DISTRIBUTOR GROUND SWITCH CONNECTOR
CURB IDLE SPEED ADJUSTING SCREW

CHOKE OPERATING LEVER
FAST IDLE CONNECTOR ROD
FAST IDLE SPEED ADJUSTING SCREW
CURB IDLE SPEED ADJUSTING SCREWS
CARBURETOR AIR CLEANER VENT TUBE FITTING
CHOKE VALVE
VENTURI
LONG AIR HORN SCREW
BOWL VENT VALVE
BOWL VENT VALVE OPERATING LEVER
ACCELERATOR PUMP SHAFT
ACCELERATOR PUMP PLUNGER STEM
BOWL VENT VALVE ADJUSTING TANG
ACCELERATOR PUMP ROCKER ARM

Holley 2210

Barracuda and Challenger Carburetor Assemblies

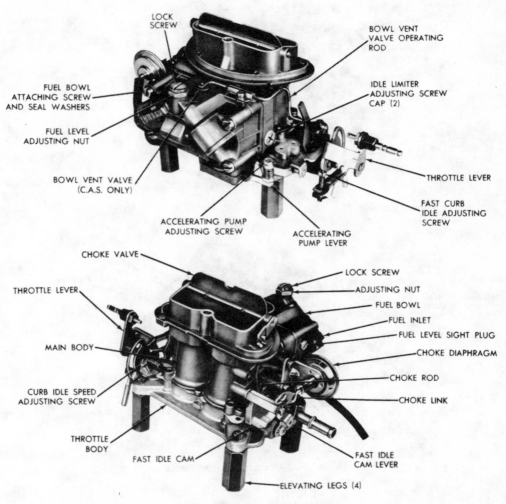

Holley 2300—center carburetor

Barracuda and Challenger Carburetor Assemblies

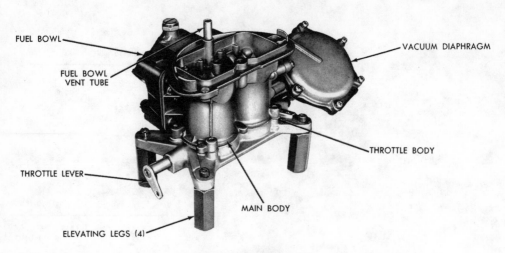

FUEL BOWL

FUEL BOWL
VENT TUBE

VACUUM DIAPHRAGM

THROTTLE BODY

THROTTLE LEVER

MAIN BODY

ELEVATING LEGS (4)

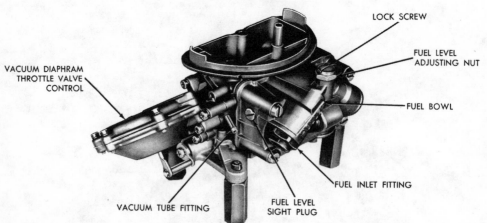

LOCK SCREW

VACUUM DIAPHRAM
THROTTLE VALVE
CONTROL

FUEL LEVEL
ADJUSTING NUT

FUEL BOWL

FUEL INLET FITTING

VACUUM TUBE FITTING

FUEL LEVEL
SIGHT PLUG

Holley 2300—front or rear carburetor

Barracuda and Challenger Carburetor Assemblies

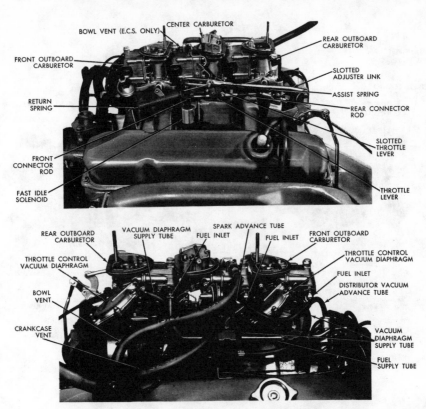

Holley 2300 Six Pack installation

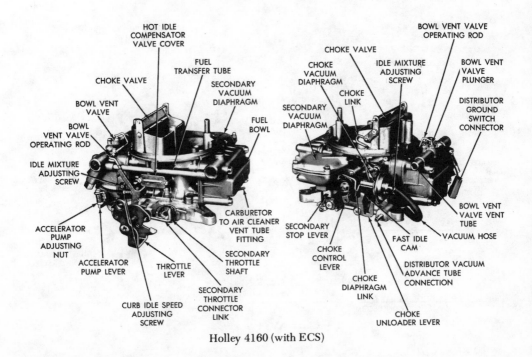

Holley 4160 (with ECS)

Barracuda and Challenger Carburetor Assemblies

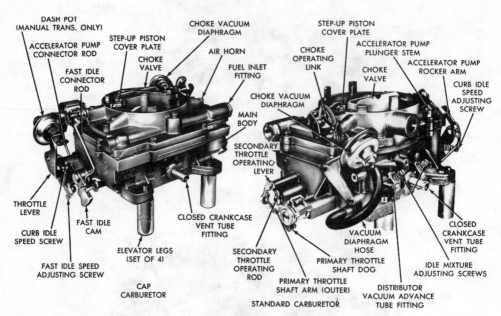

DASH POT
(MANUAL TRANS. ONLY)

ACCELERATOR PUMP
CONNECTOR ROD

FAST IDLE
CONNECTOR
ROD

STEP-UP PISTON
COVER PLATE

CHOKE
VALVE

CHOKE VACUUM
DIAPHRAGM

AIR HORN

FUEL INLET
FITTING

CHOKE VACUUM
DIAPHRAGM

MAIN
BODY

SECONDARY
THROTTLE
OPERATING
LEVER

THROTTLE
LEVER

CURB IDLE
SPEED SCREW

FAST IDLE
CAM

FAST IDLE SPEED
ADJUSTING SCREW

ELEVATOR LEGS
(SET OF 4)

CAP
CARBURETOR

CLOSED CRANKCASE
VENT TUBE
FITTING

SECONDARY
THROTTLE
OPERATING
ROD

PRIMARY THROTTLE
SHAFT ARM (OUTER)

STANDARD CARBURETOR

STEP-UP PISTON
COVER PLATE

ACCELERATOR PUMP
PLUNGER STEM

ACCELERATOR PUMP
ROCKER ARM

CHOKE
OPERATING
LINK

CHOKE
VALVE

CURB IDLE
SPEED
ADJUSTING
SCREW

VACUUM
DIAPHRAGM
HOSE

PRIMARY THROTTLE
SHAFT DOG

CLOSED
CRANKCASE
VENT TUBE
FITTING

IDLE MIXTURE
ADJUSTING SCREWS

DISTRIBUTOR
VACUUM ADVANCE
TUBE FITTING

Carter AFB—1965–67 273 and 383 cu in. engine

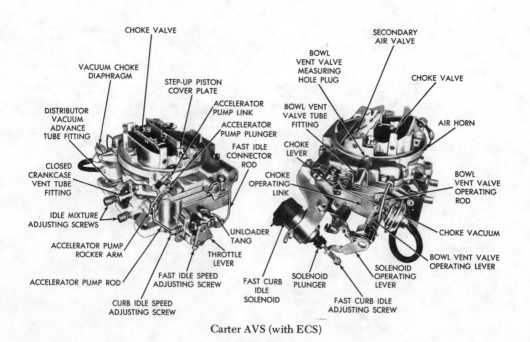

CHOKE VALVE

VACUUM CHOKE
DIAPHRAGM

STEP-UP PISTON
COVER PLATE

ACCELERATOR
PUMP LINK

ACCELERATOR
PUMP PLUNGER

DISTRIBUTOR
VACUUM
ADVANCE
TUBE FITTING

FAST IDLE
CONNECTOR
ROD

CHOKE
OPERATING
LINK

CLOSED
CRANKCASE
VENT TUBE
FITTING

IDLE MIXTURE
ADJUSTING SCREWS

ACCELERATOR PUMP
ROCKER ARM

ACCELERATOR PUMP ROD

CURB IDLE SPEED
ADJUSTING SCREW

FAST IDLE SPEED
ADJUSTING SCREW

THROTTLE
LEVER

UNLOADER
TANG

FAST CURB
IDLE
SOLENOID

SOLENOID
PLUNGER

FAST CURB IDLE
ADJUSTING SCREW

SECONDARY
AIR VALVE

BOWL
VENT VALVE
MEASURING
HOLE PLUG

CHOKE VALVE

AIR HORN

BOWL VENT
VALVE TUBE
FITTING

CHOKE
LEVER

BOWL
VENT VALVE
OPERATING
ROD

CHOKE VACUUM

BOWL VENT VALVE
OPERATING LEVER

SOLENOID
OPERATING
LEVER

Carter AVS (with ECS)

Barracuda and Challenger Carburetor Assemblies

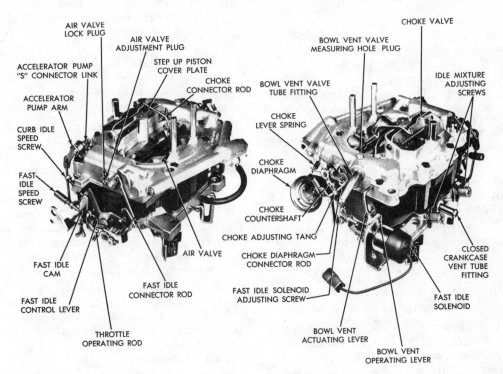

Carter Thermo-Quad

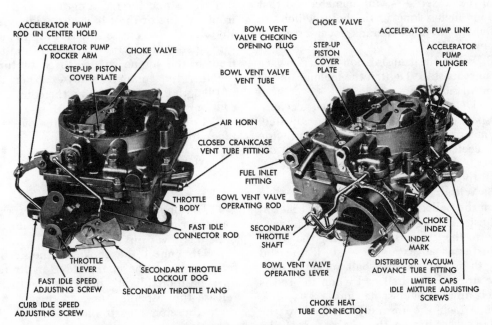

Carter AFB—1970–71 426 Hemi

Throttle Linkage Adjustment

6 Cylinder Engine—1965–66 with Manual Transmission

1. Disconnect the choke at the carburetor. Open the throttle just enough to release the fast idle cam, then return the throttle to its curb idle position.

2. Detach the upper end of the accelerator pedal rod. The length of the rod should be adjusted to provide a pedal angle of 111–113 degrees. The rod length is adjusted by means of a screw adjustment. Increasing the rod length increases the pedal angle and vice versa.

3. Connect the upper end of the accelerator pedal rod and the choke at the carburetor.

4. Lubricate the outer edges of the carburetor lever isolator, the plastic torque shaft bushing, and the torque shaft ball stud.

6 Cylinder Engine—1965–66 with Automatic Transmission

1. Disconnect the choke at the carburetor. Open the throttle just enough to release the fast idle cam, then return the throttle to its curb idle position. Detach the torque shaft ball from the ball socket.

2. Loosen the locknut on the transmission rod. Insert a $3/16$ in. diameter rod that is four inches long in the holes which are provided in the bellcrank/lever assembly bracket.

3. Bring the transmission lever forward against its stop. Tighten the locknut on the transmission rod.

4. Detach the upper end of the accelerator pedal rod. The rod should be adjusted, by means of its adjusting screw, to provide an accelerator pedal angle of 111–113 degrees. After completing the adjustment, attach the upper end of the rod.

5. Withdraw the $3/16$ in. diameter rod from the bellcrank/lever assembly bracket. Adjust the length of the bellcrank in relation to the torque shaft by using the screw adjustment at its upper end. If the rod length is correct, the ball socket should line up with the ball end when the rod is lifted upward against its stop.

6. Attach the torque shaft ball to the ball socket. Fasten the choke rod at the carburetor.

7. Lubricate the outer surface of the carburetor lever isolator, the plastic bushing on the torque shaft, the torque shaft ball stud, and the bellcrank pin.

6 Cylinder Engine—1966 with Manual Transmission and Air Conditioning
V8 Engine—1965–66 with Manual Transmission
All Engines—1967–72 with Manual Transmission

1. Disconnect the choke (not on Hemi) at the carburetor or block the choke valve in its fully opened position.

2. Slightly open the throttle to release the fast idle cam and then return the carburetor to curb idle.

3. Loosen the cable clamp nut. Position the cable housing adjuster in the clamp so that there is no slack in the cable at curb idle. To decrease cable slack, move the adjuster away from the carburetor lever.

4. Back off the adjuster $1/4$ in. to allow $1/4$ in. of cable slack at idle. Torque the clamp nut to 45 in. lbs.

5. On the Hemi, mount the carburetor connector rod between the carburetors so that the carburetor rod slotted end is connected to the inner lever of the rear carburetor. The slotted end should be on the outward side of the carburetor lever. Fully open the rear carburetor throttle and adjust the connector rod length so that the front carburetor throttle is also wide open. Rod length is increased by turning the adjusting stud clockwise (as viewed from the front of the engine) or decreased by turning the stud counterclockwise. When the rod length is correct, tighten the connector rod locknut.

6. Connect the choke or remove the block from the choke valve.

6 Cylinder Engine—1966 with Automatic Transmission and Air Conditioning

1. Disconnect the linkage return spring and the slotted transmission link from the bellcrank lever pin.

2. Disconnect the choke at the carburetor or block the choke valve in its full open position. Slightly open the throttle to release the fast idle cam and then return the carburetor to curb idle.

3. Move the transmission lever forward against its stop. The lever must remain in this position during the remainder of the adjustment procedure. Either wire the

lever to secure it or have an assistant hold the lever against its stop.

4. Adjust the length of the transmission rod by using the threaded adjuster which is located at its upper end. The rear end of the slot should contact the bellcrank lever pin without exerting any forward force. Lengthen the rod by one full turn of the adjustment.

5. Attach the slotted adjuster to the bellcrank lever pin. Fit the washer and retaining pin, then position the linkage return spring.

6. Check the transmission linkage operation by releasing the transmission lever, moving the adjuster link to its full rearward position, and then allowing the link to slowly return. If the linkage is operating correctly, the adjuster link should return to its full forward position.

7. Loosen the throttle cable clamp nut. Position the cable housing adjuster in the clamp so that there is no slack in the cable at curb idle. To decrease the cable slack, move the adjuster away from the carburetor lever.

8. Back off the adjuster one-fourth inch to allow one-fourth inch of cable free-play at idle. Tighten the clamp nut.

9. Connect the choke or remove the block from the choke valve.

6 Cylinder Engine—1967 with Automatic Transmission

This procedure is essentially the same as for the 1966 six-cylinder automatic with air conditioning (see above). When adjusting the transmission rod, apply light pressure to the rod while turning the threaded adjuster. The ball socket and the ball end must be aligned and at the same height.

V8 Engine—1965–66 with Automatic Transmission

1. Disconnect the linkage return spring and the carburetor rod ball socket from the carburetor, or disconnect the transmission intermediate rod ball socket from the upper bellcrank ball end.

2. Disconnect the choke at the carburetor or block the choke valve in its fully open position. Slightly open the throttle to release the fast idle cam and then return the carburetor to curb idle.

3. Insert a 6 in. long $3/16$ in. diameter rod in the holes provided in the upper bellcrank and lever. Adjust the length of the intermediate transmission rod by turning its threaded adjuster located at the upper end of the rod. For the rod length to be correct, the ball socket must line up with the ball end with the rod held downward against the transmission stop.

4. Attach the ball socket to the ball end. Remove the $3/16$ in. diameter rod from the upper bellcrank and lever.

5. Hold the carburetor rod forward against the transmission stop. Turn the threaded adjuster at the front of the carburetor rod to adjust the length of the rod so that the ball socket lines up with the ball end of the carburetor lever. Then lengthen the carburetor rod four turns by turning the ball socket counterclockwise.

6. Attach the ball socket to the ball end and connect the return spring.

7. Loosen the throttle cable clamp nut. Position the cable housing adjuster in the clamp so that there is no slack in the cable at curb idle. To decrease the cable slack, move the adjuster away from the carburetor lever.

8. Back off the adjuster $1/4$ in. to allow $1/4$ in. of cable free-play at idle. Tighten the clamp nut.

9. Connect the choke or remove the block from the choke valve.

6 Cylinder Engine—1968–72 with Automatic Transmission

1. Disconnect the choke at the carburetor or block the choke valve in its fully opened position.

2. Slightly open the throttle to release the fast idle cam and then return the carburetor to curb idle.

3. Move the transmission lever forward against its stop. The lever must remain in this position during the remainder of the adjustment procedure. Either wire the lever to secure it or have an assistant hold the lever against its stop.

4. Loosen the adjuster link lockbolt and pull the adjuster link forward so that its side slots contact the carburetor lever pin without any backlash. Tighten the lockbolt to 100 in. lbs.

5. Check the transmission linkage operation by releasing the transmission lever, moving the adjuster link to its full rearward position, and then allowing the link to slowly return. If the linkage is operating correctly, the adjuster link should return to its full forward position.

6. Connect the choke or remove the block from the choke valve.

V8 Engines—1967–72 with Automatic Transmission

1. Disconnect the choke at the carburetor (not on Hemi) or block the choke valve in its fully open position.

2. Slightly open the throttle to release the fast idle cam and then return the carburetor to curb idle.

3. Move the transmission lever forward against its stop. The lever must remain in this position during the remainder of the adjustment procedure. Either wire the lever to secure it or have an assistant hold the lever against its stop.

4. Place a $\frac{3}{16}$ in. diameter rod in the holes provided in the upper bellcrank and lever. Adjust the length of the intermediate transmission rod by means of the threaded adjuster at its upper end. The ball socket must line up with the ball end with a slight downward effort on the rod.

5. Assemble the ball socket to the ball end and remove the $\frac{3}{16}$ in. rod from the upper bellcrank and lever.

6. Disconnect the linkage return spring. Adjust the length of the carburetor rod by lightly pushing the rod rearward to remove all backlash and turning the threaded slotted adjuster link. When the slotted adjuster link is in its normal operating position, the rear end of the slot should contact the carburetor lever pin without exerting any force on the pin.

7. Assemble the slotted adjuster link to the carburetor lever pin and install the washer and retainer clip. Refit the linkage return spring.

8. Check the transmission linkage operation by releasing the transmission lever, moving the adjuster link to its full rearward position, and then allowing the link to slowly return. If the linkage is operating correctly, the adjuster link should return to its full forward position.

9. Loosen the throttle cable clamp nut. Position the cable housing adjuster in the clamp so that there is no slack in the cable at curb idle. To decrease cable slack, move the adjuster away from the carburetor lever.

10. Back off the adjuster one-fourth inch to allow one-fourth inch of cable free-play between the front edge of the accelerator shaft lever and the dash bracket. Torque the clamp nut to 45 in. lbs.

11. On the Hemi, mount the carburetor connector rod between the carburetors so that the carburetor rod slotted end is connected to the inner lever of the rear carburetor. The slotted end should be on the outward side of the carburetor lever. Fully open the rear carburetor throttle and adjust the connector rod length so that the front carburetor throttle is also wide open. Rod length is increased by turning the adjusting stud clockwise (as viewed from the front of the engine) or decreased by turning the stud counterclockwise. When the rod length is correct, tighten the connector rod locknut.

12. Connect the choke or remove the block from the choke valve.

V8 Engine—1970–71 with Automatic Transmission and Single-Section Throttle Rod

1. Disconnect the choke at the carburetor or block the choke valve in its fully opened position.

2. Slightly open the throttle to release the fast idle cam and then return the carburetor to curb idle. On engines fitted with solenoid idle stops, the solenoid plunger must also be in its fully extended position.

3. Loosen the transmission throttle rod adjustment lockscrew.

4. Move the transmission lever forward against its stop. The lever must remain in this position during the remainder of the adjustment procedure. Either wire the lever to secure it or have an assistant hold the lever against its stop.

5. Adjust the transmission rod at the carburetor by pushing the rod rearward while pushing the retainer (through which the lockscrew passes) forward to remove all backlash. The rear edge of the throttle rod link slot must be against the carburetor lever pin during this adjustment. Tighten the lockscrew after all backlash has been removed.

6. Check the transmission linkage operation by releasing the transmission lever, moving the throttle rod link at the carburetor to its full rearward position, and then allowing the link to slowly return. If the linkage is operating correctly, the link should return to its full forward position.

7. Connect the choke or remove the block from the choke valve.

Throttle Linkage Adjustments

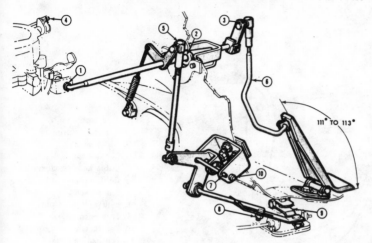

1   Isolator
2   Plastic bushing
3   Ball stud
4   Choke rod
5   Ball joint socket
6   Accelerator pedal rod
7   $\frac{3}{16}$ in. diameter rod *
8   Locknut *
9   Transmission lever *
10 Bellcrank pin *

* Automatic transmission only

1965–66 Six-cylinder

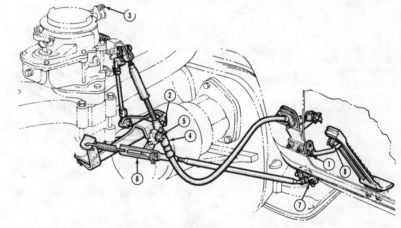

1   Accelerator shaft
2   Bellcrank pin
3   Choke rod
4   Cable housing adjuster
5   Cable housing clamp nut
6   Slotted transmission rod *
7   Transmission lever *
8   Nylon roller

* Automatic transmission only

1966 Six-cylinder with air conditioning

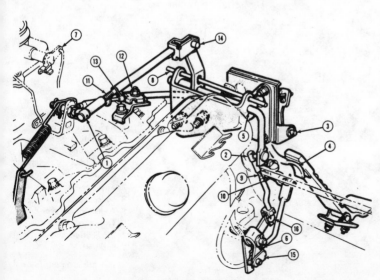

1   Ball
2   Ball socket
3   Shaft
4   Lubrication point
5   Lubrication point
6   Lubrication point *
7   Choke rod
8   $\frac{3}{16}$ in. diameter rod *
9   Transmission rod *
10 Stop *
11 Throttle rod
12 Cable clamp
13 Cable adjuster
14 Lubrication point
15 Lubrication point *
16 Lubrication point *

* Automatic transmission only

1965–66 Eight-cylinder

Throttle Linkage Adjustments

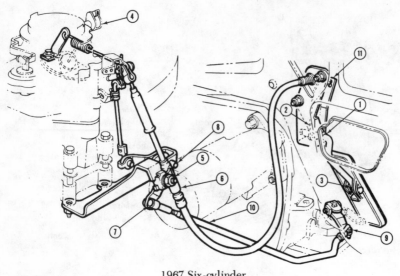

1 Accelerator shaft
2 Anti-rattle spring
3 Pedal pivot
4 Choke rod
5 Cable housing clamp nut
6 Cable housing adjuster
7 Ball socket *
8 Bellcrank pivot pin *
9 Transmission lever *
10 Transmission rod *
11 Lubrication pocket

* Automatic transmission only

1967 Six-cylinder

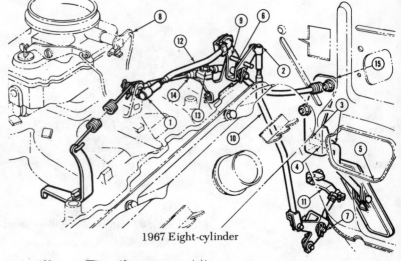

1 Threaded adjuster
2 Ball socket *
3 Lubrication point
4 Lubrication point
5 Lubrication point *
6 Bellcrank *
7 Lubrication point *
8 Choke rod
9 ³⁄₁₆ in. diameter rod
10 Transmission rod *
11 Transmission lever *
12 Carburetor rod
13 Cable housing clamp nut
14 Cable housing adjuster
15 Lubrication pocket

* Automatic transmission only

1967 Eight-cylinder

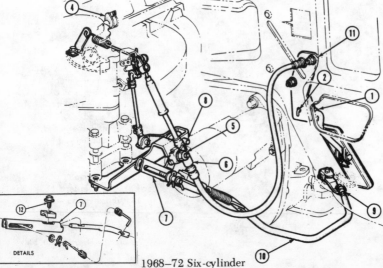

DETAILS

1 Lubrication point
2 Anti-rattle spring
3 Lubrication point
4 Choke rod
5 Cable housing clamp nut
6 Cable housing adjuster
7 Adjuster link *
8 Bellcrank pivot pin *
9 Transmission lever *
10 Transmission rod *
11 Lubrication pocket
12 Lockbolt *

* Automatic transmission only

1968–72 Six-cylinder

Throttle Linkage Adjustments

1 Adjuster link
2 Ball socket *
3 Accelerator shaft
4 Cable housing clamp nut
5 Cable housing adjuster
6 Lubrication point
7 Lubrication point *
8 Choke rod
9 $\frac{3}{16}$ in. diameter rod *
10 Transmission rod *
11 Transmission lever *
12 Carburetor rod
13 Return spring
14 Lubrication pocket
15 Anti-rattle spring

* Automatic transmission only

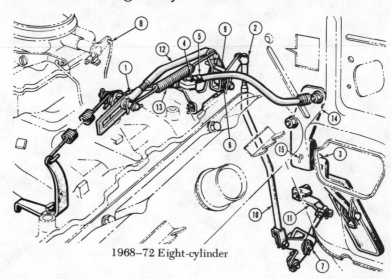

1968–72 Eight-cylinder

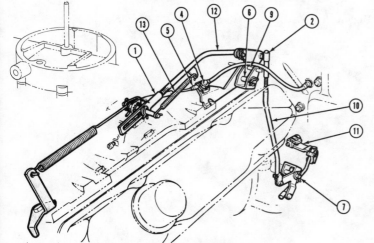

1 Adjuster link
2 Ball socket *
4 Cable housing clamp nut
5 Cable housing adjuster
6 Lubrication point
7 Lubrication point *
9 $\frac{3}{16}$ in. diameter rod *
10 Transmission rod *
11 Transmission lever *
12 Carburetor rod
13 Linkage return spring

* Automatic transmission only

1967–69 383 cu in. engine

1 Lubrication point
2 Adjuster link
3 Carburetor lever stud
4 Carburetor connector rod assembly
5 Lubrication point
6 Lubrication point
7 Lubrication point *
8 $\frac{3}{16}$ in. diameter rod *
9 Intermediate transmission rod *
10 Transmission lever *
11 Linkage return spring
12 Cable housing clamp nut
13 Cable housing adjuster
14 Cable clamp
15 Upper bellcrank and lever
16 Carburetor connector rod slotted end
17 Connector rod adjusting stud
18 Connector rod locknut

19 Lubrication point
20 Carburetor rod

* Automatic transmission only

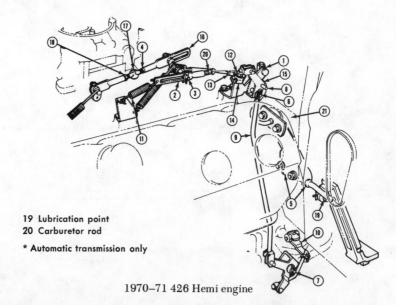

1970–71 426 Hemi engine

Throttle Linkage Adjustments

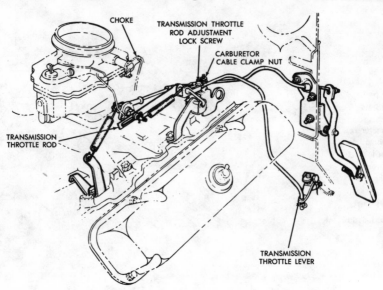

1970–71 Eight-cylinder engine with single section throttle rod

5 · Chassis Electrical

Heater System

All Barracuda and Challenger models are equipped with a blended-air type of heater. Fresh air flows through the cowl grille (beneath the windshield) and enters a plenum chamber. A door in the plenum chamber, which is controlled by the temperature lever on the instrument panel, directs the air either through or past the heater core. The heater/defroster lever selects the direction of the blended air.

A blower motor is used to increase the velocity of the air entering the interior of the car through the heater/defroster outlets. The motor speed is determined by its instrument panel switch.

NOTE: *On 1970–72 models, the heater inlet hose is ½ in. diameter on all engines. The return hose to the engine is ⅝ in. diameter.*

HEATER ASSEMBLY

Removal and Installation

1965–69 BARRACUDA

1. Drain the radiator. Disconnect the battery.
2. Disconnect the heater hoses from the heater and remove the heater hoses-to-dash panel seal and retainer plate.
3. Disconnect the wires from the heater motor.
4. Remove the heater motor seal retainer plate from the dash panel.
5. Disconnect the heater and defroster control cables from the heater assembly.
6. Remove the heater motor resistor wire from the resistor.
7. Remove the defroster tubes from the heater assembly.
8. Disconnect the heater housing support rod from the fresh air duct.
9. Remove the heater assembly.
10. Installation is the reverse of the above.

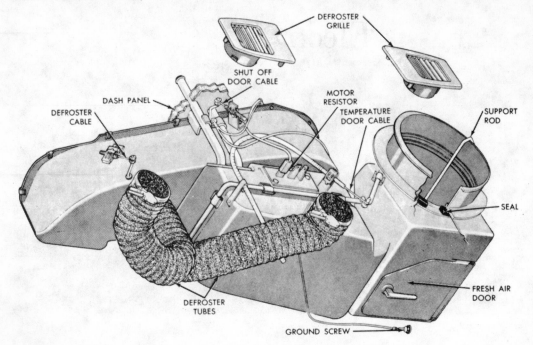

DEFROSTER
GRILLE

SHUT OFF
DOOR CABLE

MOTOR
RESISTOR

DASH PANEL

TEMPERATURE
DOOR CABLE

DEFROSTER
CABLE

SUPPORT
ROD

SEAL

FRESH AIR
DOOR

DEFROSTER
TUBES

GROUND SCREW

Heater assembly—1965–69 Barracuda

1970–72 Barracuda and Challenger

1. Disconnect the battery.
2. Drain the radiator.
3. Disconnect the heater hoses from the core tubes at the dash panel. Plug the core tubes to prevent spilling coolant on the car interior.
4. Remove the three mounting nuts from the studs around the blower motor and remove the flange and air seal.
5. Unplug the antenna lead from the radio and move the lead out of the way.
6. Remove the screw, which is located at the right side of the heater housing above the fresh air opening, from the housing-to-plenum support rod.
7. Disconnect the three cables at the air door.
8. Disconnect the wires from the blower motor resistor.
9. Move the heater assembly down and out from under the instrument panel.
10. Installation is the reverse of the above.

HEATER BLOWER

Removal and Installation

1965 Barracuda

1. Disconnect the battery.
2. Disconnect the heater ground wire.

3. Loosen the fresh air intake duct clamp at the blower end and remove the duct from the blower assembly.
4. Withdraw the screw which secures the blower to the plenum.
5. Remove the heater blower assembly from the heater housing.
6. From inside the heater housing, disconnect the blower assembly wires.
7. Withdraw the blower assembly from the car.
8. Installation is the reverse of the above.

1966–69 Barracuda

1. Remove the heater assembly as described above.
2. Remove the seal from around the heater blower motor mounting studs.
3. Remove the spring clips that retain the spacers and the blower motor to the heater housing.
4. Withdraw the blower motor from the heater housing.
5. Installation is the reverse of the above.

1970–72 Barracuda and Challenger

1. Remove the heater assembly as described above.

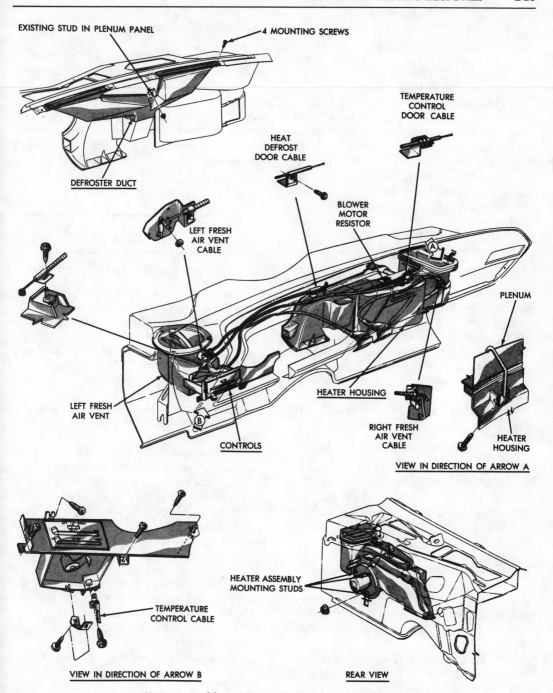

EXISTING STUD IN PLENUM PANEL

4 MOUNTING SCREWS

TEMPERATURE CONTROL DOOR CABLE

DEFROSTER DUCT

HEAT DEFROST DOOR CABLE

LEFT FRESH AIR VENT CABLE

BLOWER MOTOR RESISTOR

A

PLENUM

LEFT FRESH AIR VENT

HEATER HOUSING

B

RIGHT FRESH AIR VENT CABLE

HEATER HOUSING

CONTROLS

VIEW IN DIRECTION OF ARROW A

HEATER ASSEMBLY MOUNTING STUDS

TEMPERATURE CONTROL CABLE

VIEW IN DIRECTION OF ARROW B

REAR VIEW

Heater assembly—1970–72 Barracuda and Challenger

2. Disconnect the blower motor lead from the resistor block and the ground wire from the mounting plate.

3. Withdraw the six sheet metal screws and the six retaining clips, which secure the blower motor assembly, from the housing.

4. Remove the blower wheel from the motor shaft.

5. Remove the two retaining nuts and separate the motor from the mounting plate.

6. Installation is the reverse of the above.

HEATER CORE

Removal and Installation

1965 Barracuda

1. Drain the cooling system.
2. Disconnect the heater hoses at the heater core and temperature control valve.
3. Withdraw the screws which secure the temperature control valve cover to the heater housing.
4. Carefully withdraw the control valve from the opening in the heater housing and disconnect the valve control cable.
5. Disconnect the hose which connects the water valve to the heater core.
6. Remove the water valve and valve cover.
7. Withdraw the screws which secure the core housing to the cowl panel and remove the housing.
8. Insert a screwdriver between the cowl and the heater housing, and carefully pry the heater housing from the cowl.
9. Withdraw the screws which secure the core to the housing and remove the core.
10. Installation is the reverse of the above.

1966–69 Barracuda

1. Remove the heater assembly and the heater blower motor as described above.
2. Remove the fresh air door seal from either the inner or outer heater housing half only.
3. Remove the clips which retain the heater housing halves together.
4. Separate the heater housing halves.
5. Withdraw the screw that attaches the seal retainer and seal around the heater core tubes.
6. Remove the heater core tube support clamp.
7. Withdraw the screws that attach the heater core to the heater housing and remove the heater core.
8. Installation is the reverse of the above.

1970–72 Barracuda and Challenger

1. Remove the heater assembly as described above.
2. Remove the nine spring clips and the four screws which secure the front cover to the heater housing.
3. Cut the sponge-rubber plenum-to-heater housing air seal in two places where

the front cover separates the cover from the housing.
4. Remove the core tube retaining screw from behind the housing, between the core tubes.
5. Remove the two sponge-rubber gaskets from the heater core tubes and remove the core from the heater housing.
6. Installation is the reverse of the above.

Radio

Removal and Installation

CAUTION: *Never operate the radio without its speaker connected or severe damage to the output transistors will result. If the speaker must be replaced, be sure to use one of the proper impedance (ohms) for the particular radio.*

1965–67 Barracuda

1. Disconnect the battery.
2. Remove the control knobs from the front of the radio.
3. Disconnect the radio feed wire at its connector under the instrument panel.
4. Remove the bottom screw from the radio mounting bracket.
5. Remove the left defroster tube.
6. Loosen the top screw on the radio mounting bracket and remove the bracket.
7. Disconnect the antenna and speaker leads.
8. Remove the mounting nuts from the front of the radio and remove the radio bezel.
9. Remove the radio from below the instrument panel.
10. Installation is the reverse of the above.

1968 Barracuda

1. Disconnect the battery.
2. Remove the control knobs from the front of the radio and unscrew the mounting nuts.
3. On those cars that are equipped with air conditioning, remove the two outlet duct retaining bolts and remove the duct. Remove the right defroster hose and hose bracket.
4. From under the instrument panel,

withdraw the lower screw and upper stud nut for the radio support bracket. Remove the bracket.

5. Lower the radio to a position under the panel and disconnect the feed and speaker wires and the antenna cable. Remove the radio.

6. Installation is the reverse of the above.

1969 BARRACUDA

1. Disconnect the battery.

2. From under the instrument panel, disconnect the speaker and feed wires and the antenna cable.

3. Withdraw the two radio mounting nuts from the radio mounting bracket.

4. Remove the radio from below the instrument panel.

5. Installation is the reverse of the above.

1970–72 BARRACUDA AND CHALLENGER

1. Disconnect the battery.

2. From under the instrument panel, disconnect the speaker and feed wires, and the antenna cable.

3. Remove the channel selector shaft and knobs (if so equipped).

4. Withdraw the two radio mounting screws from under the panel and loosen

the radio-to-lower support bracket mounting nut.

5. Move the radio rearward, down, and out from under the instrument panel.

6. Installation is the reverse of the above.

Windshield Wiper System

WINDSHIELD WIPER MOTOR

Removal and Installation

1965–66 BARRACUDA

1. Disconnect the wiper link at the wiper motor. For variable-speed wiper motors, note the position of the follower cam.

2. Disconnect the wiper motor lead wires at the wiper motor.

3. Remove the three nuts which secure the wiper motor and wiper motor bracket assembly to the cowl panel.

4. Pull the motor bracket assembly down from the bracket mounting studs and out from underneath the instrument panel.

5. Installation is the reverse of the above.

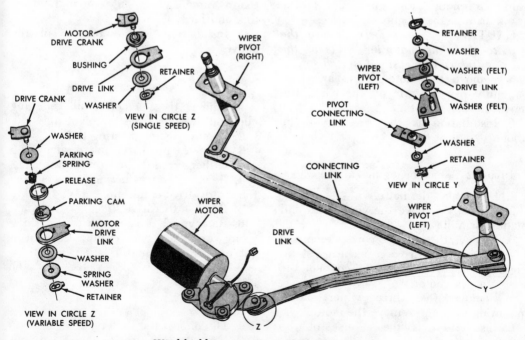

Windshield wiper system—1965–66 Barracuda

1967–69 Barracuda

1. Disconnect the battery.
2. Disconnect the wiper motor wiring harness.
3. Remove the three wiper motor mounting nuts. On cars that are equipped with air conditioning, it is easier to first remove the crank arm nut and crank arm from under the instrument panel and omit steps 4 and 5.

WINDSHIELD WIPER LINKAGE

Removal and Installation

1965–66 Barracuda with Single-Speed Wipers

1. From under the instrument panel, remove the retaining clip and core washer from the pivot arm pins.
2. Remove the link and pin from the motor crank.

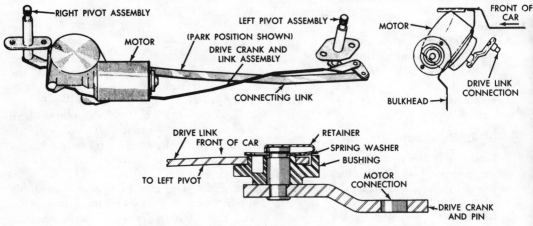

Windshield wiper system—1967–72 Barracuda and Challenger

4. Work the motor off its mounting studs far enough to gain access to the crank arm mounting nuts.

CAUTION: *Do not force or pry the motor from its mounting studs as the drive link can be easily distorted.*

5. Remove the motor crank arm nut. Carefully pry the arm off the shaft. Remove the wiper motor.
6. Installation is the reverse of the above.

1970–72 Barracuda and Challenger

1. Disconnect the battery.
2. Carefully remove the wiper arm and blade assemblies.
3. Remove the left-side cowl screen.
4. Remove the drive crank arm retaining nut and drive crank. Disconnect the wiring at the motor.
5. Remove the three wiper motor mounting nuts and remove the motor.
6. Installation is the reverse of the above.

3. Withdraw the assembly from under the instrument panel and remove the drive link and bushing.
4. Installation is the reverse of the above.

1965–66 Barracuda with Variable Speed Wipers

1. Remove the connecting link retaining clips and washers from the pivot pins.
2. Remove the connecting link.
3. Remove the drive link retainer clip and washers from the left pivot pin.
4. Remove the retainer and washer from the motor drive crank pin.
5. Remove the drive link.
6. Remove the cam, release, parking spring, and washer for examination, lubrication, or replacement.
7. Installation is the reverse of the above.

1967–69 Barracuda

1. Disconnect the battery.
2. On cars that are equipped with air

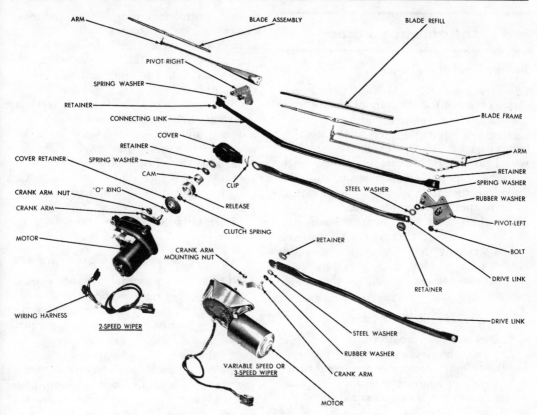

Windshield wiper system—1970–72 Barracuda and Challenger with concealed wipers

conditioning, remove the duct supplying the left spot cooler to provide easier access to the left wiper pivot. Insert a wide blade screwdriver between the plastic link bushing and the pivot crank arm. Gently twist the screwdriver to force the bushing and link from the pivot pin. Remove the three motor mounting nuts, pull the motor away from the bulkhead, and remove the motor crank arm retaining nut. After the crank arm has been removed from the motor shaft, remove the drive link assembly from under the left side of the instrument panel.

3. On cars without air conditioning, remove the motor drive crank arm retaining nut and pry the crank arm off the motor shaft. Gently pry the drive link and bushing from the left pivot crank arm pin and withdraw the assembly from under the instrument panel. After removing the assembly from the car, remove the motor drive crank arm from the drive link.

4. To remove the connecting link from the pivots, remove the glove compartment.

Reaching through the glove compartment opening, gently pry the bushing and link from the right pivot pin. Lift the link from the pivot crank arm pin and repeat this operation at the left pivot.

5. Withdraw the assembly from under the left side of the instrument panel.

6. Installation is the reverse of the above.

1970–72 Barracuda and Challenger

1. Remove the wiper arm and blade assemblies.

2. Remove the left cowl screen to gain access to the wiper linkage.

3. Disconnect the battery.

4. Remove the crank arm nut and crank from the motor shaft.

5. Remove the bolts which secure the left and right pivots to the body.

6. Remove the links and pivots through the top cowl opening.

7. Installation is the reverse of the above.

Instrument Cluster

Removal and Installation

To service the instruments, it is necessary to remove the instrument cluster from the car. Before removing the instrument cluster, it is advisable to cover the steering column jacket tube, between the steering wheel and the instrument panel, with masking tape to avoid scratching the finish. Be sure to label all of the electrical leads to the instrument cluster before disconnecting them so that the leads can be reconnected at their correct locations. When servicing the instruments, place the cluster on a padded work area to protect the instruments and the face of the cluster panel.

1965–66 BARRACUDA

1. Disconnect the battery.
2. Lower the steering column by loosening the column clamp screws several turns.
3. Reach up under the instrument panel to disconnect the speedometer cable at the speedometer.
4. Withdraw the four instrument cluster mounting screws and pull the cluster out far enough to disconnect the printed circuit board and ignition switch multiple connectors. Disconnect all the electrical leads at the instrument cluster.
5. Remove the cluster from the car.
6. Reverse the above for installation.

1967–69 BARRACUDA

1. Disconnect the battery.
2. Reach up under the instrument panel to disconnect the multiple connector at the left printed circuit board and the speedometer cable at the speedometer.
3. Withdraw the four instrument cluster mounting screws from underneath the dash pad and the four retaining screws from the lower front face of the cluster.
4. Remove the clock reset cable.
5. Pull the cluster out far enough to reach behind and disconnect the right printed circuit board multiple connector, ammeter wires, vacuum gauge hose or tachometer wire, and emergency flasher switch connector.
6. Loosen the air conditioner or heater control knobs and remove from the slide control. Withdraw the air conditioner or

heater control mounting screws and move the control out of the way.
7. Depress the headlight switch knob release button on the bottom side of the switch and pull the knob and shaft out of the switch.
8. Pull the windshield wiper knob from the shaft. Remove the wiper switch bezel nut and allow the switch to remain connected to the wiring harness.
9. Pull the cluster out from the panel opening, tilt it face down, and move it to the right to remove it completely.
10. Remove the cluster from the car.
11. Installation is the reverse of the above.

1970–72 BARRACUDA AND CHALLENGER

NOTE: *This procedure requires lowering of the very delicate collapsible steering column. It is recommended that the job be done by an authorized dealer's shop.*

1. Disconnect the battery.
2. Withdraw the six lamp panel mounting screws. Carefully slide the lamp panel out and lay it on top of the instrument panel.
3. Withdraw the four switch bezel mounting screws and let the bezel hang loose. It is not necessary to disconnect the switches.
4. Withdraw the retaining screws from the steering column floor plate and the two securing nuts from the column support clamp. Allow the steering column to rest on the seat.
5. Reach up under the instrument

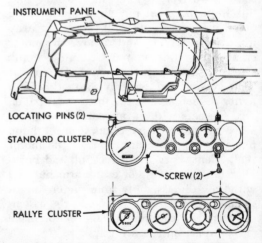

Instrument cluster removal and installation—1970–72 Barracuda and Challenger

panel to disconnect the speedometer cable at the speedometer.

6. Withdraw the six instrument cluster bezel mounting screws. Angle the bezel out in such a manner as to clear the clock reset button.

7. Reach between the bezel and the panel to disconnect the stereo control wiring harness (if so equipped).

8. On the Rallye cluster, remove the clock and odometer reset buttons from the cluster bezel so that the clock may be removed.

9. Withdraw the four screws which secure the cluster to the panel.

10. Disconnect all the wiring harnesses and remove the instrument cluster.

11. Reverse the above for installation.

Light Bulb Specifications

	1965	1966	1967	1968	1969	1970	1971	1972
Air conditioner and Auto-Temp	——	1893	——	1445①	1445	1815	1815	1815
Ash tray	——	57	——	1445①	1445	1445	1445	1445
Back-up lamps	1073	1073	1073	1073	1156	1156	1156	1156
Brake system warning light	——	57	57	158	158	158	57	57
Clock	——	57	1816	1816	1816	①	①	①
Courtesy lamp	——	90	90	89	89	1445	89	89
C-pillar lamp	——	——	1004	211—1	211—1	——	——	——
Dome lamp	1004	1004	1004	211—1	1004	1004②	1004③	1004④
Door, pocket panel, and/or reading lamp	90	90	90	90	90	90	90	90
Door ajar indicator	——	——	——	——	——	1892	1892	1892
Emergency flasher	57	57	552	552	552	552	552	552
Gear selector indicator (column)	1445	1445	1445	1445	1445	161	161	161
Gear selector indicator (console)	53X	57	57	57	57	57	57	57
Glove compartment lamp	1891	1891	1891	1891	1891	1891	1891	1891
High beam indicator	158	158	158	158	158	57	57	57
Ignition lamp	1445	1445	1445	1445	1445	1445	1445	1445
Instrument cluster and speedometer	158	158	158	158	158	1893	1816	1816
License plate lamp	67	67	67	67	67	67	67	67

Light Bulb Specifications

	1965	1966	1967	1968	1969	1970	1971	1972
Low fuel indicator	—	—	—	—	—	1892	1892	1892
Map and courtesy lamp	90	90	90	89	89	89	89	89
Oil pressure indicator	158	158	57	57	57	57	57	57
Park and turn signal lamps (front)	1034	1034A	1034A	1034A	1157A	1157	1157NA	1157NA
Parking brake indicator	57	57	57	—	—	—	—	—
Radio—AM and/or tape deck	1893	1893	1893	1816	1816	1816	1816	1816
Radio—AM/FM stereo	—	—	—	—	—	1815	1815	1815
Reverse indicator (4 speed transmission)	—	—	—	—	53	53	53	53
Sealed beam (single)	6012	6012	6012	6012	6012	6012	6012	6012
Sealed beam (dual) High/low beam High-beam	— —	— —	— —	— —	— —	4002 4001	4000 4001	4000 4001
Seat belt indicator	—	—	—	—	—	1892	1892	—
Side marker lamp	—	—	—	1895	1895	1895	1895	194
Stereo indicator	—	—	—	—	—	1445	1445	1445
Tachometer	—	57	—	①	①	①	①	①
Tail, stop, and turn signal	1034	1034	1034	1034	1157	1157	1157	1157
Trunk and/or under hood lamp	1004	1004	1004	1004	1004	1004	1003	1003⑤
Turn signal indicator (fender-mounted)	—	330	330	330	330	330	330	330
Turn signal indicator (panel-mounted)	158	158	158	158	158	57	57	57

① Included in instrument cluster lighting.
② 1004 or 550.
③ 1004 or 211—1.
④ 1004 or 211—1 or 551.
⑤ 1003 or 1004.

Fuses and Circuit Breakers

1965–66

Fuses

	Amps
Accessories	20
Cigar lighter	20
Heater or air conditioner	20
Instrument panel lamps	2
Radio	5
Stop, tail, and dome lamps	20

Circuit Breakers

	Amps
Electric door locks (behind left front kick panel)	15
Lighting system (integral with headlamp switch)	15
Power windows, power seats, and convertible top lift (behind left front kick panel)	30
Windshield wipers—single-speed (integral with wiper switch)	5
Windshield wipers—variable-speed (integral with wiper switch)	6

1967

Fuses

	Amps
Accessories	20
Cigar lighter	20
Console (inline fuse)	20
Emergency flasher	20
Heater or air conditioner	20
Instrument panel lights	2
Radio	5
Stop, tail, and dome lamps	20

Circuit Breakers

	Amps
Convertible top lift (integral with top lift switch)	30
Headlamps (integral with headlamp switch)	15
Windshield wipers (integral with wiper switch)	6

1968

Fuses

	Amps
Accessories	20
Cigar lighter and dome lamp	20
Heater or air conditioner	20
Instrument panel lamps	2
Radio and back-up lamps	5
Stop, tail, and emergency flasher lamps	20

Circuit Breakers

	Amps
Convertible top lift (integral with top lift switch)	30
Headlamps (integral with headlamp switch)	15
Windshield wipers (integral with wiper switch)	6

1969

Fuses

	Amps
Accessories	20
Heater or air conditioner	20
Instrument panel lamps	3
Radio and back-up lamps	7.5
Stop and dome lamps	20
Taillamps and cigar lighter	20

Circuit Breakers

	Amps
Convertible top lift (integral with top lift switch)	30
Headlamps (integral with headlamp switch)	15
Windshield wipers (integral with wiper switch)	6

1970

Fuses

	Amps
Accessories	20
Emergency flasher	20
Heater or air conditioner	20
Instrument panel lamps	3
Radio and back-up lamps	20
Stop and dome lamps	20
Taillamps and cigar lighter	20

Circuit Breakers

	Amps
Convertible top lift (on fuse block)	30
Headlamps (integral with headlamp switch)	20
Windshield wipers (integral with wiper switch)	
2-speed motor	6
3-speed motor	7.5
Variable-speed motor	7.5

1971

Fuses

	Amps
Accessories	20
Console	20
Emergency flasher	20
Headlamp delay relay (inline)	20
Heater or air conditioner	20
Instrument panel lamps	3
Radio and back-up lamps	20
Stop and dome lamps	20
Taillamps and cigar lighter	20

Circuit Breakers

	Amps
Convertible top lift (on fuse block)	30
Headlamps (integral with headlamp switch)	20
Power windows (on fuse block)	30
Windshield wipers (integral with wiper switch)	
2-speed motor	6
Variable-speed motor	7.5

Fuses and Circuit Breakers

1972

Fuses

	Amps
Accessories	20
Brake lamps and power windows	5
Heater or air conditioner	20
Horn	20
Instrument panel lamps	5
Miscellaneous	20
Radio and back-up lamps	20
Stop and emergency flasher lamps	20

Circuit Breakers

	Amps
Headlamps (integral with headlamp switch)	20
Power windows (on fuse block)	30
Windshield wipers (integral with wiper switch)	
2-speed motor	60
3-speed motor, variable speed	75

Engine Compartment Wiring Diagrams

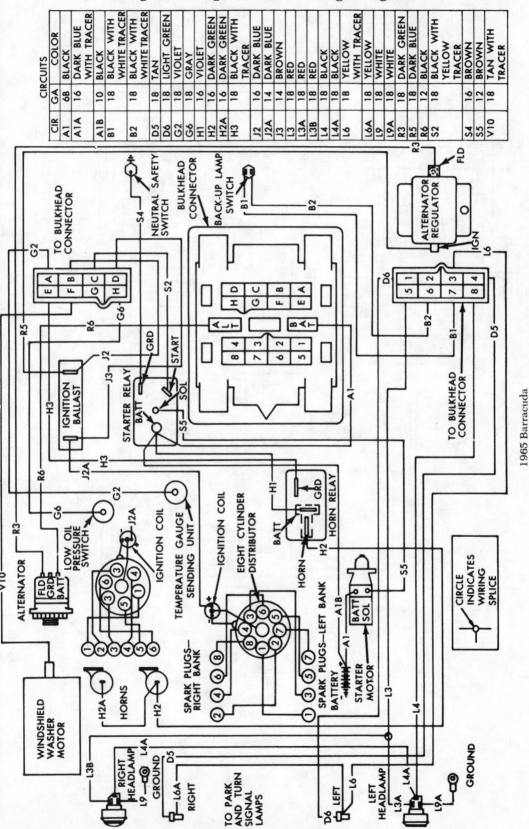

CIRCUITS		
CIR	GA	COLOR
A1	6B	BLACK
A1A	16	DARK BLUE WITH TRACER
A1B	10	BLACK
B1	18	BLACK WITH WHITE TRACER
B2	18	BLACK WITH WHITE TRACER
D5	18	TAN
D6	18	LIGHT GREEN
G2	18	VIOLET
G6	18	GRAY
H1	16	VIOLET
H2	16	DARK GREEN
H2A	16	DARK GREEN
H3	18	BLACK WITH TRACER
J2	16	DARK BLUE
J2A	14	DARK BLUE
J3	14	BROWN
L3	18	RED
L3A	18	RED
L3B	18	RED
L4	18	BLACK
L4A	18	BLACK
L6	18	YELLOW WITH TRACER
L6A	18	YELLOW
L9	18	WHITE
L9A	18	WHITE
R3	18	DARK GREEN
R5	18	DARK BLUE
R6	12	BLACK
S2	18	BLACK WITH YELLOW TRACER
S4	16	BROWN
S5	12	BROWN
V10	18	TAN WITH TRACER

1965 Barracuda

CIRCUITS		
CIR	GA	COLOR
A1	6B	RED
A1A	10	BLACK
A1B	16	DARK BLUE WITH TRACER
B1	18	VIOLET
B1A	18	VIOLET
B2	18	VIOLET
B2A	18	VIOLET
C2	18	DARK BLUE
C5	18	DARK BLUE
D5	18	TAN
D6	18	LIGHT GREEN
G2	18	VIOLET
G6	18	GRAY
H1	16	VIOLET
H2	16	DARK GREEN
H2A	16	DARK GREEN
H3	18	BLACK WITH TRACER
J2	16	DARK BLUE WITH TRACER
J2A	14	DARK BLUE
J3	14	BROWN
L3A	18	RED
L4	18	BLACK
L4A	18	BLACK
L6	18	YELLOW WITH TRACER
L6A	18	YELLOW
L9	18	WHITE
L9A	18	WHITE
R3	18	DARK GREEN
R5	18	DARK BLUE
R6	12	BLACK
S2	18	BLACK WITH YEL. TRACER
S4	16	BLACK
S5	12	BROWN
T11	18	GRAY WITH TRACER
V10	18	BROWN

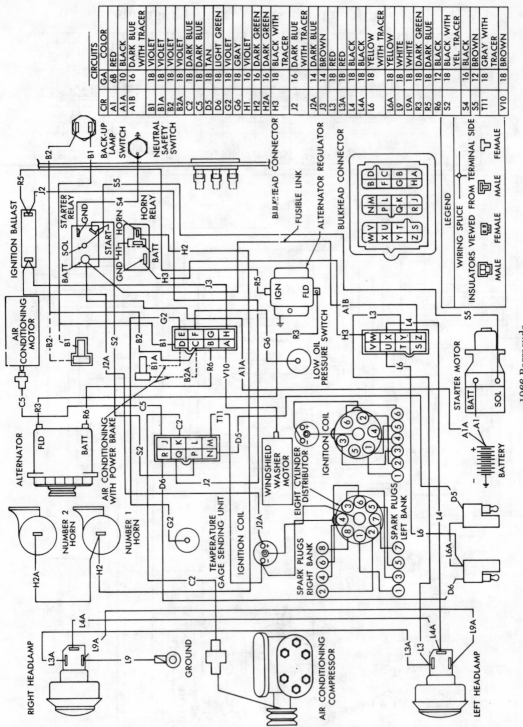

1966 Barracuda

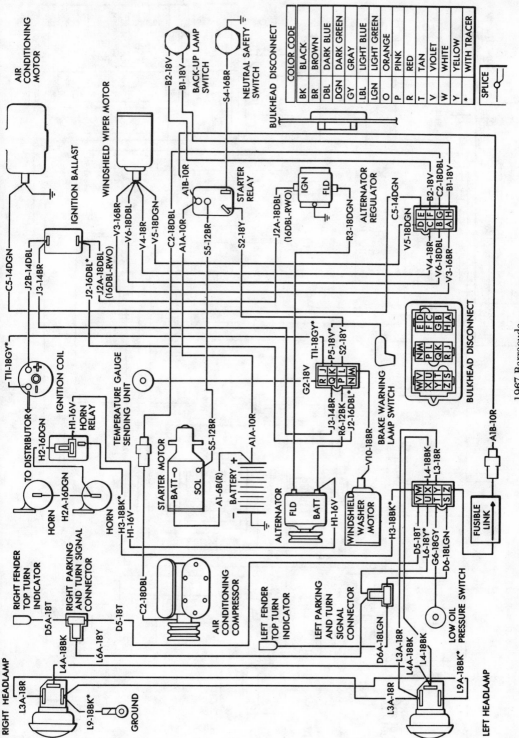

COLOR CODE	
BK	BLACK
BR	BROWN
DBL	DARK BLUE
DGN	DARK GREEN
GY	GRAY
LBL	LIGHT BLUE
LGN	LIGHT GREEN
O	ORANGE
P	PINK
R	RED
T	TAN
V	VIOLET
W	WHITE
Y	YELLOW
*	WITH TRACER

SPLICE

1967 Barracuda

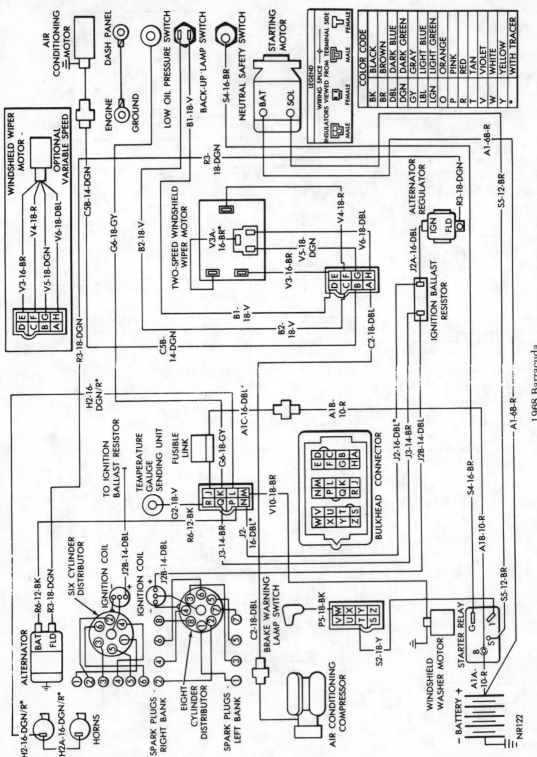

1968 Barracuda

NR122

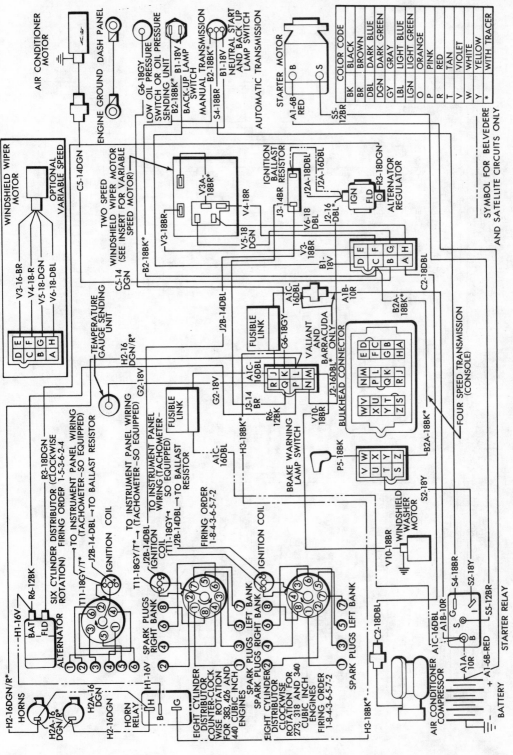

1969 Barracuda

COLOR CODE	
BK	BLACK
BR	BROWN
DBL	DARK BLUE
DGN	DARK GREEN
GY	GRAY
LBL	LIGHT BLUE
LGN	LIGHT GREEN
O	ORANGE
P	PINK
R	RED
T	TAN
V	VIOLET
W	WHITE
Y	YELLOW
*	WITH TRACER

SYMBOL FOR BELVEDERE AND SATELLITE CIRCUITS ONLY

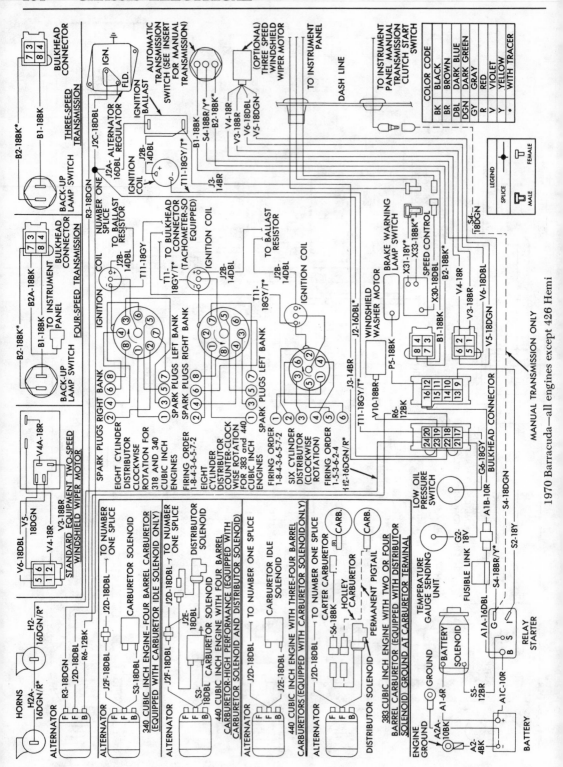

1970 Barracuda—all engines except 426 Hemi

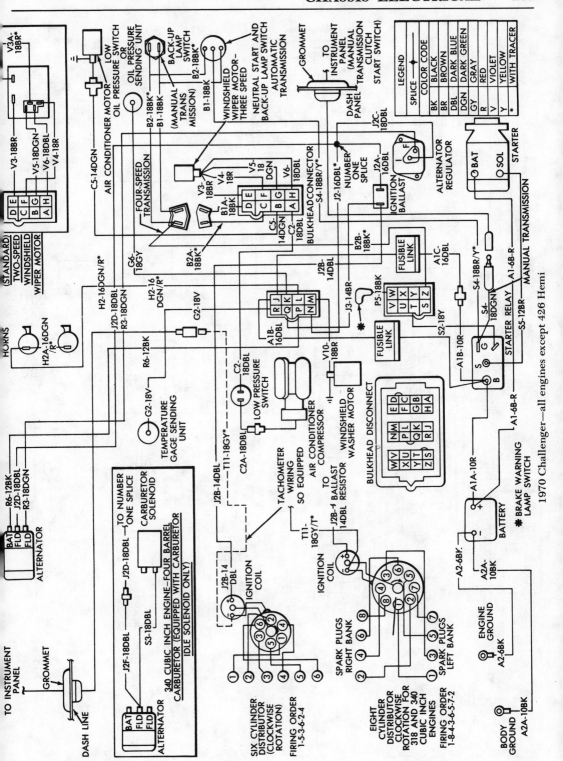

1970 Challenger—all engines except 426 Hemi

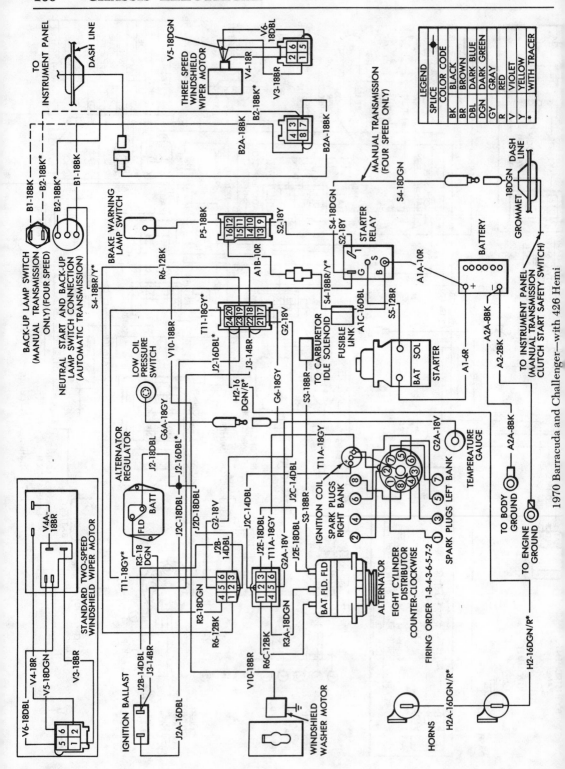

1970 Barracuda and Challenger—with 426 Hemi

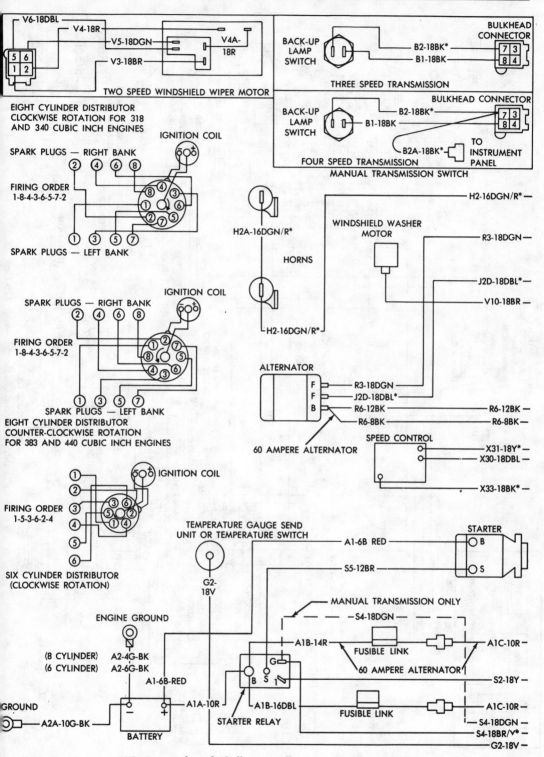

1971 Barracuda and Challenger—all engines except 426 Hemi

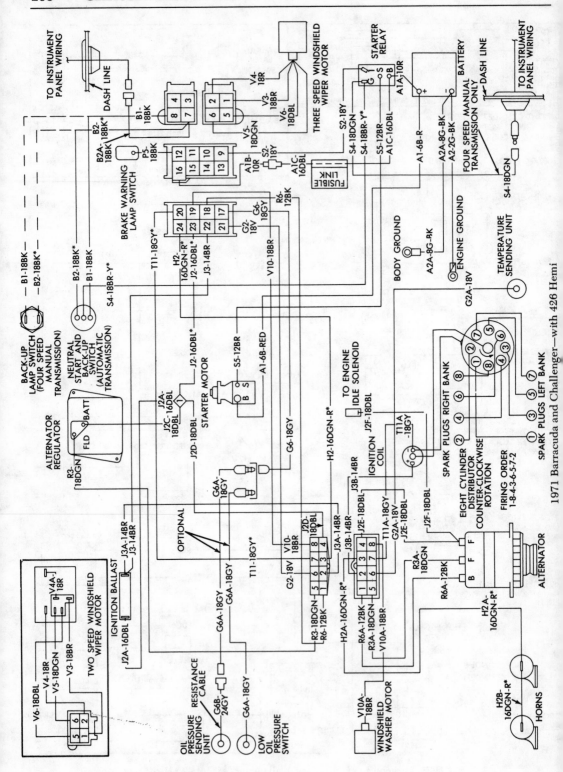

1971 Barracuda and Challenger—with 426 Hemi

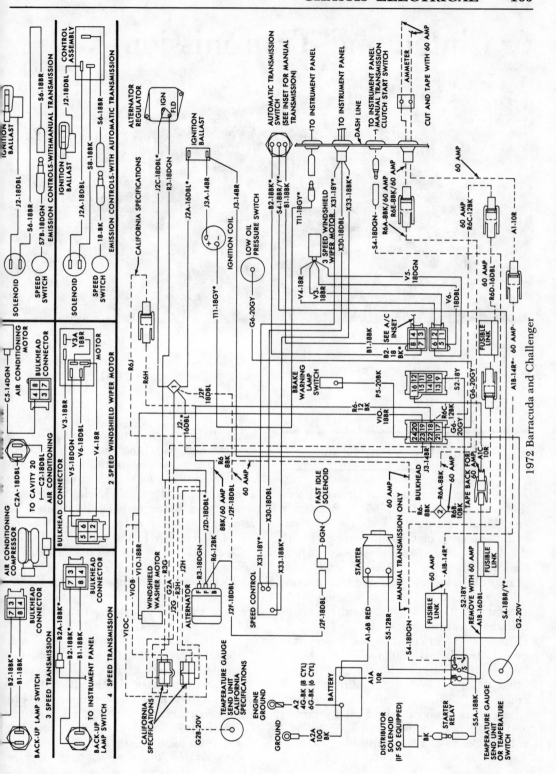

1972 Barracuda and Challenger

6 · Clutch and Transmission

Manual Transmission

There are four manual transmissions that have been used in 1965–72 Barracuda and Challenger models. All 1965–72 six-cylinder-engine models are equipped with the A—903 three-speed transmission which has synchromesh on second and third gears only. The A—745 three-speed transmission, which also has synchromesh on second and third only, is used on eight-cylinder Barracudas from 1965 to 1969. In 1970, the A—745 transmission was succeeded by the A—230 model which has full synchromesh on all three gears and is fitted to all 1970–72 eight-cylinder Barracuda and Challenger models. The four-speed transmission used on all Barracuda and Challenger models from 1965 to 1972 is the type A—833 transmission.

Removal and Installation

ALL MANUAL TRANSMISSIONS

Removal and installation is essentially the same for all Chrysler manual transmissions. It is necessary to loosen the engine mounts and raise the engine slightly in order to remove and install the transmission. In addition, on models equipped with a floor-mounted gearshift, the shifter assembly and the console (if fitted) must be removed before the transmission can be withdrawn. Refer to the procedure below.

To remove the transmission, proceed as follows:

1. Loosen the engine mount bolts. Raise the car on a hoist or jack up the front of the car and support it with suitable stands.
2. Drain the transmission lubricant.
3. Disconnect the shift rods from the transmission levers.
4. Disconnect the driveshaft at its rear universal joint after marking both parts to ensure assembly in the original position. Carefully pull the driveshaft front yoke out of the transmission extension housing.

   CAUTION: *Take care not to scratch or nick the sliding spline yoke ground surface while removing and installing the driveshaft.*
5. Disconnect the speedometer cable, the back-up lamp switch leads, and the gearshift and interlock control rods.

6. On some models it will be necessary to remove part of the exhaust system if it interferes with transmission removal.

7. Install a suitable engine support tool on the side frame members or attach a lifting tool to the engine. Use the support or the lifting tool to raise the engine slightly.

8. Disconnect the transmission extension housing from the removable center crossmember.

9. Place a suitable support or jack under the transmission and remove the center crossmember.

10. Withdraw the bolts which secure the transmission to the bellhousing. Slide the transmission rearward until the pinion shaft clears the clutch disc before lowering the transmission.

11. Lower the transmission and remove it from under the car.

Install the transmission using the reverse of the above. When engaging the pinion shaft with the clutch disc, put the transmission in gear. Install the transmission mounting bolts immediately after the pinion shaft and clutch disc are correctly engaged. *Do not allow the transmission to hang on the pinion shaft.*

FLOOR-MOUNTED GEARSHIFT

1. Disconnect the battery.
2. Remove the gearshift lever knob.
3. If a console is fitted, withdraw the console mounting screws, label and disconnect the electrical leads, and remove the console.

Transmission Specifications

Transmission Type	Year	Engine Displacement (cu in.)	Gear Ratios				
			1st	2nd	3rd	4th	Reverse
A—903	1965	170	3.22	1.84	1.00	——	4.14
	1965–68	225	2.95	1.83	1.00	——	3.80
	1969–72	198, 225	2.95	1.83	1.00	——	3.80
A—745	1965–68	273, 318	3.02	1.76	1.00	——	3.95
	1969	318	3.02	1.76	1.00	——	3.95
	1967–68	383	2.55	1.49	1.00	——	3.34
	1969	383	2.55	1.49	1.00	——	3.34
A—230	1970–72	198, 225, 318	3.08	1.70	1.00	——	2.90
	1970–72	340, 383	2.55	1.49	1.00	——	3.34
A—833	1965	225, 273	3.09	1.92	1.40	1.00	3.00
	1966–68	273, 318, 340, 383	2.66	1.91	1.39	1.00	2.58
	1969–70	Standard	2.66	1.91	1.39	1.00	2.58
	1969–70	Heavy Duty	2.65	1.93	1.39	1.00	2.57
	1971–72	Standard	2.47	1.77	1.34	1.00	2.40
	1971–72	Heavy Duty	2.44	1.77	1.34	1.00	2.36

4. Withdraw the floor pan boot retaining screws and slide the boot up and off the shift lever.

5. Slide a knife blade or feeler gauge down along the driver's side of the shift lever to release the spring clip which retains the shift lever and then withdraw the lever. Some levers must be unbolted.

6. Remove the retaining clips, washers, and control rods from the transmission shift levers.

7. Remove the bolts and washers which hold the shifter assembly to its transmission mounting plate and withdraw the shifter assembly.

8. Installation is the reverse of the above.

Linkage Adjustment

COLUMN-MOUNTED 1965–67

With the Second and Third control rod disconnected from the lever on the column, and the First and Reverse control rod disconnected at the transmission, with the levers in Neutral:

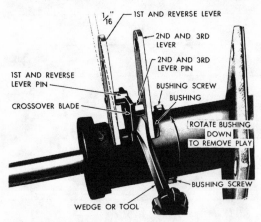

Adjusting column gearshift lever—1965–67 Barracuda

1. Check for axial freedom of the shift levers in the column. If the outer ends of the levers move up or down along the column axis over $1/16$ in., loosen the two upper bushing screws and rotate the plastic bushing, downward, until all of the axial play is eliminated. Retighten the bushing screws.

2. Wedge a screwdriver between the crossover blade and the Second and Third lever, so that the crossover blade is engaged with both lever crossover pins.

3. Adjust the swivel on the end of the Second and Third control rod until the stub shaft of the swivel enters the hole in the column lever. Install washers and a clip. Tighten the swivel locknut to 70 in. lbs.

4. Slide the clamp and swivel, on the end of the First and Reverse control rod, until the swivel stub shaft enters the hole in the transmission lever. Install washers and a clip. Tighten the swivel clamp bolt to 100 in. lbs.

COLUMN-MOUNTED 1968–69

1. Remove both shift rod lever swivels at the transmission levers.

2. Make sure that both transmission levers are in the Neutral (middle) position.

3. Adjust the Second-Third shift rod swivel so it will enter the Second-Third (forward) lever at the transmission while the hand lever on the steering column is held 10° above the horizontal (Neutral) position. Position the swivel in the lever and install the washer and clip and tighten the attaching nut to 70 in. lbs.

Adjusting column gearshift lever—1968–69 Barracuda

4. Place a screwdriver or other suitable tool between the crossover blade and the Second-Third lever at the base of the steering column, so that both lever pins are engaged by the crossover blade.

5. Adjust the First-Reverse shift rod swivel so it will freely enter the lever on the transmission. Position the swivel in the transmission lever and install the washer and clip and tighten the attaching nut to 100 in. lbs.

6. Remove the tool from the crossover blade at the steering column and check the linkage operation.

FOUR-SPEED—1965

1. Remove the boot attaching screws and slide the boot up the shift lever.

2. Disconnect the shift rods from the levers at the adjusting swivels.

3. Slide tool C—3951, or equivalent, over the levers to align the three levers in the shift control assembly and hold them in the Neutral position.

4. With the shift operating levers in the Neutral position, adjust the three shift rods

equipped with a Hurst shifter assembly, refer to the adjustment procedures for the Hurst linkages which follow.

1. Using a $\frac{1}{16}$ in. piece of metal, fabricate a shift lever aligning tool.

2. Place the transmission in Neutral and disconnect all the control rods from the transmission levers.

3. Insert the lever aligning tool through the slots in the levers, making sure that it passes through all the levers and against the back plate.

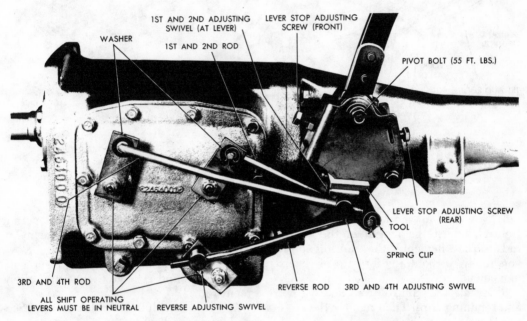

Gearshift linkage adjustment—1965 four-speed transmission

by turning the swivels until the swivel stubs match the lever holes.

5. Remove the aligning tool.

6. With the hand-shift lever in Third or Fourth position, adjust the lever stop screw (front and rear) to provide 0.020–0.040 in. between the lever and the stops.

CAUTION: *Because there is no Reverse gear interlock, it is very important that the transmission linkage adjustments be correctly performed in order to prevent the possibility of engaging two gears at once.*

FLOOR-MOUNTED THREE AND FOUR-SPEED—1966–72

This procedure is for the Chrysler Corporation linkage only. For cars that are

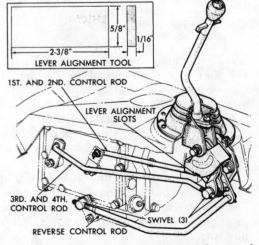

Gearshift linkage adjustment—1966–68 four-speed transmission

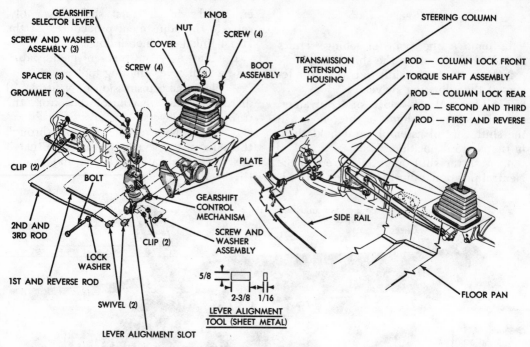

Floor-mounted gearshift linkage—1970–72 three-speed transmission

4. Now that all the levers are locked in Neutral, adjust the length of the control rods so that they enter the transmission levers freely, without any forward or reverse movement.

5. Install the control rod flat washers and retaining clips. Then remove the aligning tool.

6. Check the linkage for ease of shifting into all gears and for crossover smoothness.

FLOOR-MOUNTED THREE-SPEED— HURST SHIFT LINKAGE

This linkage uses two shift rods and levers. Adjustments can be made with the aid of a neutral alignment rod, which is supplied with the shift linkage kit, or by using a ¼ in. diameter rod.

1. Place the shifter unit in Neutral.

2. Back both shifter stop bolts out of the shifter frame until only a few threads remain engaged.

3. Remove both shifting rods and the rod adjusting buttons from the shifter unit.

4. Place the Neutral alignment rod through the alignment holes in the shifter unit and levers.

5. Be doubly sure that both transmission levers are in the Neutral position and ad-

just the rod adjusting buttons to permit each button to slip easily into the nylon bushing of its corresponding lever.

6. Fasten the buttons in the lever with spring clips and remove the Neutral alignment rod.

7. Push the shift lever firmly into Second gear and hold it in this position. Screw the Second gear stop bolt in until contact is felt. Back the bolt out one full turn and tighten the locknut.

8. Pull the shift lever firmly back into Third gear. Screw the Third gear stop bolt in until contact is made, then back the stop bolt out one full turn and tighten the locknut.

FLOOR-MOUNTED FOUR-SPEED— HURST SHIFT LINKAGE

The four-speed transmission gearshift linkage uses three shift rods and levers. The adjustment can be made with the aid of a Neutral alignment rod, which is supplied with the shift linkage kit, or by using a ¼ in. diameter rod.

1. Place the shifter unit in Neutral.

2. Back both shifter stop bolts out of the shifter frame until only a few threads remain engaged.

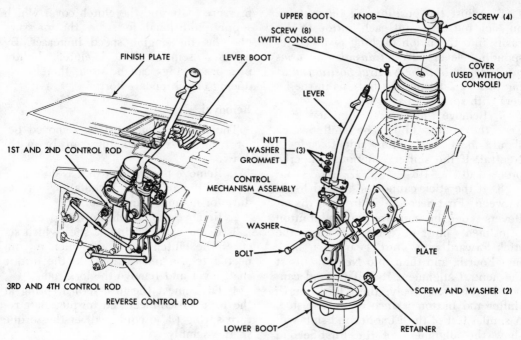

Gearshift linkage—1966–68 four-speed transmission

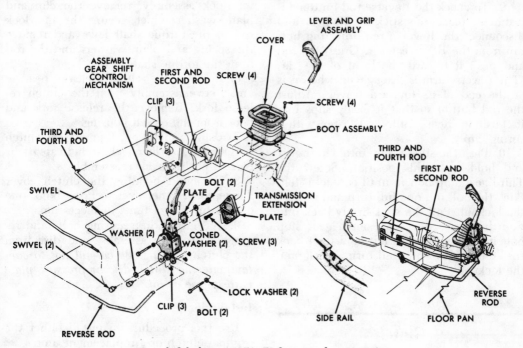

Gearshift linkage—1970–72 four-speed transmission

3. Remove the shifting rods and the rod adjusting buttons from the shifter unit.

4. Align the levers with the shifter frame and insert the neutral alignment rod through the notches in the frame and the holes in the levers.

5. Rotate the transmission arms backward and forward. The Neutral position for each arm can be felt at the mid-position of full travel. The Reverse arm must be moved to the end of its travel toward the front (disengaged position).

6. Adjust the positions of the buttons on each rod to permit each button to slip easily into the nylon bushing of its corresponding lever. *The transmission arms must remain in their Neutral positions during this step.* Fasten the buttons in the levers with spring clips.

7. Remove the neutral alignment rod. Test the shifter unit. The shifter stick should move freely from side to side in Neutral. If the shifter functions properly, proceed to step 10.

8. If the stick cannot be moved freely between First-Second, Third-Fourth, or Reverse, one or more of the rod button adjustments must be corrected. Move the stick forward into Third gear, then back into Fourth, and then into Neutral. Insert the neutral alignment rod. If the rod cannot be inserted freely, the Third-Fourth shifter rod button is incorrectly adjusted. A similar test of the First-Second shift will show the alignment of the First-Second adjustment.

9. To check the Reverse rod button adjustment, place the stick in Neutral and disconnect the Reverse rod adjusting button from the Reverse lever. Grasp the rod and push it toward the front of the car. (The Reverse arm is disengaged when it is at the end of its forward travel.) Adjust the rod button so that it easily slips into its bushing. Reassemble and fasten with a spring clip.

10. Push the stick firmly into Third gear and hold it in this position. Screw the Third gear stop bolt in until contact is felt. Back the bolt out one full turn and tighten the locknut. Pull the stick firmly back into Fourth gear, screw the Fourth gear stop bolt in until contact is felt, and then back the stop bolt out one full turn and tighten the locknut.

Clutch

All Barracuda and Challenger models that are equipped with manual transmissions use a single, dry plate type of clutch. Six-cylinder and small eight-cylinder engines are fitted with a standard clutch while the larger engines are equipped with a semi-centrifugal clutch. This clutch has several centrifugal rollers between the

pressure plate and the clutch cover which supply additional force to the pressure plate as the engine speed increases. By using a semi-centrifugal clutch, lighter pressure springs can be used, thereby reducing clutch pedal effort.

Removal

The transmission must be removed before the clutch assembly can be withdrawn.

1. Remove the transmission as described in the "Removal and Installation" procedure for manual transmissions.

2. Remove the clutch housing pan.

3. Remove the spring washer which secures the clutch fork rod (which is connected to the release fork) to the torque shaft lever and remove the fork rod.

4. Disconnect the fork return spring at the fork. Disconnect the torque shaft return spring (if so equipped) at the torque shaft assembly.

5. On 1968–72 models with a gearshift interlock assembly, remove the clip and plain washer which secure the interlock rod to the torque shaft lever and remove the spring and plain washers and the rod from the torque shaft.

6. Remove the clutch release bearing and sleeve assembly from the clutch release fork. Remove the release fork and boot from the clutch housing.

7. Using a metal punch, mark the clutch cover and the flywheel to indicate their correct positions for reassembly.

8. To avoid bending the clutch cover flange, loosen the cover securing bolts, one or two turns at a time, in succession.

9. Withdraw the securing bolts and remove the clutch assembly and disc from the clutch housing. *Be careful not to contaminate the clutch disc or pressure plate with grease or oil.*

Installation

Use this procedure to install either the original clutch or a replacement unit.

1. Lightly lubricate the drive pinion bushing in the end of the crankshaft. Use about one-half teaspoonful of chassis grease and insert the lubricant in the radius back of the bushing.

2. Thoroughly clean the surfaces of the flywheel and pressure plate with fine sandpaper. Be sure that all oil and grease have been removed.

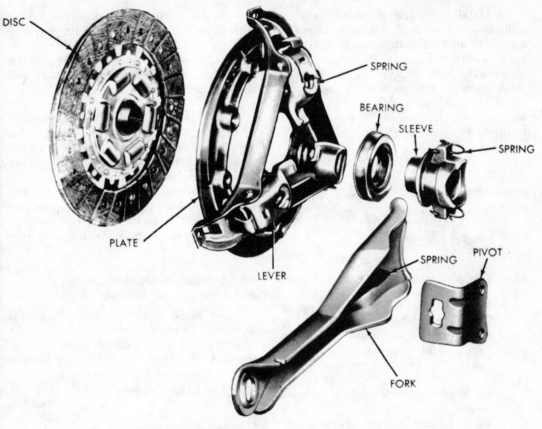

Standard clutch components

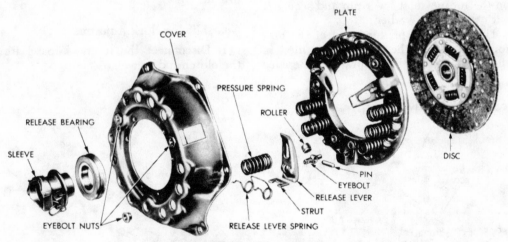

Semi-centrifugal clutch components

3. Position the clutch disc, pressure plate, and cover in the mounting position, with the springs on the disc damper facing away from the flywheel. Do not touch the disc facing at any time.

4. Insert a clutch disc aligning arbor or a spare transmission drive pinion through the disc hub and into the drive pinion bushing to assist in aligning the assembly.

5. Align the punch marks, that were made before removal, in the flywheel and the clutch cover.

6. Install the clutch cover securing bolts and tighten each bolt a few turns at a time, in an alternating sequence. Torque $5/16$ in. securing bolts to 200 in. lbs and $3/8$ in. securing bolts to 30 ft lbs.

7. Pack the release bearing sleeve cavity and release fork pads with an appropriate grease (NLGI Grade 2 EP grease is recommended).

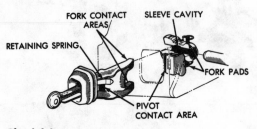

Clutch lubrication points

8. Insert the release bearing and sleeve assembly into the clutch housing as far forward as possible. Lightly lubricate the fork fingers and retaining spring.

9. Insert the fork fingers under the clutch sleeve retaining springs. The retaining springs must have lateral freedom on the sleeve.

10. Be sure that the groove in the seal is properly seated in the seal opening flange of the clutch housing. Refit the pedal rod on the torque shaft lever pin and secure it with the spring washer.

11. Insert the threaded end of the fork rod assembly in the opening provided in the end of the release fork rod. Replace the eye end of the fork rod on the torque shaft lever pin and lock it with a spring washer.

12. Connect the fork return spring to the fork. If so equipped, connect the torque shaft return spring to the torque shaft assembly.

13. On 1968–72 models with a gearshift interlock assembly, install the spring and plain washers with the interlock rod in the torque shaft lever and lock it in position with the washer and clip.

14. Install the transmission. Be sure not to allow grease to settle on the splines or the pilot end of the transmission drive pinion. Adjust the clutch pedal free-play (see below).

Clutch Linkage Adjustment— Pedal Height and Free-play

If the car is equipped with a gearshift interlock, disconnect it by loosening the interlock rod swivel clamp screw. Adjust the fork rod by rotating the self-locking nut to provide $5/32$ in. of free-play at the fork end. This adjustment will give the proper one inch of free-play at the clutch pedal.

If the gearshift interlock was disconnected, refer to the procedure below to adjust it.

Gearshift Interlock Adjustment

1. Disconnect the interlock pawl from the clutch rod swivel.

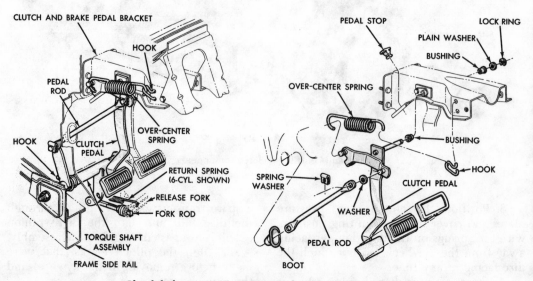

Clutch linkage—1967–69 Barracuda with 225 cu in. engine

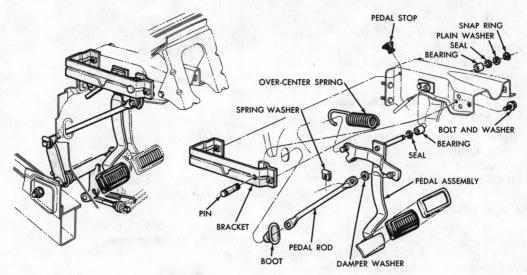

Clutch linkage—1967–69 Barracuda with eight-cylinder engine

2. Adjust the clutch linkage as described above.

3. With the First-Reverse lever on the transmission in the Neutral (middle detent) position, the interlock pawl should enter the slot in the First-Reverse lever.

4. Loosen the swivel clamp bolt and move the swivel on the rod so that it will enter the pawl. Install the washers and clip. Hold the interlock pawl forward and torque the swivel clamp bolt to 100–125 in. lbs. The clutch pedal must be in the fully returned position during this adjustment. The clutch rod should *never* be pulled rearward to engage the pawl swivel.

5. Check the adjustment by making a normal shift from Neutral to First, disengaging and engaging the clutch. Check again by shifting from Neutral to Reverse. The clutch action should be normal.

6. Disengage the clutch and shift halfway to First or Reverse. The clutch should be held down by the interlock to within one to two inches of the floor. If necessary, readjust the interlock and repeat steps 5 and 6.

Automatic Transmission

The Chrysler Torqueflite automatic transmission combines a torque converter with a fully automatic three-speed gear system, mounted in an integral aluminum casing. The transmission consists of two multiple disc clutches, an overrunning clutch, two servos and bands, and two planetary gear sets to provide three forward and reverse gear ratios. The transmission hydraulic system is composed of an oil pump (front and rear pumps on 1965 models only) and a single valve body which contains all of the control valves except the governor valve. The torque converter assembly is sealed and cannot be disassembled.

The transmission fluid is filtered by an

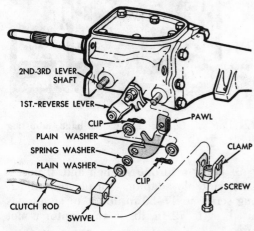

Gearshift interlock

internal, Dacron-type filter which is attached to the lower side of the valve body assembly. The fluid is cooled by circulating the fluid through the cooler in the lower radiator tank.

Oil Pan Removal and Transmission Filter Service

Refer to the section concerning "Transmission Lubricant Changes" in chapter 1 for removing and installing the transmission oil pan and filter.

Band Adjustments

KICK-DOWN BAND

The kick-down band adjusting screw is located on the left-hand side of the transmission case near the throttle lever shaft. Refer to chapter 1 for transmission model applications.

1. Loosen the locknut and back it off about five turns. Be sure that the adjusting screw is free in the case.

2. Using a torque wrench and, if necessary, suitable adaptors, torque the adjusting screw to 50 in. lbs, if an adaptor is used, or to 72 in. lbs if an adaptor is not used.

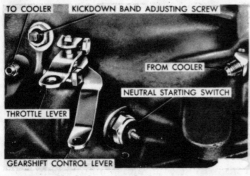

Location of kick-down band adjusting screw

3. Back off the adjusting screw the exact number of turns specified below. Then, keep the screw from turning and torque the locknut to the value specified below.

Kick-down Band Adjustment Specifications

A—904

1965 170 cu in.	2⅝ turns
1965–70 225 cu in.	2 turns
1965–67 273 cu in.	2 turns
1968–72 318 cu in.	2 turns

A—727

1965–70 six and eight-cylinder engines except Hemi	2 turns
1970–71 Hemi and 440 Six Pack	1½ turns
1971–72 225, 318, 340, 383 and 440 cu in.	2½ turns
A—904 (1965–70) kick-down adjusting screw locknut torque	25 ft lbs
A—904 (1971–72) kick-down adjusting screw locknut torque	29 ft lbs
A—727 (1965–72) kick-down adjusting screw locknut torque	29 ft lbs

FIRST AND REVERSE BAND

The oil pan must be removed from the transmission to gain access to the First and Reverse band adjusting screw. Refer to chapter 1 for transmission model applications.

1. Drain the transmission and remove the oil pan as described in the "Transmission Lubricant Changes" section in chapter 1.

2. Loosen the band adjusting screw locknut and back it off about five turns. Be sure that the adjusting screw turns freely in the lever.

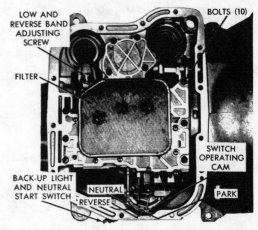

Location of Low and Reverse band adjusting screw

3. Using a torque wrench and, if necessary, suitable adaptors, torque the adjusting screw to 47–50 in. lbs if an adaptor is used, or to 72 in. lbs if an adaptor is not used.

4. Back off the adjusting screw the exact number of turns specified below. Then, keep the screw from turning and torque the locknut to the value specified below.

5. Using a new gasket, refit the oil pan and torque the pan bolts to 150 in. lbs. Refill the transmission to the proper fluid level.

*First and Reverse Band
Adjustment Specifications*

A—904

1965–66 All	5¼ turns
1967–72 All except 318 cu in.	3¼ turns
1968–72 318 cu in.	4 turns

A—727

1965–66 All	3 turns
1967–72 All	2 turns
A—904 (1965–70) First and Reverse band adjusting screw locknut torque	20 ft lbs
A—904 (1971–72) First and Reverse band adjusting screw locknut torque	35 ft lbs
A—727 (1965–72) First and Reverse band adjusting screw locknut torque	35 ft lbs

Shift Linkage Adjustment

1965 STEERING COLUMN AND CONSOLE GEARSHIFT

The gearshift control cable is adjusted at the transmission as follows:

1. Remove the gearshift control cable-to-transmission adjusting wheel lockscrew. Position a container under the transmission at the cable opening and pull the cable outward just enough to allow the transmission fluid to drain into the container.

2. Place the gearshift lever firmly in the number one (Low) position and have an assistant hold the lever in position.

3. Hold the control cable so that it is centered in the hole in the transmission case and pull the cable outward to bottom the assembly in the Low detent.

4. While holding the cable outward, rotate the adjusting wheel clockwise until it just contacts the transmission case.

5. Now turn the adjusting wheel coun-

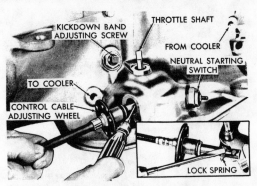

Gearshift control cable—1965 Torqueflite

terclockwise just enough to allow the next adjustment hole in the wheel to line up with the screw hole in the transmission case. Counting this hole as number one, continue turning the wheel counterclockwise until the fifth hole lines up with the screw hole in the case.

6. Push the cable and the adjusting wheel tight against the case, install the lockscrew and torque it to 75 in. lbs.

7. Refill the transmission to the correct fluid level.

1966–72 STEERING COLUMN GEARSHIFT

1. Place the gearshift lever in the Park position.

2. Loosen the swivel assembly clamp screw a few turns.

3. Move the transmission control lever all the way to the rear (into the Park detent).

4. With the gearshift lever in the Park position and the transmission control lever in the Park detent, tighten the swivel assembly clamp screw securely.

1966–68 CONSOLE GEARSHIFT

1. Place the gearshift lever in the Park position.

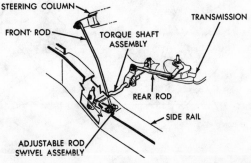

Column gearshift linkage—1970–72 Torqueflite

2. Loosen the bolt in the lower rod adjusting lever.

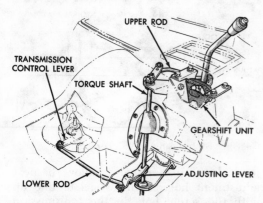

Console gearshift linkage—1966–68 Torqueflite

3. Move the transmission control lever all the way to the rear (into the Park detent).

4. With the gearshift lever in the Park position and the transmission control lever in the Park detent, tighten the adjusting lever bolt securely.

1969–72 Console Gearshift

Use the adjustment procedure described above for 1966–72 models with a column gearshift.

Throttle Linkage Adjustment

Refer to the throttle linkage adjustment procedures described in the "Carburetor" section in chapter 4.

Neutral Safety Switch

The neutral safety switch is mounted in the transmission case on all models. When the gearshift lever is placed in either the Park or Neutral position, a cam, which is attached to the transmission throttle lever inside the transmission, contacts the neutral safety switch and provides a ground to complete the starter solenoid circuit.

On late model cars, the back-up lamp switch has been incorporated into the neutral safety switch. This combination switch can be identified by the three electrical terminals on the rear of the switch. On this type of switch, the center terminal is for the neutral safety switch and the two outer terminals are for the back-up lamps.

There is no adjustment provided for the neutral safety switch. If a malfunction occurs, first check to make sure that the transmission gearshift linkage is properly adjusted and that the actuator cam is centered in the switch mounting hole in the transmission. If the malfunction continues, the switch must be removed and replaced with a new unit.

To remove the switch, disconnect the electrical leads and, using the proper wrench, unscrew the switch. Place a suitable container under the switch to catch the transmission fluid which will drain as the switch is withdrawn. Using a new seal, install the new switch and torque it to 24 ft lbs. Refill the transmission to the correct fluid level.

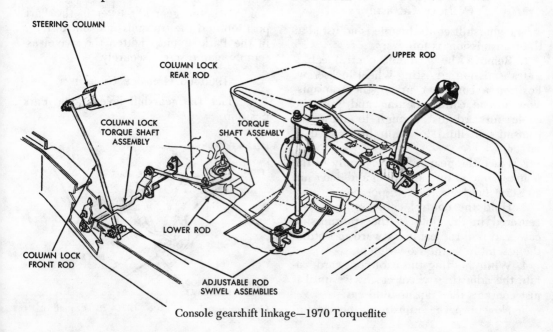

Console gearshift linkage—1970 Torqueflite

7 · Drive Train

Driveline

Two types of driveshaft are used on Barracuda and Challenger models; either a solid tube-type or an internally damped type which has a vibration absorber located near the front universal joint. Driveshaft application for a particular car is determined by its engine, transmission, and axle ratio. However, service to both types is identical.

The driveshaft is connected to the transmission on 1965 Barracudas by means of a ball and trunnion universal joint. Barracuda and Challenger models for 1966–72 use a cross and roller type of front universal joint, incorporating an internally splined yoke which can slide on the transmission output shaft. Both types of universal joint allow the driveshaft to move fore and aft to compensate for the movement of the rear axle. The rear universal joint on all models is the cross and roller type.

All Barracuda and Challenger models are equipped with a conventional semi-floating rear axle assembly. The axle size depends upon the particular engine and transmission combination for each model.

DRIVESHAFT AND U-JOINTS

Removal and Installation

Scribe alignment marks on the driveshaft, rear U-joint, and the drive pinion flange, before removing them, to ensure proper drive train balance upon installation.

DRIVESHAFT WITH BALL AND TRUNNION U-JOINT

1. Remove the rear U-joint roller and bushing assembly clamps from the drive pinion flange. Be sure not to disturb the retaining strap which holds the bushings on the U-joint cross. Do not allow the driveshaft to hang loose while removing either U-joint.

2. Disconnect the ball and trunnion U-joint from the transmission flange by removing the attaching bolts. Remove the driveshaft and protect the sliding yoke from damage.

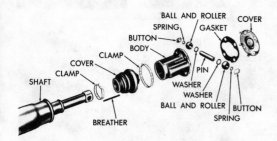

Ball and trunnion front U-joint

3. To install the driveshaft, first attach the front U-joint to the transmission flange. Torque the clamp bolts to 32 ft lbs.

4. At the rear, align the scribe marks and install the U-joint cross and roller bushings in the drive pinion flange. Fit the bushing clamps and securing screws and torque the screws to 170 in. lbs.

DRIVESHAFT WITH CROSS AND ROLLER U-JOINT

1. Remove both U-joint roller and bushing assembly clamps from the rear axle drive pinion flange. Be sure not to disturb the retaining strap (if so equipped) which holds the bushing assemblies on the U-joint cross. Do not allow the driveshaft to hang loose while removing either U-joint.

2. Slide the driveshaft with the front yoke from the transmission output shaft. Be careful not to damage the splines on the output shaft and the yoke. Do not disturb the yoke seal unless the seal is damaged or leaking. Remove the driveshaft and protect the sliding yoke from damage.

3. To install the driveshaft, clean the sliding yoke and inspect its machined surface. File off burrs if necessary. Carefully engage the yoke splines with the splines on the end of the transmission output shaft.

4. At the rear, align the scribe marks and install the U-joint cross and roller bushings in the drive pinion flange. Fit the bushing clamps and securing screws and torque the screws to 170 in. lbs.

U-Joint Overhaul

The driveshaft must be removed before the U-joints can be serviced.

BALL AND TRUNNION TYPE

1. Straighten the cover tabs and remove the gasket and cover. Slide the body back on the driveshaft and remove the buttons, springs, ball and rollers, and washers from both ends of the trunnion pin.

2. Take off the cover clamps and loosen the dust cover. Remove the cover with the polished jute breather. The breather is located between the driveshaft and the rear end of the cover. Save the breather for reassembly.

3. Clean the trunnion pin and races, and examine them for wear. If wear is excessive, the body must be replaced. A press is necessary to remove the pin and body from the driveshaft.

4. If the pin and body have not been removed, coat all parts with grease. Without using any tools, fit a new dust cover over the pins and install it through the body

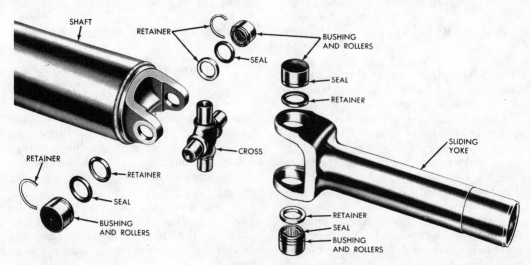

Cross and roller front U-joint

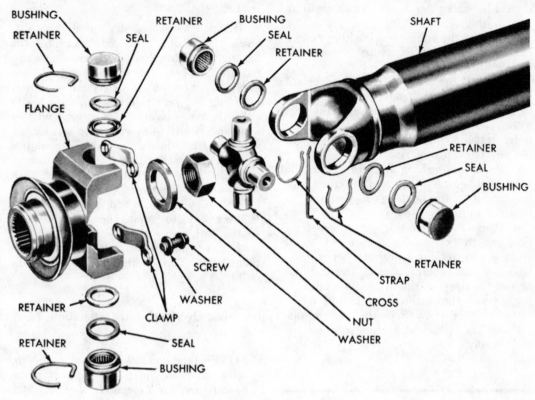

BUSHING
RETAINER
SEAL
RETAINER
BUSHING
SEAL
RETAINER
SHAFT
FLANGE
RETAINER
SEAL
BUSHING
RETAINER
STRAP
CROSS
NUT
WASHER
SCREW
WASHER
RETAINER
CLAMP
RETAINER
SEAL
BUSHING

Cross and roller rear U-joint

into its proper position on the driveshaft.

5. If the pin and body were removed, install the new body on the driveshaft and fit a new pin in the shaft. Press the pin into position.

6. Pack the ball and rollers with grease. Install the thrust washer, ball and rollers, button spring, and centering button on each end of the trunnion pin.

7. Place the dust cover on the driveshaft with the jute breather parallel to the shaft and extending one-half inch outside of the small end of the dust cover. Place the dust cover on the body and install the large clamp.

8. Lubricate the joint with about two ounces of grease. Apply the grease evenly to both races. Be careful not to use too much grease or to put grease in the dust cover.

9. Install a new gasket on the cover and position the cover and gasket on the body, locating the cover tabs in the body grooves. Bend the tabs to secure the cover.

Cross and Roller

1. If the original parts are to be reused, mark the yoke, cross, and bushings to indicate correct alignment for reassembly.

2. Remove the four bushing retainers from the U-joint cross assembly. With the aid of a socket of nearly the same size as the bushings, press one bushing and roller assembly from the yoke by pressing the opposite bushing in. Press the remaining bushings out by applying pressure to the cross end.

3. Remove the cross assembly from the yoke. Do not remove the seal retainers from the cross assembly as the cross and retainers are serviced as a single unit.

4. Use an appropriate solvent to clean all of the parts and dry them thoroughly. Examine the cross bearing surfaces for smoothness. If the bearing surfaces or the seal retainers are damaged, replace the cross assembly. Check the rollers in the bushings. If the rollers have been used on a worn cross, replace them. The rollers

should be smooth and should roll easily in the bushings.

5. Grease the roller and bushing assemblies, and pack the reservoirs in the cross ends with grease.

6. Install the cross in the driveshaft yoke. If the original parts are reinstalled, be sure to align the reference marks that were made before disassembly. Install the roller and bushing assemblies, again aligning any reference marks.

7. Press the bushing assemblies into the yoke while guiding the cross into the bushings. Position the bushings so that the retainers can be installed.

8. Place the remaining bushing assemblies on the cross. On the rear U-joint, replace the retainer strap to secure the bushings on the cross during the installation of the strap on the drive pinion flange. Lightly tap the bushing outer ends while turning the cross to check the bushing operation. The cross and bushings should operate freely.

Rear Axle

For all Barracuda and Challenger models, there are only three different types of rear axle assembly. The type that is used depends upon the choice of engine and transmission, and the intended usage of the car. A "Rear Axle Identification" chart is included in the first chapter of this book.

The axle ratio may be determined on $7\frac{1}{4}$ in. axles by checking the code number, which is stamped on the front face of the pad at the bottom of the axle housing, at an authorized dealership. The $8\frac{3}{4}$ in. and $9\frac{3}{4}$ in. axle ratios may be checked in a similar manner. Their code numbers can be found on a metal tag which is attached to one of the rear axle to housing carrier bolts on the $8\frac{3}{4}$ in. axle, or to one of the cover screws on the $9\frac{3}{4}$ in. axle.

All of the rear axle assemblies have some type of breather arrangement. If the rear axle is submerged in water, or if water is suspected to have entered the rear axle, the rear axle lubricant should be changed immediately.

A Sure-Grip differential assembly is optional on $7\frac{1}{4}$ and $8\frac{3}{4}$ in. axles and is standard on the $9\frac{3}{4}$ in. heavy-duty axle.

AXLE SHAFTS

Because the axle shafts are slightly different from one rear axle assembly to another, individual service procedures are required for each axle shaft assembly. Two very important points to remember when servicing any rear axle assembly are:

1. Always elevate both rear wheels when performing any rear axle service, or when rotating the axle by using the engine or other means.

2. On those cars that are equipped with a Sure-Grip differential, never rotate one axle shaft without rotating the other. If it is necessary to rotate one of the axle shafts, both shafts must be in position and both must be rotated. Otherwise, alignment of the axle shafts will be very difficult.

Removal, Overhaul, and Installation

$7\frac{1}{4}$ IN. AXLE

NOTE: *Whenever this axle assembly is serviced, both the brake support plate gaskets and the inner axle shaft oil seal must be renewed.*

1. Jack up the rear of the car and remove the rear wheels.

2. Detach the clips which secure the brake drum to the axle shaft studs and remove the brake drum.

3. Disconnect the brake lines at the wheel cylinders and block off the lines.

4. Through the access hole in the axle shaft flange, remove the axle shaft retaining nuts.

5. Attach a suitable puller to the axle shaft flange and remove the axle shaft.

6. Remove the brake assembly from the axle housing.

7. Remove the axle shaft oil seal from the axle housing.

CAUTION: *Never use a torch or other heat source as an aid in removing any axle shaft components as this will result in serious damage to the axle assembly.*

8. Place the axle shaft housing retaining collar in a vise. With a chisel, cut deeply into the retaining collar at 90° intervals. Remove the bearing with a suitable puller.

9. To assemble and install the axle shaft, replace the retainer plate, bearing, and bearing retainer collar on the axle shaft, using a suitable press or puller.

10. Insert new axle shaft oil seals in the axle housing and lightly grease the outside diameter of the bearing.

11. Replace the foam gasket on the studs of the axle housing and install the brake support plate assembly on the axle housing studs. Refit the outer gasket.

12. Very carefully slide the axle shaft assembly through the oil seal and engage the splines of the differential side gear. Using a non-metallic hammer, lightly tap the end of the axle shaft to position the axle shaft bearing in the recess of the axle housing. Install the retainer plate over the axle housing studs and torque the securing nuts to 35 ft lbs.

13. Reconnect the brake lines to the wheel cylinders and bleed the hydraulic system.

14. Install the brake drum and retaining clips.

15. Refit the rear wheels and lower the car.

8¾ In. and 9¾ In. Axles

NOTE: *Whenever this axle assembly is serviced, both the brake support plate gaskets and the inner axle shaft oil seal must be renewed.*

1. Jack up the rear of the car and remove the rear wheels.

2. Detach the clips which secure the brake drum to the axle shaft studs and remove the brake drum.

3. Through the access hole in the axle shaft flange, remove the axle shaft retaining nuts. The right-side axle shaft has a threaded adjuster in the retainer plate and a lock under one of its studs which should be removed at this time.

4. Remove the parking brake strut.

5. Attach a suitable puller to the axle shaft flange and remove the axle shaft.

6. Remove the brake assembly from the axle housing.

7. Remove the axle shaft oil seal from the axle housing.

CAUTION: *It is advisable to position some sort of a protective sleeve over the axle shaft seal surface next to the bearing collar to protect the seal surface. Never use a torch or other heat source as an aid in removing any axle shaft components as this will result in serious damage to the axle assembly.*

8. Wipe the axle housing seal bore clean. Install a new axle shaft oil seal.

9. Place the axle shaft housing retaining collar in a vise. With a chisel, cut deeply into the retaining collar at 90° intervals. Remove the bearing with a suitable puller.

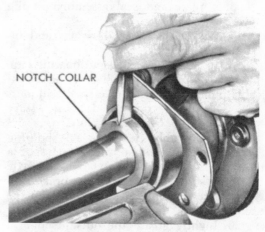

Removing rear axle shaft retaining collar—all axles

10. Remove the bearing roller retainer flange by cutting off the lower edge with a chisel.

11. Grind or file a section off the flange of the inner bearing cone and remove the bearing rollers.

Ground off inner bearing cone flange for roller removal—8¾ in. and 9¾ in. axles

12. Pull the bearing roller retainer down as much as possible and cut it off with side cutters.

13. Remove the roller bearing cup with its protective sleeves.

14. To prevent damage to the seal journal when the bearing cone is removed, protect the journal with a single wrap of shim stock that is 0.002 in. thick and is held in place by a rubber band.

15. Using a suitable puller, remove the bearing cone. Remove the seal in the bearing retainer plate and replace it with a new seal.

16. To assemble the axle, first install the retainer plate and seal assembly on the axle shaft.

17. Grease the wheel bearings and install them.

18. Install a new axle shaft bearing cup, cone, and collar on the shaft, using a suitable puller. Check the axle shaft seal journal for imperfections and if necessary polish with no. 600 crocus cloth.

19. Thoroughly clean the axle housing flange face and brake support. Install a new rubber asbestos gasket onto the axle housing studs. Next, install the brake support plate assembly on the left side of the axle housing.

20. Lightly grease the outside edge of the bearing cup. Install the bearing cup in the bearing bore.

21. Replace the foam gasket on the studs of the left-side axle housing and very carefully slide the axle shaft assembly through the oil seal and engage the splines of the differential side gear.

22. Using a non-metallic hammer, lightly tap the end of the axle shaft to position the axle shaft bearing in the recess of the axle housing. Install the retainer plate over the axle housing studs and, starting with the bottom securing nut, torque the nuts to 30–35 ft lbs.

23. Repeat step 19 for the right-side axle housing.

24. At the right side of the axle housing, back off the threaded adjuster until the inner face of the adjuster is flush with the inner face of the retainer plate. Very carefully slide the axle shaft assembly through the oil seal and engage the splines of the differential side gear. Then repeat step 22.

25. Mount a dial indicator on the left brake support. Turn the adjuster clockwise until both wheel bearings are seated and there is zero end-play in the axle shafts. Back off the adjuster about four notches to establish an end-play of 0.013–0.023 in. for models through 1968 and 0.008–0.018 in. for 1969 and later models (0.008–0.012 in. for 9¾ in. axle).

26. Lightly tap the end of the left axle shaft with a non-metallic hammer. This will seat the right wheel bearing cup against the adjuster. Turn the axle shaft several times so that a true end-play reading is obtained.

27. Remove one retainer plate nut and install the adjuster lock. If the lock tab does not mate with the notch in the adjuster, turn the adjuster slightly until it does. Refit the nut and torque it to 30–35 ft lbs.

28. Recheck the axle shaft end-play. If it is not within 0.013–0.023 in. for models through 1968 and 0.008–0.018 in. for 1969 and later models. (0.008–0.012 in. for 9¾ in. axle), repeat the adjustment. When the adjustment is complete, remove the dial indicator.

29. Install the parking brake strut. Refit the brake drum and retaining clips.

30. Install the rear wheels and lower the car.

8 · Suspension and Steering

Rear Suspension

The rear suspension on all Barracuda and Challenger models consists of semi-elliptical leaf springs and double-acting shock absorbers. Each leaf spring is fitted with zinc interleaves between the normal leaves to reduce corrosion and lengthen spring life. The springs are designed to operate with little or no camber under very light or no loads. Heavy-duty rear springs, which have a higher spring rate, are available on all models as a part of the heavy-duty suspension option.

The sole purpose of the rear shock absorbers is to control ride motion. They are matched to the particular suspension used on the car. Heavy-duty shock absorbers are included in the heavy-duty suspension option. A slight fluid weep, from a Chrysler-built shock absorber, during cold weather, is normal and does not affect the shock absorber performance. Replace the shock absorbers if they are broken, leaking badly, or have lost their resistance in one or both directions.

REAR SPRINGS

Removal and Installation

1. Jack up the rear of the car and position jack stands under the rear axle so that the stands will relieve the weight on the rear springs.

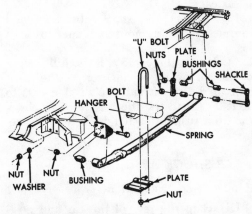

Rear spring assembly—all models

2. Remove the rear shock absorber lower mounting bolts and disconnect the shock absorbers. Lower the axle assembly to allow the rear springs to hang free.

3. Remove the U-bolt nuts and withdraw the U-bolts and spring plates. Remove the nuts which secure the front spring hanger to the body mounting bracket.

4. Remove the bolts from the rear spring hanger and allow the spring to drop far enough that the front spring hanger bolts can be removed.

5. Remove the pivot bolt from the front spring hanger.

6. Remove the shackle nuts and remove the shackles from the rear springs.

7. To install the rear springs, begin by assembling the shackles and bushings in the rear of the springs and hangers. Start each shackle bolt nut. Do not lubricate the rubber bushings to ease installation and do not tighten the shackle bolt nut.

8. Install the front spring hanger to the front spring eye and insert the pivot bolt. Fit the nut but do not tighten it.

9. Install the rear spring hanger to the body bracket and torque the mounting bolts to 30 ft lbs.

10. Raise the spring and have an assistant hold it in place. Insert the bolts into the spring hanger mounting bracket holes. Install the nuts and torque them to 30 ft lbs.

11. Position the axle assembly so that it is correctly aligned with the spring center bolt.

12. Position the center bolt over the lower spring plate. Install the U-bolt and nuts. Torque the nuts to 40 ft lbs for 7¼ in. axles, or to 45 ft lbs for 8¾ in. and 9¾ in. axles.

13. Connect the shock absorbers and torque the lower mounting nuts to 50 ft lbs.

14. Lower the car. With the full weight of the car on its wheels, torque the pivot bolts to 125 ft lbs and the shackle nuts to 40 ft lbs. Road-test the car and then check the front suspension height. Adjust as necessary.

REAR SHOCK ABSORBERS

Removal and Installation

1. Jackup the rear of the car and position jack stands under the rear axle so that

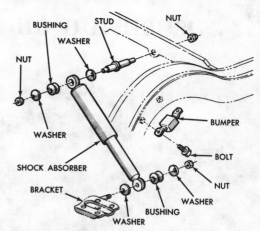

Rear shock absorber assembly—1965–69 Barracuda

the stands will relieve the load on the shock absorbers.

2. Remove the lower mount bolt and disconnect the shock absorber from the spring mounting plate.

3. Remove the upper mounting bolt and withdraw the shock absorber. On 1970–72 models, it is necessary to first remove the rubber plug in the trunk to gain access to the upper mounting bolt nut.

4. To install the shock absorber, position it so that the upper mounting bolt can be inserted and hand-tighten the nut.

5. Align the shock absorber with the spring mount plate stud and install the bolt and nut. Hand-tighten the nut.

6. Lower the car so that the full weight of the car is on its wheels. Torque the upper and lower mounting bolt nuts to 50 ft lbs. Refit the rubber plug in the trunk (if so equipped).

Front Suspension

All Barracuda and Challenger cars are equipped with a torsion bar, front suspension. Each torsion bar is attached to the lower control arm at the front and to the engine support crossmember at the rear. A compression-type ball joint, integral with the steering arm, is used to connect the lower control arm to the steering knuckle. The upper control arm is attached to the steering knuckle by means of a separate ball joint. The tie rods, which connect the steering arms to the center tie rod link, have removable tie rod ends and can be serviced separately.

When performing any service or adjustments to the front suspension, the following points should always be noted:

1. Never lubricate the rubber bushings which are used in some of the front suspension components.

2. Before tightening any front suspension components which contain rubber, be sure that the front suspension height is set according to specification and that the full weight of the car is resting on its wheels.

FRONT SUSPENSION HEIGHT

Checking and Adjusting

1. Be sure that the car has a full tank of fuel, the tire pressures are correct, and the car is positioned on a level floor.

2. Clean the road dirt from the bottom of the steering knuckle assemblies and from the height adjusting blades which are located directly below the center of each lower control arm inner pivot assembly.

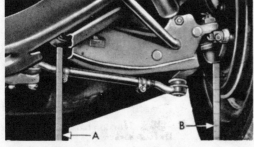

Checking front suspension height

3. Bounce the front of the car at least five times and release on the fifth downward motion.

4. Measure the distance from the bottom of one adjusting blade to the floor. This is measurement A. Then measure the distance

from the lowest point of the steering knuckle at its centerline to the floor. This is measurement B. The difference between A and B is the front suspension height.

5. Repeat step 4 for the other side of the suspension.

6. Refer to the specifications for the front suspension height and adjust as necessary. Adjustment is made by rotating the adjusting bolt clockwise to increase suspension height or counterclockwise to decrease the height. After each adjustment, bounce the front of the car as described above before measuring the suspension height. Both sides must be measured even if only one side has been adjusted. Be certain that the suspension height does not vary more than 1/8 in. from one side of the car to the other.

TORSION BARS

Removal and Installation

Contrary to appearance, the torsion bars are not interchangeable from right to left. They are marked with an "R" or an "L," according to their location.

1. Remove the upper control arm rebound bumper (if so equipped).

2. If the car is to be raised on a hoist, lift only the body so the front suspension is free of all load. If the car is to be raised with a jack, place the jack under the center crossmember with a support between the jack and the crossmember. Use the jack to raise the car until the front suspension is free of all load.

3. Release the load from the torsion bar by backing off the anchor adjusting nuts.

4. Remove the lockring from the torsion bar rear anchor.

5. Attach a suitable clamp toward the rear of the torsion bar. Move the torsion

Front Suspension Height Specifications

Height * (in.)

Suspension Type	1965	1966	1967	1968	1969	1970	1971	1972
Standard	2	2	1⅜	1⅜	1⅜	1³⁄₁₆	1	1
Heavy Duty	2⅜	2⅜	1⅜	1⅜	1⅜	1³⁄₁₆	1	1

* All measurements (±) 1/8 in.

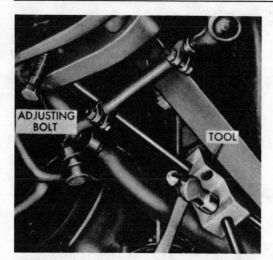

Torsion bar removal

bar rearward by striking the clamping tool and detach the bar from its mount.

CAUTION: *Do not apply heat to the front or rear anchors. Do not scratch or otherwise mar the surface of the torsion bar during removal or installation.*

6. Remove the clamp and slide the rear anchor balloon seal off the front end of the torsion bar.

7. Remove the torsion bar by sliding the bar rearward and out through the rear anchor.

8. Examine the balloon seal and replace it if necessary. Examine the torsion bar for scores and scratches, and smooth off any nicks and scratches from the sharp edges. Coat all repaired areas with a good rust preventive.

9. Be sure that the hex ends of the torsion bar and the hex openings in the anchors are clean. Examine the adjusting bolt and swivel for damage and replace parts as necessary. Grease the swivel for ease of operation.

10. To install the torsion bar, slide the bar through the rear anchor. Slide the ballon seal over the torsion bar with its large, cupped side facing the rear.

11. Grease both ends of the torsion bar and slide the front end of the torsion bar into the hex opening of the anchor on the lower control arm.

12. Install the lockring in the rear anchor and pack the annular opening in the rear anchor with grease.

13. Install the balloon seal on the rear anchor so that the seal lip engages the anchor groove.

14. Load the torsion bar by turning the adjusting bolt clockwise.

15. Lower the car and adjust the front suspension height. Refit the upper control arm rebound bumper (if so equipped) and torque the nut to 200 in. lbs.

FRONT SHOCK ABSORBERS

Removal and Installation

1. Remove the nut and washer from the upper end of the shock absorber. Note the positions of all the small parts.

2. Jackup the front of the car until the wheels are clear of the floor. Remove the shock absorber lower mounting bolt. Allow the control arm mounting bracket to lower itself.

3. Fully compress the shock absorber by pushing upward. Pull the shock firmly downward and remove it from the car.

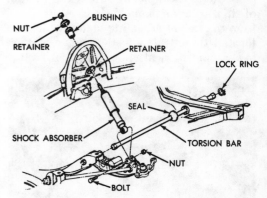

Front shock absorber and torsion bar

4. To install the shock absorber, fully compress it and insert the upper end through the upper bushing. Fit the washer and nut and torque the nut to 25 ft lbs. Be sure that all of the retainers are installed with the concave side in contact with the rubber.

5. Position and align the shock absorber lower mount. Install the bolt and tighten it finger-tight. Lower the car and torque the lower mounting bolt to 50 ft lbs.

BALL JOINTS

Inspection

LOWER BALL JOINT

1. Raise the front of the vehicle by placing a floor jack under the lower control arm. Position the lifting point of the jack as close to the wheel as possible.

2. Have an assistant raise and lower the tire and wheel assembly and observe any movement at the lower ball joint.

3. On 1965–67 models, replace the ball joint if the axial (up and down) play of the ball joint housing arm in relation to the ball joint stud exceeds 0.050 in. On 1968–72 models, replace the ball joint if the axial play exceeds 0.070 in.

Removal and Installation

LOWER BALL JOINT AND STEERING ARM

The lower ball joint is integral with the steering arm and is not serviced separately.

1. Raise the vehicle on a hoist so the front suspension will drop to the downward limit of its travel.

2. Remove the upper control arm rebound bumper if the car is so equipped.

3. Remove all load from the torsion bar, that is attached to the same side of the vehicle as the ball joint to be replaced, by turning the torsion bar adjusting bolt in a counterclockwise direction.

4. Remove the tire, wheel, and brake drum from the vehicle as an assembly. If the car is equipped with disc brakes, remove the tire and wheel, remove the brake pads, and remove the caliper from the steering knuckle and position it out of the way with the brake line attached. Remove the rotor from the spindle.

5. Remove the two lower bolts that attach the steering arm-ball joint assembly to the brake assembly mounting plate.

6. Using a suitable tool, disconnect the tie-rod end from the steering arm.

7. Remove the ball joint stud retaining nut and cotter pin.

8. Using a suitable tool, separate and remove the ball joint from the lower control arm.

9. Position the ball joint/steering arm assembly on the steering knuckle and install the two retaining bolts.

10. Insert the ball joint stud in the lower control arm and install the retaining nut and cotter pin.

11. Position the tie rod end in the steering knuckle and install the retaining nut and cotter pin.

12. Place a load on the torsion bar by turning the adjusting bolt in a clockwise direction.

13. Install the tire, wheel, and brake drum assembly. If the car is equipped with disc brakes, install the rotor, caliper, brake pads, and tire and wheel assembly.

14. Lower the vehicle and install the upper control arm rebound bumper if the car is so equipped.

15. Check and adjust the front suspension height and alignment as required.

UPPER BALL JOINT

1. Raise the vehicle by placing a floor jack under the lower control arm. Place the lifting point of the jack as close as possible to the wheel.

2. Remove the wheel, tire, and drum as an assembly. On models with disc brakes, remove the tire and wheel, remove the disc brake pads, remove the disc brake caliper from the steering knuckle, and position the caliper out of the way with the brake line attached. Remove the brake rotor from the steering knuckle.

3. Remove the nut that attaches the upper ball joint to the steering knuckle and, using a suitable tool, loosen the ball joint stud from the steering knuckle.

4. Unscrew the upper ball joint from the upper control arm and remove it from the vehicle.

5. Position a new ball joint on the upper control arm, screw the ball joint into the control arm until it bottoms on the control arm, and tighten the ball joint to a minimum of 125 ft lbs.

NOTE: *When installing a ball joint, make certain that the ball joint threads engage those of the upper control arm squarely if the original control arm is being used.*

6. Position a new seal on the ball joint stud and install the seal in the ball joint making sure that the seal is fully seated on the ball joint housing.

7. Position the ball joint stud in the steering knuckle and install the retaining nut.

8. Lubricate the ball joint and, if the replacement ball joint is equipped with a knock-off type grease fitting, break off that portion of the fitting over which the lubrication gun was installed.

9. If the car is equipped with disc brakes, install the rotor, caliper, and brake pads. Install the tire and wheel.

10. Lower the car and adjust the front

suspension height and alignment as required.

LOWER CONTROL ARM AND STEERING ARM

Removal and Installation

1. Remove the wheel, tire, and brake drum as an assembly. On cars that are equipped with disc brakes, remove the disc brake assembly as described in chapter 9.

2. Disconnect the shock absorber at its lower mount and swing the shock absorber up and out of the way. Detach the torsion bar from the lower control arm.

3. Using a suitable puller, remove the tie rod end from the steering arm. Be careful not to damage the seal during this operation.

4. Detach the sway bar link from the lower control arm. Remove the steering arm-to-brake support bolts and detach the arm. Position the brake support assembly to one side.

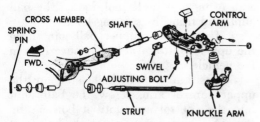

Lower control arm assembly

5. Using a suitable puller, remove the ball joint stud from the lower control arm. Be careful not to damage the seal during this operation.

6. At the forward end of the crossmember, remove the strut spring pin, nut, and bushings. Note their relative positions. Remove the nut and washer from the lower control arm shaft.

7. Using a non-metallic hammer, tap the end of the lower control arm shaft to aid in removing the shaft from the crossmember. Remove the lower control arm, strut, and shaft as an assembly.

8. To install the lower control arm, begin by inserting a new strut bushing into the crossmember (use a twisting motion). Use water as a lubricant to aid installation. Grease or oil must not be used.

9. Position the strut bushing inner retainer on the strut and install the control arm, strut, and shaft assembly. Replace the shaft bushing outer retainer and tighten the nut finger-tight.

10. Replace the lower control arm shaft washer and tighten the nut finger-tight.

11. Replace the lower ball joint stud in the lower control arm and torque the stud nut to 100 ft lbs on 1965–69 models, or to 85 ft lbs on 1970–72 models. Install the cotter pin.

12. Install the brake support on the steering knuckle and replace the two upper bolts and nuts. Tighten the nuts finger-tight.

13. Fit the steering arm to the steering knuckle, insert the two lower bolts, and fit the nuts. Torque the upper bolts to 55 ft lbs and the lower bolts to 100 ft lbs on 1965–66 models, or to 120 ft lbs on 1967–72 models.

14. Inspect the tie rod end seal and replace it if necessary. Install the tie rod end on the steering arm and torque it to 40 ft lbs. Install the cotter pin.

15. Connect the shock absorber by installing the rear bolt only, and tighten it finger-tight.

16. Refit the torsion bar to the lower control arm.

17. Install the wheel, tire, and brake drum assembly. Refit the disc brake assembly (if so equipped).

18. Lower the car and adjust the front suspension height if necessary. Torque the strut nut at the crossmember to 45 ft lbs and insert the strut pin. Torque the lower control arm shaft nut to 130 ft lbs on 1965–69 models, or to 145 ft lbs on 1970–72 models. Complete the installation of the shock absorber.

19. Align the front suspension as necessary.

UPPER CONTROL ARM

Removal and Installation

1. Position a jack under the lower control arm as close to the wheel as possible. Use this jack to raise the front of the car.

2. Remove the wheel, tire, and brake drum as an assembly. On those cars that are equipped with disc brakes, remove the disc brake assembly as described in chapter 9.

3. Using a suitable tool, remove the upper and lower ball joint studs.

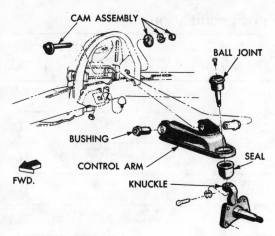

Upper control arm assembly

Front Suspension Torque Specifications

Ball joint-to-upper control arm nut,
  1965–72: 125 ft lbs
Ball joint-to-upper stud nut, 1965–66: 55 ft lbs
                             1967–72: 100 ft lbs
Ball joint-to-lower stud nut, 1965–69: 100 ft lbs
                             1970–72: 85 ft lbs
Control arm pivot shaft nut, 1965–69: 130 ft lbs
                             1970–72: 145 ft lbs
Crossmember bolts, 1965–70: 150 ft lbs
Idler arm stud nut (at center link),
  1965–69: 40 ft lbs
  (at mounting bracket),
  1965–66: 45 ft lbs
  1967–68: 40 ft lbs
  1969–72: 65 ft lbs
Rebound bumper, 1965–72: 200 in. lbs
Steering knuckle bolts (upper), 1965–66: 100 ft lbs
                           1967–72: 120 ft lbs
            (lower), 1965–72: 55 ft lbs
Tie rod ends (sleeve clamp bolt), 1965–66: 15 ft lbs
                           1967–68: 150 ft lbs
                           1969–72: 115 ft lbs
          (stud nuts), 1965–72: 40 ft lbs

4. Remove the nuts, lockwashers, cams, and cam bolts which secure the upper control arm and bushings to the support brackets. Lift the control arm up and away from the support.

5. Using a suitable puller, remove the ball joint and seal.

6. The upper control arm bushing can be pressed out of the arm if necessary. To install a new bushing, support the control arm at the point where the bushing is to be inserted and press it in place. Do not lubricate the bushing to aid in installation.

7. Place the ball joints in the control arm and tighten or press the joints in until they are properly seated. Be sure that a torque of at least 125 ft lbs is applied to the ball joint. Install the ball joint seal.

8. Place the control arm in position and install the cam bolts, cams, lockwashers, and nuts. Insert the upper ball joint stud in the steering knuckle and refit the nut, torqueing it to 55 ft lbs.

9. Install the wheel, tire, and brake drum assembly. Refit the disc brake assembly (if so equipped).

10. Lower the car. Check and adjust the front suspension height and alignment as necessary. Torque the cam bolts to 65 ft lbs.

FRONT SUSPENSION ALIGNMENT

Because of the special equipment necessary to perform the front suspension alignment adjustments, it is not possible to describe the exact procedures for these adjustments. In all cases, follow the procedures recommended by the manufacturer of the alignment equipment that is used.

Before the front suspension is aligned, the following components should be checked and corrected as required.

1. Front wheel bearings.
2. Front wheel and tire for both radial and lateral runout.
3. Wheel and tire balance.
4. Ball joints and steering linkage pivots.
5. Tire wear and inflation pressure.
6. Shock absorbers.
7. Steering gear operation.
8. Rear springs.
9. Front suspension height.

Caster and Camber Adjustment

Caster and camber are adjusted by rotating the adjusting cams located in the upper control arms. Caster should be as nearly equal as possible for both front wheels.

Toe-in Adjustment

Toe-in is adjusted by rotating the tie rod sleeves which are located at the ends of the tie rods. Before adjusting them, be sure that the steering wheel is centered and that the front wheels are in the straight-ahead position. Both tie rod sleeves should be rotated an equal amount. When torqueing the sleeve clamp bolts, be sure that the clamp bolt nuts are at the bottom. Otherwise, the nuts may interfere with the other front suspension components.

Wheel Alignment Specifications

Year	Steering Type	Caster		Camber		Toe-in (in.)	King Pin Inclination (deg)	Wheel Pivot Ratio	
		Range (deg)	Pref Setting (deg)	Range (deg)	Pref Setting (deg)			Inner Wheel	Outer Wheel
1965	Manual	1N to 0	½N	①	①	⅛	7½	20	17.6
	Power	¼P to 1¼P	¾P	①	①	⅛	7½	20	17.6
1966–68	Manual	1N to 0	½N	②	②	³⁄₃₂–⁵⁄₃₂	7½	20	17.6
	Power	¼P to 1¼P	¾P	②	②	³⁄₃₂–⁵⁄₃₂	7½	20	17.6
1969	Manual	1N to 0	½N	②	②	³⁄₃₂–⁵⁄₃₂	7½	20	17.6
	Power	¼P to 1¼P	¾P	②	②	³⁄₃₂–⁵⁄₃₂	7½	20	17.6
	Manual	1⁵⁄₁₆N to ¹⁵⁄₁₆N	1N	③	③	¹⁄₃₂–⁷⁄₃₂	7½	20	17.8
	Power	¹⁵⁄₁₆P to ⅜N	¹⁄₁₆N	③	③	¹⁄₃₂–⁷⁄₃₂	7½	20	17.8
1971–72	Manual	1N to 0	½N	③	③	⅛ ±¹⁄₃₂	7½	20	17.5
	Power	¼P to 1¼P	¾P	③	③	⅛ ±¹⁄₃₂	7½	20	17.5

N—Negative
P—Positive
① Right wheel: ⅛N to ⅜P; left wheel: ⅛P to ⅝P.
② Right wheel: 0 to ½P, ¼P preferred; left wheel: ¼P to ¾P, ½P preferred.
③ Right wheel: ¼P ± ¼, ¼P preferred; left wheel: ½P ± ¼, ½P preferred.

Steering

A worm and recirculating ball-type steering gear is used with the manual steering system.

The worm shaft is supported at each end by ball-type thrust bearings.

The sector shaft includes an integral sector gear which meshes with helical grooves on the worm shaft ball nut.

The sector shaft is supported, and rotates, in two needle bearings in the housing and one in the housing cover.

Constant-Control power steering is an option on all models. Hydraulic power is provided by a vane-type, belt-driven pump. A double-groove pump pulley is

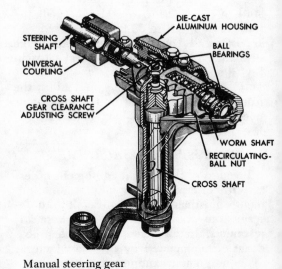

Manual steering gear

used. The power steering gear and pump are essentially the same as those used on other Chrysler Corporation cars.

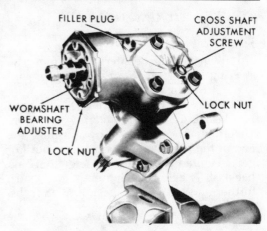

Manual steering gear adjustment locations

STEERING WHEEL

Removal and Installation

CAUTION: *Be very careful when removing the steering wheel from a car that is equipped with a collapsible steering column. A sharp blow or excessive pressure on the column could cause it to collapse, thereby destroying the steering column.*

1. Disconnect the battery.
2. Using a screwdriver, carefully remove the center assembly from the steering wheel.
3. Remove the large center nut. Using a puller, remove the steering wheel from the column.
4. Reverse the above to install the steering wheel. Torque the steering wheel nut to 28 ft lbs.

Turn Signal Switch Replacement

1. Remove the steering wheel as described above.
2. Remove the horn wiring and the turn signal lever.
3. Tie a piece of string to the turn signal switch wires. While holding the other end of the string to prevent the wires from falling down inside the steering column, remove the turn signal switch.
4. Reverse the above to install the new turn signal switch.

MANUAL STEERING GEAR

Worm Bearing Preload Adjustment

1. Remove the steering gear arm using a suitable gear puller.
2. Remove the horn button or horn ring.
3. Loosen the cross-shaft adjusting screw locknut and back out the adjusting screw about two turns.
4. Turn the steering wheel two complete turns from the straight-ahead position, and place an in. lb torque wrench on the steering shaft nut.
5. Rotate the steering shaft at least one turn toward the straight-ahead position while measuring the torque on the torque wrench. The torque should be between 1½ and 4½ in. lbs to move the steering wheel. If torque is not within these limits, loosen

the worm shaft bearing adjuster locknut and turn the adjuster clockwise to increase the preload or counterclockwise to decrease the preload. When the preload is correct, hold the adjuster screw steady and tighten the locknut. Recheck the preload.

Ball Nut Rack and Sector Mesh (Cross-Shaft) Adjustment

NOTE: *This adjustment can be accurately made only after proper preloading of the worm bearing.*

1. Turn the steering wheel gently from one stop to the other, counting the number of turns. Turn the steering wheel back exactly half-way, to the center position.
2. Turn the cross-shaft adjusting screw clockwise to remove all lash between the ball nut rack and the sector gear teeth, then tighten the adjusting screw locknut to 35 ft lbs.
3. Turn the steering wheel about one-fourth turn away from the center or high spot position. With an inch-pound torque wrench on the steering wheel nut, measure the torque required to turn the steering wheel through the high spot at the center position. The reading should be between 8 and 11 in. lbs. This is the total of the worm shaft bearing preload and the ball nut rack and sector gear mesh load. Readjust the cross-shaft adjustment screw if necessary to obtain a correct torque reading.
4. After completing the adjustments, place the front wheels in a straight-ahead position and with the steering wheel and steering gear centered, install the steering arm on the cross-shaft. Tighten the steering arm retaining nut to 180 ft lbs.

POWER STEERING GEAR

Cross-shaft Adjustment

1. Remove the center link from the steering gear arm. Start the engine and allow it to run at idle speed.

2. Back off the adjusting screw until backlash is felt in the steering gear arm. Determine the backlash by grasping the end of the steering gear arm with your fingers. Tighten the adjusting screw until no backlash is evident. Tighten ⅜ to ½ turn further and torque the locknut to 28 ft lbs.

POWER STEERING PUMP

Chrysler Corporation has utilized four different power steering pumps over the years. These include 0.94, 0.96, 1.06, and 1.20 cu in. displacement models. Usage varies with the particular vehicle, engine, and rear axle combination. The 0.94 and 1.06 cu in. pumps may be identified by the differences in the filler tube shape. (The 0.94 pump has an oval-shaped filler tube and the 1.06 pump has a round filler tube.) The 0.96 cu in. pump may be identified by the plain end of the pump driveshaft while the 1.20 cu in. pump may be identified by the hexagonal hole in the driveshaft pulley end.

The 0.96 and 1.20 cu in. pumps were last installed on production models in 1968. After that date, only the 0.94 and 1.06 cu in. pumps have been utilized.

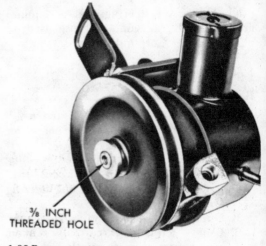

3/8 INCH THREADED HOLE

1.06 Power steering pump

side the reservoir. These only require service when they are completely clogged or when the pump is disassembled. Servicing is by replacement only.

Power Steering Pump Removal and Installation

NOTE: *Before beginning removal, carefully take notice of the exact hose routing. Hoses must be routed and installed in the exact same manner as they were removed. Read the entire procedure before beginning pump service.*

1. Back off the pump mounting and locking bolts and remove the pump drive belt.

2. Disconnect all hoses at the pump.

3. Remove the pump bolts and remove the pump with its bracket.

4. To install the pump, place it in position and install the mounting bolts.

5. Install the pump drive belt and adjust it to specification. Torque the mounting bolts to 25–30 ft lbs.

6. Connect the pressure and return hoses. On the 1.06 cu in. pump, install a new pressure hose O-ring.

7. Fill the pump with power steering fluid.

8. Start the engine and rotate the steering wheel from stop to stop at least ten times. This will help to bleed the system. Check the pump oil level and fill as required.

9. The pump end hose fitting torque is 24 ft lbs. The gear end fitting torque is 160 in. lbs. Be certain that the hoses are at least two inches from the exhaust manifolds and are not kinked or twisted.

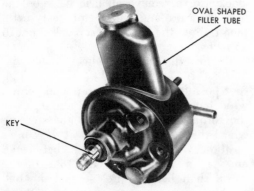

OVAL SHAPED FILLER TUBE

KEY

0.94 Power steering pump

Some power steering pumps were equipped from the factory with oil coolers. These were used on vehicles with high-performance engines and/or vehicles equipped with special axle ratios.

Up to, and including, 1968, most power steering pumps utilized an oil filter screen that was located in the oil return tube in-

9 · Brakes

Brake System

The older Barracuda models are equipped with drum brakes at all four wheels. Since 1966, front disc brakes have been offered as an option. In both cases, the brake system is hydraulically operated, with a power assist being offered as an option.

The year 1967 marked the beginning of the use of a dual-tandem master cylinder and separate brake circuits to the front and rear wheels. In case of a hydraulic failure in one set of wheels, the other set remains operable.

MASTER CYLINDER

Removal and Installation

If the master cylinder requires removal for replacement or overhauling, proceed in the following manner.

1. Disconnect the brake line(s) from the master cylinder.
2. Remove the nuts that attach the mas-

ter cylinder to the cowl panel or brake booster.

3. On those models that are fitted with standard brakes, disconnect the master cylinder pushrod from the brake pedal.
4. Slide the master cylinder straight out and off the cowl panel or brake booster.
5. Reverse the above procedure to install, and bleed brake system.

Overhaul

1965–66 BARRACUDA

To overhaul the master cylinder, begin by removing it from the car as detailed above. Clean the outside of the cylinder carefully and drain the brake fluid from it. Then proceed in the following manner.

1. Remove the bolts which hold the piston flange in place. Withdraw the boot and then the pushrod/piston assembly from the cylinder, but do not separate the pushrod from the piston.
2. Take off the brass washer that fits between the piston and the cup. Extract the cup, spring, valve, and seal from the cylinder bore.

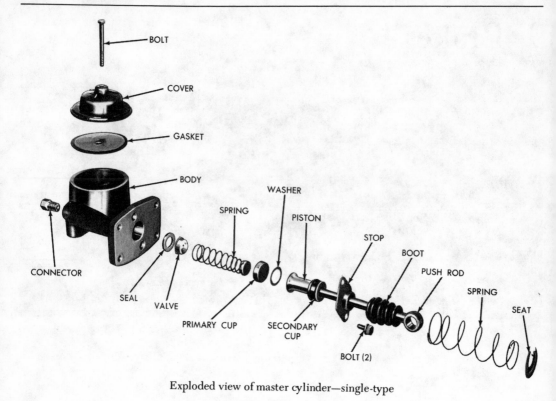

Exploded view of master cylinder—single-type

3. Wash out the cylinder bore with fresh brake fluid. Examine it for signs of wear or damage. If the piston shows signs of wear or corrosion, it should be replaced with a new one. Always replace both of the cups and the valve assembly when overhauling the master cylinder.

4. If the walls of the cylinder are corroded or scratched, clean them with a polishing cloth. If this does not remove the scratches, then the walls must be honed to remove them.

CAUTION: *Do not increase the bore more than 0.002 in. when honing. If the cylinder still shows signs of damage, discard it and use a new assembly.*

5. After completing the overhaul, clean the cylinder by flushing it out with denatured alcohol and then dry it with a clean, lint-free cloth. Finish drying it with compressed air and run clean brake fluid through it.

1967–72 BARRACUDA AND CHALLENGER

NOTE: *Over the years, various manufacturers' master cylinders have been employed. Except for very minor differences, service procedures are identical.*

1. Thoroughly clean the outside of the housing. Remove the cover and drain the fluid.

2. Loosen the rear piston retainer screw in the flange below the piston and flip the retainer down to release the piston assembly for removal.

3. Remove the front piston. If the piston sticks in the cylinder, air pressure may be used to remove it. If air pressure is used, it is mandatory to install new cups. (New cups are recommended in any event.)

4. Note the position of the rubber cups and remove them from the pistons. Do not remove the primary cup of the rear piston. If the cup is damaged or worn, install a new piston assembly.

5. With the aid of an easy out, remove the tube seats.

6. Remove the residual pressure valves and springs.

7. Thoroughly clean the inside of the master cylinder. Use a non-petroleum solvent for this procedure.

8. Closely inspect the inside of the master cylinder. If necessary, hone the bores with a crocus cloth. Be sure not to increase the bore size by more than 0.002 in. Discard the master cylinder if scores

cannot be eliminated by honing to this depth.

9. If a master cylinder repair kit is available, use all of the parts furnished. Do not attempt to reuse parts if new ones are available.

10. Before assembly, thoroughly lubricate all of the parts in clean brake fluid.

11. Replace the primary cup on the front piston end with the lip away from the piston.

12. Carefully slide the second seal cup over the piston rear and into the second land. The cup lip must face the piston front.

13. Slowly work the rear secondary cup over the piston and position it in the rear land. The lip must face the rear.

14. Slide the retainer cup over the front piston stem with the beveled side facing away from the piston cup.

15. Replace the small end of the pressure spring into the retainer.

16. Position the assembly in the bore. Be sure that the cups are not canted.

in the seated position. Insert the piston retaining screws with their gaskets. Tighten them securely.

20. Replace the residual pressure valves and spring. Position them in the front outlet. Install the tube seats.

NOTE: *When the bleeding tubes are attached, the tube seats will be correctly positioned.*

Bleeding the Dual Tandem Master Cylinder

Before installing the reconditioned master cylinder, it will be necessary to bleed it as follows:

1. Insert bleeding tubes into the tube seats and fill both brake reservoirs with brake fluid.

2. Depress the rod slowly (using a dowel for power brakes) and allow the pistons to return under the pressure of their own springs. Repeat this operation until all of the air bubbles are expelled.

3. Remove the bleeding tubes and install the cover and the gasket.

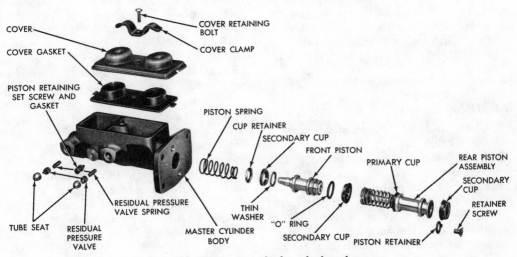

Exploded view of master cylinder—dual tandem-type

17. Slowly work the secondary cup over the back of the rear piston with the cup lip facing forward.

18. Position the spring retainer in the center of the rear piston assembly. It should be over the shoulder of the front piston. Position the piston assembly in the bore. Slowly work the cup lips into the bore, then seat the piston assembly.

19. With your fingers, hold the pistons

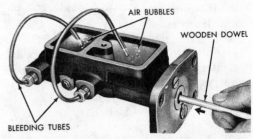

Bleeding dual tandem master cylinder

4. Install the master cylinder on the vehicle.

POWER BRAKE BOOSTER

Removal and Installation

1. Remove the nuts that attach the master cylinder to the brake booster and position the master cylinder out of the way without disconnecting the lines. Be careful not to kink the brake lines.

2. Disconnect the vacuum hose from the brake booster.

3. Working under the dash, remove the nut and bolt that attach the brake booster pushrod to the brake pedal. On linkage-type brake boosters, remove the lower pivot retaining bolt.

4. Remove the four brake booster attaching nuts and washers.

5. Remove booster assembly from the vehicle.

6. Reverse the above procedure to install.

The power brake booster is replaced as an entire unit because there are no replacement components available for it. Save the old unit as it may be used as a trade-in when purchasing a rebuilt unit.

BLEEDING BRAKES

1. Clean and fill the master cylinder with clean brake fluid.

2. Jack up the car to allow access to the bleeder valves which are located on the inside of the brake plate.

3. Starting at the right rear wheel, attach a tube to the bleeder valve and insert the other end of the tube into a glass jar which is partially filled with brake fluid (to check for air bubbles).

4. Open the valve and have someone slowly push the brake pedal several times until the fluid coming out of the tube has no air bubbles.

5. Tighten the valve while steady pressure is being applied to the brake pedal.

6. Repeat the above steps for the rest of the wheels; first the left rear, then the right front, and finally the left front.

7. Throw away the fluid in the jar because it is full of microscopic air bubbles. Refill the master cylinder.

Front Disc Brakes

DISC BRAKE CALIPERS

Removal and Installation

Fixed Caliper Disc Brakes

1. Jack up the front of the car and support it with jack stands. Remove the front wheel.

2. Detach the flexible hydraulic line from the tube at the frame mount. Be sure to plug the tube to prevent fluid loss.

3. Unfasten the bolts which attach the caliper to the steering knuckle.

4. If a new flexible hydraulic line is to be installed, mark the bracket where the line enters it and the position of its clip underneath. *The open end of the clip should face away from the caliper assembly.*

5. Withdraw the caliper by slowly sliding it upward and away from the disc assembly.

6. The thickness and the runout of the brake disc should be checked as described in the "Brake Disc Inspection" procedure before the caliper is installed.

7. To install the caliper, place it over the brake disc and torque the attaching bolts to 45–60 ft lbs on 1966–68 models, or to 50–80 ft lbs for 1969–72 models.

8. Check to see that the disc is running evenly between the halves of the caliper. The clearance should be 0.090–0.120 in. between the disc and the caliper, and a minimum of 0.050 in. from each disc surface to the groove in the outboard caliper.

9. Install the pad assemblies between the disc and the caliper. Fasten the pad retainers on the caliper.

10. Loosen the bleed screw and attach the brake line at the caliper housing. After the caliper has filled with brake fluid, close the bleed screw after making sure that there are no bubbles remaining. Fill the master cylinder and pump the brake pedal.

11. Check for leaks with maximum pedal pressure applied. Recheck the master cylinder reservoir level.

NOTE: *Be sure that the lower shock absorber mounting bolt has been installed from the rear, with the nut toward the front of the car.*

12. Install the wheel and lower the car.

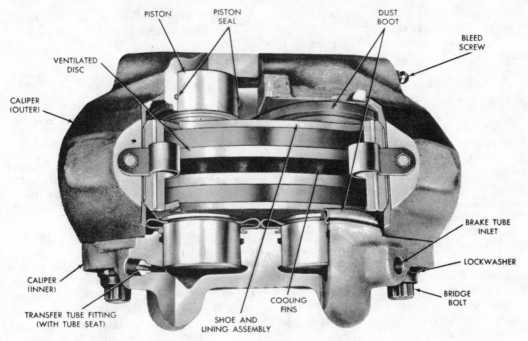

PISTON   PISTON SEAL   DUST BOOT   BLEED SCREW

VENTILATED DISC

CALIPER (OUTER)

BRAKE TUBE INLET

LOCKWASHER

CALIPER (INNER)

BRIDGE BOLT

TRANSFER TUBE FITTING (WITH TUBE SEAT)   SHOE AND LINING ASSEMBLY   COOLING FINS

Sectional view of fixed caliper disc brake assembly

CAUTION: *Road-test the car. Make several stops to seat the brake pads, but be careful because the car may pull to one side until the pads are properly seated.*

FLOATING CALIPER DISC BRAKES

1. Jack up the front of the car and support it with jack stands. Remove the front wheel.

2. If the caliper will not be disassembled, detach the flexible hydraulic line

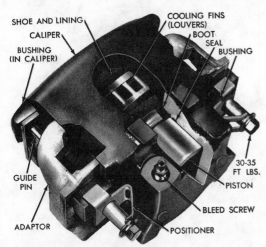

SHOE AND LINING   COOLING FINS (LOUVERS)
CALIPER   BOOT SEAL
BUSHING (IN CALIPER)   BUSHING

30-35 FT LBS.
PISTON

GUIDE PIN

BLEED SCREW

ADAPTOR   POSITIONER

Sectional view of floating caliper disc brake assembly

from the tube at the frame mount. Be sure to plug the tube to prevent fluid loss. If the caliper will be disassembled, leave the flexible hose in position because it will be necessary to remove the piston from the caliper while the caliper is still on the car, as described in the overhaul procedure for the floating caliper.

3. Disconnect the other end of the hose from the caliper.

4. Withdraw the guide pins and positioners which secure the caliper to the adaptor. While holding the outboard shoe and lining assembly, withdraw the caliper by slowly sliding it out away from the disc assembly. Withdraw the inboard shoe and lining assembly.

5. The thickness and the runout of the brake disc should be checked as described in the "Brake Disc Inspection" procedure before the caliper is installed.

6. To install the caliper, connect the flexible hydraulic line, with a new gasket, to the caliper and torque the hose fitting to 25 ft lbs. Connect the hose to the frame bracket (if it had been removed).

CAUTION: *Always connect the brake hose to the caliper and tighten the hose fitting before attaching the other end of the hose to the frame bracket. Twist the* hose as little as possible when fitting it to the frame bracket.

7. Fit the inboard shoe and lining to the adaptor. Carefully slide the caliper down into position in the adaptor and over the disc, while holding the outboard shoe and lining in position in the caliper.

8. Align the guide pin holes in the caliper, adaptor, and both shoes. Fit the positioners over the guide pins with the open ends toward the outside and the arrows pointing upward. Insert the guide pins with their positioners through the bushing, caliper, adaptor, and both shoes, and into the outer bushings in the caliper and anti-rattle spring.

9. Make sure that the positioner tabs are in place, press in on the guide pins, and carefully screw the pins into the adaptor. Torque the pins to 25–35 ft lbs.

10. Connect the flexible hydraulic line to the tube at the frame mount (if it had been removed).

11. Loosen the caliper bleed screw. After the caliper has filled with brake fluid, close the bleed screw after making sure that there are no bubbles remaining. Fill the master cylinder and pump the brake pedal.

12. Check for leaks with maximum pedal pressure applied. Recheck the master cylinder reservoir level.

13. Install the wheel and lower the car. CAUTION: *Road-test the car. Make several stops to seat the brake pads, but be* careful because the car may pull to one side until the pads are properly seated.

Overhaul

FIXED CALIPER

Remove the caliper assembly from the car as described previously and continue with the procedure below.

1. Unfasten the disc pad retaining clips and the transfer tube from the caliper. Place the assembly in a vise with brass jaws, using the caliper lugs to mount it. Detach the transfer tube and withdraw the pad assemblies.

2. Separate the halves of the caliper by removing the bridge bolts.

3. Peel the dust boots off the caliper housing and piston groove. Using compressed air, carefully force the pistons out of both halves of the caliper. Be careful not to scratch the pistons or their bores. CAUTION: *Do not try to pry out the pistons as their surfaces will be damaged and they will not seal properly.*

4. Using a small pointed tool made of wood or plastic, remove the piston seals from the bore grooves and discard the seals. Be careful not to scratch the bore or the seal grooves.

5. Clean all parts in brake fluid. Wipe them dry with a clean, lint-free cloth. Blow out the passages and bores with compressed air. If the dust boots show any signs of tearing or deterioration, they must

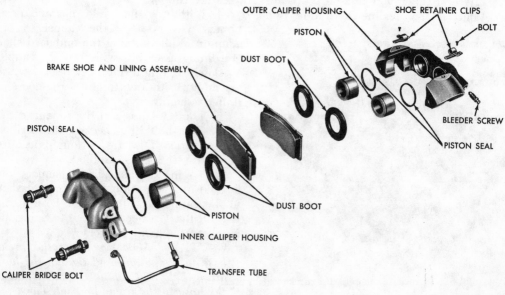

Exploded view of fixed caliper assembly

be replaced. Inspect the pistons and their bores for evidence of pitting or scoring. Replace any pitted, worn, or scored pistons with new parts.

6. If light scratches or corrosion are evident, clean the bores with a crocus cloth. If the bores do not come clean, or if deep scratches are present, use a hone to clean out the piston bore.

CAUTION: *Do not increase the bore diameter by more than 0.002 in. If the bore is still not clean after honing this amount, replace the caliper housing with a new unit. Disregard any black stains; these are caused by the piston seals and are harmless.*

7. Clean out the honed bore with a stiff, but non-metallic, rotary brush. Clean the caliper completely after honing by flushing it out with the brake fluid and wiping it dry with a clean, lint-free cloth. Repeat this operation.

8. Begin assembly by placing the inner caliper housing in a vise with brass jaws, using the caliper lugs to mount it.

9. Place the new piston seals in clean brake fluid. Install the seals in the caliper grooves by positioning each seal over one area, and using a finger to work it into a groove until it has been properly seated. Be careful not to pinch, roll, or twist the new seal when seating it. Never use an old seal.

10. Coat the outside piston surface with clean brake fluid. Fit the pistons into their bores, with the open end and boot groove of each piston facing toward the outside of the cylinder.

11. Squarely place the piston in the bore and push it home with a slow, steady pressure. If the piston will not seat properly, remove it and check the seal for correct groove positioning. After checking to make sure that the piston is properly seated, install a new dust boot in the caliper and piston grooves. Repeat this procedure for the three remaining pistons.

12. Position the other caliper half on the one in the vise and refit the bridge bolts. Torque the bolts to 70–80 ft lbs.

CAUTION: *Do not replace the original bridge bolts with ones which are not specified for this purpose. This could weaken the caliper, resulting in brake failure.*

13. Attach the transfer tube under its protective moulded lip. Insert the bleed screw but do not tighten it. Install the caliper assembly as described previously.

FLOATING CALIPER

Refer to steps 1 and 2 of the floating caliper disc brakes, "Removal and Installation" procedure and continue as follows:

1. Withdraw the guide pins and positioners which secure the caliper to the adaptor. While holding the outboard shoe and lining assembly, withdraw the caliper by slowly sliding it out away from the disc assembly. Withdraw the inboard shoe and lining assembly.

2. Remove the piston dust boot from the caliper.

3. Place several rags on top of the upper control arm and position the caliper on the rags. The rags are necessary to absorb any hydraulic fluid which may be lost while removing the piston.

CAUTION: *Be careful not to allow any brake fluid to contact the exterior finish because the fluid will destroy the paint.*

4. Depress the brake pedal very slowly. This will cause the piston to be pushed hydraulically out of its bore. The pedal will drop as soon as the piston has been pushed out. *Using air pressure to remove the piston is not recommended.* To prevent brake fluid loss, prop the brake pedal to any position below the first inch of pedal travel.

5. If it is necessary to remove the pistons from both calipers, disconnect the flexible hydraulic line at the frame bracket after removing the first piston. Plug the brake tube to prevent fluid loss and then repeat steps 1 through 4 to remove the other piston.

6. Disconnect the flexible hose from the tube at the frame bracket.

7. Place the caliper assembly in a vise with brass jaws. Using a small pointed tool made of wood or plastic, remove the piston seal from the bore groove and discard the seal. Be careful not to scratch the bore or the seal groove.

8. Use the tool described above to push out the inner and outer guide pin bushings and discard the old bushings.

9. Clean all parts in brake fluid. Wipe them dry with a clean, lint-free cloth. Blow out the passages and bores with compressed air. If the dust boots show any signs of tearing or deterioration, they must be replaced. Inspect the pistons and their

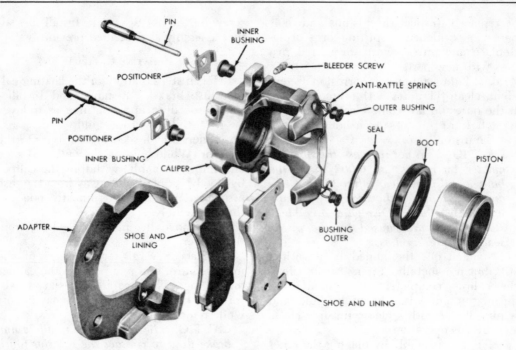

Exploded view of floating caliper assembly

bores for evidence of pitting or scoring. Replace any pitted, worn, or scored pistons with new parts.

10. If light scratches or corrosion are evident, clean the bores with a crocus cloth. If the bores do not come clean, or if deep scratches are present, use a hone to clean out the piston bore.

CAUTION: *Do not increase the bore diameter by more than 0.002 in. If the bore is still not clean after honing this amount, replace the caliper housing with a new unit. Disregard any black stains; these are caused by the piston seals and are harmless.*

11. Clean the honed bore out with a stiff, but non-metallic, rotary brush. Clean the caliper completely, after honing, by flushing it out with brake fluid and wiping it dry with a clean, lint-free cloth. Repeat this operation.

12. Begin assembly by placing the caliper in a vise with brass jaws. Place the new piston seal in clean brake fluid. Install the seal in the caliper groove by positioning the seal over the groove and using a finger to work it into the groove until it has been properly seated. Be careful not to pinch, roll, or twist the new seal when seating it. Never use an old seal.

13. Coat the new piston boot with clean brake fluid. Install the boot in the caliper

by using your finger to work it into the outer groove until it snaps into position.

14. Liberally coat the piston surface with clean brake fluid. Spread the piston boot, fit the piston in the boot, and slowly press the piston into the boot. Pressure must be applied uniformly to the piston to position it correctly in the boot and the caliper bore.

15. Fit a new inner guide pin bushing into the caliper with the flanged end of the bushing on the inboard side of the caliper. Install a new outer guide pin bushing by pressing the bushing into the caliper from the outboard side. Install the bleeder screw.

16. Install the caliper assembly as described previously.

DISC BRAKE PADS

Removal and Installation

FIXED CALIPER

1. Jack up the front of the car and support it with jack stands. Remove the front wheel.

2. Withdraw the clips which secure the brake pads to the caliper.

3. Use a pair of pliers to grasp the tabs located on the outer ends of the brake pads. Pull outward to remove the pads. If

the pads do not come out easily, force the pistons back with a pair of water pump pliers. The pads should now be free for removal.

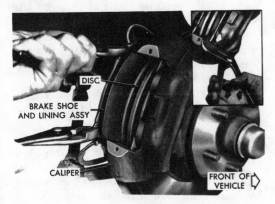

Removing brake pads from fixed caliper disc brake

4. Inspect the caliper assembly for any signs of leaks or damage. If there is any fluid leakage, the caliper piston boots and seals must be replaced as detailed in the "Fixed Caliper Overhaul" procedure. Wipe the area between the housing halves with a clean, dry cloth.

5. To install the new brake pads, push the pistons in one half of the caliper fully home in their bores by placing a flat metal bar against them and depressing the pistons with a steady force. This will allow for the additional thickness of the new pads. *Because this operation will raise the brake fluid level in the master cylinder reservoir, be sure to remove some of the fluid before proceeding with it.*

6. Slide the new pad assembly into the caliper. The ears of the pad should rest on the bridges of the caliper. The pad should face the disc and should be fully seated.

7. Repeat steps 5 and 6 for the other half of the caliper. Install all of the pad retainers on the caliper.

8. Pump the brake pedal until a firm pedal pressure is felt; the pad assembly is now properly seated.

9. Install the wheel and lower the car. Check the master cylinder reservoir level and add brake fluid if necessary.

CAUTION: *Road-test the car. Make several stops to seat the brake pads, but be careful because the car may pull to one side until the pads are properly seated.*

FLOATING CALIPER

1. Jack up the front of the car and support it with jack stands. Remove the front wheel.

2. Withdraw the guide pins and positioners which secure the caliper to the adaptor. While holding the outboard shoe and lining assembly, withdraw the caliper by slowly sliding it out away from the disc assembly. Withdraw the inboard shoe and lining assembly.

3. Using a small pointed tool made of wood or plastic, push out the outer guide pin bushings. Remove the bushings from the inner guide pins by sliding the bushings off. Remove the positioners from the guide pins. Discard all of the old bushings and positioners.

4. Inspect the caliper assembly for any signs of leaks or damage. If there is any fluid leakage, the caliper piston boot and seal must be replaced as detailed in the "Floating Caliper Overhaul" procedure. Examine the mating surfaces of the abutments on the caliper and the adaptor, and, if necessary, clean the surfaces with a wire brush.

5. To install the new brake pads, push the piston fully home in its bore by placing a flat metal bar against it and depressing the piston with a steady force. This will allow for the additional thickness of the new pads. *Because this operation will raise the brake fluid level in the master cylinder reservoir, be sure to remove some of the fluid before proceeding with it.*

6. Fit the inboard shoe and lining to the adaptor. Carefully slide the caliper down into position in the adaptor and over the disc, while holding the outboard shoe and lining in position in the caliper.

7. Align the guide pin holes in the caliper, adaptor, and both shoes. Fit the positioners over the guide pins with the open ends toward the outside and the arrow pointing upward. Insert the guide pins with their positioners through the bushing, caliper, adaptor, and both shoes, and into the outer bushings in the caliper and anti-rattle spring.

8. Make sure that the positioner tabs are in place, press in on the guide pins, and carefully screw the pins into the adaptor. Torque the pins to 25–35 ft lbs.

9. Pump the brake pedal until a firm pedal pressure is felt; the pad assembly is now properly seated.

10. Install the wheel and lower the car. Check the master cylinder reservoir level and add brake fluid if necessary.

CAUTION: *Road-test the car. Make several stops to seat the brake pads, but be careful because the car may pull to one side until the pads are properly seated.*

BRAKE DISC
Removal and Installation
FIXED CALIPER AND FLOATING CALIPER

The brake disc and hub are both removed at the same time. There is no way to remove them separately.

1. Refer to the proper caliper removal procedure and remove the brake caliper, but do not disconnect the hydraulic line. Support the caliper to avoid straining the brake line.

2. Remove the grease cap, cotter pin, locknut, adjusting nut, washer, and outer wheel bearing. Withdraw the disc/hub assembly.

3. Install the disc/hub assembly with the outer wheel bearing, washer, and adjusting nut. While rotating the hub, torque the wheel bearing adjusting nut to 90 in. lbs.

4. Measure the disc runout as described in the "Brake Disc Inspection" procedures. Perform any necessary repairs.

5. Fit the locknut on the spindle and position the locknut on the adjusting nut. Align one pair of the locknut slots with the cotter pin hole in the wheel spindle. Back off the adjusting nut/locknut assembly one slot and fit the cotter pin. The wheel bearings are now properly adjusted.

6. Clean the grease cap. Coat, but do not fill, the inside of the grease cap with grease and install the cap. Clean both sides of the brake disc with solvent to remove all traces of grease.

7. Install the brake caliper assembly and road-test the car as detailed in the proper caliper installation procedure.

Inspection

Whenever any brake service is performed, the brake discs should be inspected.

FIXED CALIPER

1. Remove the brake caliper as described in the fixed caliper removal procedure, but do not disconnect the hydraulic line.

2. Remove the grease cap, cotter pin, and locknut. Loosen the wheel bearing adjusting nut.

3. While rotating the hub, torque the wheel bearing adjusting nut to 90 in. lbs.

4. Attach a dial indicator so that its plunger contacts the disc at a point about one inch from the outer edge of the disc.

5. Measure the lateral runout of the disc. The runout should be no greater than 0.0025 in. If it is greater, the disc must be replaced.

6. Using a micrometer, measure the disc thickness at twelve different points about one inch from the outer edge of the disc. If the thickness measurements vary by more than 0.0005 in., the disc must be replaced.

7. Repeat step 3.

8. Fit the locknut on the spindle and position the locknut on the adjusting nut. Align one pair of the locknut slots with the cotter pin hole in the wheel spindle. Back off the adjusting nut/locknut assembly one slot and fit the cotter pin. The wheel bearings are now properly adjusted.

9. Clean the grease cap. Coat, but do not fill, the inside of the grease cap with grease and install the cap. Clean both sides of the brake disc with solvent to remove all traces of grease.

10. Install the brake caliper assembly.

FLOATING CALIPER

1. Remove the brake caliper as described in the floating caliper removal procedure, but do not disconnect the hydraulic line.

2. Remove the grease cap, cotter pin, and locknut. Loosen the wheel bearing adjusting nut.

3. While rotating the hub, torque the wheel bearing adjusting nut to 90 in. lbs.

4. Attach a dial indicator so that its plunger contacts the outboard side of the disc at a point about one inch from the outer edge of the disc. Measure the lateral runout of the disc.

5. Detach the dial indicator and mount it on the inboard side of the disc. Measure the lateral runout as described in the previous step.

6. The runout should be no greater than 0.0025 in. If it is greater, the disc must be replaced or resurfaced.

7. Using a micrometer, measure the disc thickness at twelve different points about one inch from the outer edge of the disc. If the thickness measurements vary by more than 0.0005 in., the disc must be replaced or resurfaced.

8. When machining the disc surface, remove equal amounts of material from each side but never more than 0.025 in. per side, or 0.050 in. total thickness per disc.

9. Repeat step 3.

10. Complete this procedure by following steps 5 through 7 of the "Removal and Installation" procedure for the brake discs.

Front Drum Brakes

BRAKE DRUMS

Removal and Installation

1. Raise the car and remove the wheel.

2. On cars that are equipped with self-adjusting brakes, loosen the brake adjusting star wheel by removing the plug from the rear adjustment hole and inserting a thin screwdriver into the hole. Push the adjusting lever away from the star wheel.

CAUTION: *Do not bend the lever by forcing it.*

3. Insert a brake adjusting tool into the hole, engage the notches of the star wheel, and pry on it to release the wheel.

4. Remove the cover, grease cap, cotter pin, adjustment nut, locknut, and outer

wheel bearing. Withdraw the wheel and drum together, from the spindle. The brake lining is now exposed for inspection.

5. Check the shoe alignment for lining wear and for traces of fluid or grease where they do not belong.

6. Installation is in the reverse order of removal. Lubricate the wheel bearings and adjust them to the proper preload.

7. Adjust the brakes.

BRAKE SHOES

Removal and Installation

Remove the wheel and brake drum as outlined above. Then proceed in the following manner.

1. Take off the shoe return springs. Detach the adjusting cable eye from the anchor and unhook the other end from the lever. Withdraw the cable, overload spring, and anchor plate.

2. Detach the adjusting lever from the spring, and separate the spring from the pivot. Take the spring completely off from the secondary shoe web and unfasten it from the primary shoe web.

3. Remove the retainer springs and nails from the shoe. Extract both shoes from the pushrods and lift them out. Withdraw the star wheel assembly from the shoes.

Install the brake shoes in the following order.

1. Lightly lubricate the shoe tab contact area at six points on the support plate. Match both the primary and secondary brake shoes with each other.

2. Before installation in the car, fit the

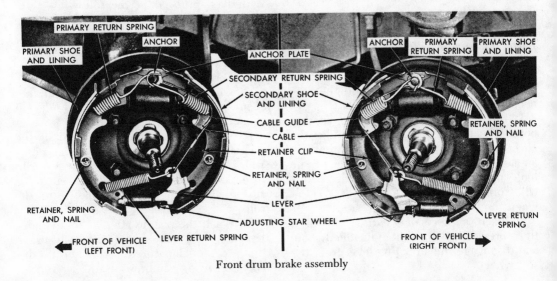
Front drum brake assembly

star wheel assembly between the shoes, with the star wheel next to the secondary shoe. The left star wheel is plated and its adjustment stud is stamped with an "L." The right star wheel is black and its stud is unmarked. Spread the anchor ends of the shoes apart to keep the star wheel assembly positioned.

3. Place the assembly on the support plate while attaching the shoe ends to the pushrods.

4. Install the shoe retaining nails, springs, and retainers. Place the anchor plate over the anchor.

5. Place the adjustment cable eye over the anchor, so that it rests against the anchor plate. Attach the primary shoe return spring shoe web and fit the other end over the anchor.

6. Place the cable guide in the secondary shoe web and fit the end over the anchor. Hold this in position while engaging the secondary shoe return spring, through the guide and into the web. Put its other end over the anchor.

NOTE: *See that the cable guide stays flat against the web and that the secondary shoe return spring overlaps that of the primary.*

Squeeze the ends of the spring loops, using pliers, until they are parallel and around the anchor.

7. The adjustment cable should be threaded over the guide, and the end of the overload spring should be hooked into the lever.

NOTE: *The eye of the adjuster cable must be tight against the anchor.*

Brake Adjustments

The self-adjusting brakes used on the Barracuda and Challenger should require no manual adjustment. If the brakes are relined or otherwise serviced, however, an initial manual adjustment will become necessary.

1. Lift up the front of the car so that both wheels are free to turn. Take the cover off the adjustment hole and insert an adjusting tool. Lift the handle of the tool upward (push downward, 1965–68). Continue this until a slight drag is felt when the wheel is rotated.

2. Insert a piece of welding rod, or a thin screwdriver, into the adjustment hole and disengage the adjusting lever from the star wheel.

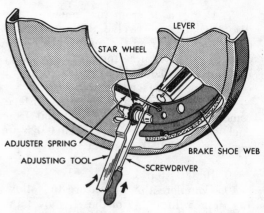

Adjusting drum brakes

CAUTION: *Do not bend the lever or stretch its spring too far.*

3. Keep the lever disengaged while backing off on the star wheel until there is no shoe drag when the wheel is rotated. Repeat the adjustment for the other front wheel.

WHEEL CYLINDERS

Overhaul

When the brake drums are removed, carry out an inspection of the wheel cylinder boots for cuts, tears, cracks, or leaks. If any of these are present, the wheel cylinder should have a complete overhaul performed.

NOTE: *Preservative fluid is used during assembly; its presence in small quantities does not indicate a leak.*

To remove and overhaul the wheel cylinders, proceed in the following manner.

1. Remove the brake shoes (see above) and check them. Replace them if they are soaked with grease or brake fluid.

2. Detach the brake hose.

3. Unfasten the wheel cylinder attachment bolts and slide the wheel cylinder off its support.

4. Pry the boots off either end of the wheel cylinder and withdraw the pushrods. Push in on one of the pistons to force out the other piston, its cup, the spring, the spring cup, and the piston, itself.

5. Wash the pistons, the wheel cylinder housing, and the spring in fresh brake fluid, or in denatured alcohol, and dry them off using compressed air.

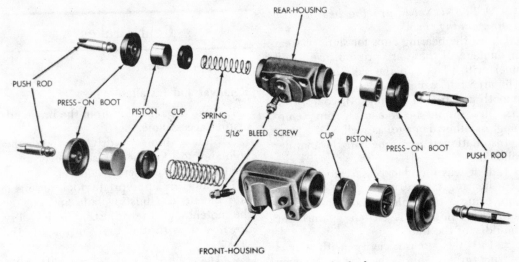

Exploded view of front and rear wheel cylinders

CAUTION: *Do not use a rag to dry them, as the lint from it will stick to the surfaces.*

Inspect the cylinder bore wall for signs of pitting, scoring, etc. If it is badly scarred or pitted, the entire cylinder should be replaced. Light scratches or corrosion should be cleaned up with crocus cloth.

NOTE: *Disregard the black stains from the piston cups that appear on the cylinder wall; they will do no damage.*

Assembly and installation are performed in the manner following:

1. Dip the pistons and the cups in clean brake fluid. Replace the boots with new ones if they show wear or deterioration. Coat the wall of the cylinder bore with clean brake fluid.

2. Place the spring in the cylinder bore. Position the cups in either end of the cylinder with the open end of the cups facing inward (toward each other).

3. Place the pistons in either end of the cylinder bore with the recessed ends facing outward (away from each other).

4. Fit the boots over the ends of the cylinder and push down until each boot is seated, being careful not to damage either boot.

5. Position the wheel cylinder on its support and torque the mounting screws to 110 in. lbs (9 in. brakes), 220 in. lbs (10 in. brakes).

6. Attach the jumper tube to the wheel cylinder and torque it to 115 in. lbs. Install the brake hose on the frame bracket. Connect the brake line to the hose, using a torque setting of 115 in. lbs also. Fit the end of the brake hose through the end of the stand-off. Attach the jumper tube to the brake hose and attach the hose to the stand-off. Torque the jumper tube to 105 in. lbs.

WHEEL BEARINGS

Removal and Installation

The procedure for removing, installing, and adjusting the bearings on cars equipped with disc brakes appears under the "Removal and Installation" procedure for brake discs, as described above.

Drum brake wheel bearings are removed in the manner following.

1. Lift the car so that both of the wheels are clear of the ground.

2. Take off the wheel disc, grease cup, cotter pin, lock, and the bearing adjustment nut. Withdraw the thrust washer and the bearing cone.

3. Remove the wheel, hub, and brake drum from the spindle.

4. Use a ¾ in. *non-metallic* rod to drift out the inner oil seal and the bearing.

Clean the hub/drum assembly and the bearings by using mineral spirits or kerosine.

CAUTION: *Never dry the bearings by air-spinning them.*

Check the bearing cups for signs of wear or damage. If these are present, use a soft steel drift, placed in the slots of the hub. The area into which the cup fits should be smooth and free of scoring. All cones, rollers, etc., should be free of scoring, chipping, or other damage, as well.

Installation is performed in the manner following.

1. If it was found necessary to install a new bearing cup, drive it flush with the hub, using a brass block and hammer. Be sure that the cup is seated against the shoulder of the hub.

2. Fill the grease cavity with wheel bearing grease, until the grease is even with the inner diameter of the bearing cups.

CAUTION: *Do not mix different brands of grease; not all of them are compatible. Because of this, new grease should never be added to that which is already in the hub.*

The grease should be forced into the bearing rollers or packed in with a bearing packer.

3. Insert the inner cone and put a new oil seal in position with its lip facing inward. Lightly tap the oil seal in place, using a wood block and a hammer, so that it is flush with the hub. Be careful not to damage the oil seal flange.

4. Clean the spindle. Coat its polished surfaces with a small amount of bearing grease. Fit the wheel and drum assembly over the spindle.

5. Position the outer bearing cone, the thrust washer, and the adjustment nut on the spindle. Adjust the preload as detailed below.

Adjustment

1. Rotate the wheel while tightening the bearing adjustment nut to 90 in. lbs.

2. Place the lock over the nut so that one pair of slots aligns with the cotter pin hole.

3. Turn the nut and lock assembly back *one* slot. Insert the cotter pin. This adjustment should yield zero preload to 0.033 in. end-play.

4. Clean the grease cap. Coat but do not fill, the cap with grease, and place it over the hub.

5. Lower the car.

Rear Brakes

BRAKE DRUMS

Removal and Installation

1. Take the rear plug from the brake adjusting access hole.

2. Slide a thin screwdriver through this hole and position the adjusting lever away from the adjusting screw notches.

3. Using an appropriate tool, insert it into the brake adjusting hole and engage the notches of the adjusting screw. Pry downward with the tool to release the brake.

4. Take off the rear wheel with clips from the wheel studs. Discard the clips and remove the drum.

5. To install, reverse removal procedure. Replacement of the clips is not necessary.

Inspection

Check the drums for signs of wear, scoring, or cracking. See that the lining is not worn, that shoe alignment is correct, and that there is no contamination from grease or brake fluid.

BRAKE SHOES

Removal and Installation

Except for the following steps, this removal procedure is identical to that for the front brake shoes.

1. With the anchor ends of both shoes spread apart, remove the parking brake lever strut, as well as the anti-rattle spring.

2. Once steps 1–3 are completed, detach the parking brake cable from the parking brake lever.

The installation procedure for the rear brake shoes is very different than that for the front shoes. This procedure must be done as follows:

1. Put a thin film of lubricant at the six points on the shoe tab contact area on the support plate.

2. Lubricate the pivot on the inner side of the secondary shoe web and install the parking brake lever on it. Fasten the lever with its washer and horseshoe clip.

3. Connect the parking brake cable to the lever. Slip the secondary shoe next to the support plate, while engaging the shoe

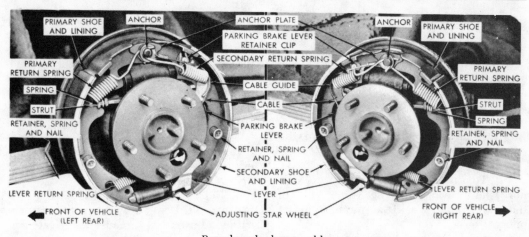

Rear drum brake assembly

web with the pushrod, and push it against the anchor.

4. Position the parking brake strut behind the hub and then slide it into the slot in the lever. Fit the anti-rattle spring over the free end of the strut.

5. Position the primary shoe, engage it in the pushrod and with the free end of the parking brake strut. Place the anchor plate over the anchor and then fit the eye of the adjustment cable over the anchor. Connect the primary shoe return spring to its web and fit its other end over the anchor as well.

6. Place the cable guide in the secondary shoe web. Hold it in this position while engaging the secondary shoe return spring, which goes through the guide and into the web. Put its other end over the anchor.

NOTE: *See that the cable guide stays flat against the web and that the secondary shoe return spring overlaps that of the primary.*

Use a pair of pliers to squeeze the spring loops around the anchor, until they are parallel.

7. Place the star wheel assembly between the shoes, with the star wheel adjacent to the secondary shoe. The left rear star wheel is plated and marked with an "L." The right rear star wheel is black and its stud is unmarked. Attach the adjuster spring, if so equipped.

8. Place the adjustment lever spring over the pivot pin on the shoe web and fit the lever *under* the spring, but *over* the

pin. To lock the lever, push it toward the rear.

9. Install the shoe retaining nails, the retainers, and the spring. Thread the adjusting cable over the guide. Hook the end of the overload spring in the adjustment lever, making sure that the cable remains tight against the anchor, and is aligned with the guide.

Adjustment

The adjustment procedures for the rear brake shoes are the same as those for cars that are equipped with front disc brakes. Should brake adjustment become necessary, check the corresponding section to this one, under "Front Drum Brakes," for adjustment procedures.

NOTE: *Be sure to release the parking brake lever fully and to back off on its cable until there is slack in it, before the rear service brakes are adjusted. Adjust the parking brake after the service brake has been adjusted. If the adjustments are not made in this order, brake drag may result.*

WHEEL CYLINDERS

Overhaul

The wheel cylinders found on the rear drum brakes are identical to those used on the models that are equipped with front drum brakes. Service procedures for the rear wheel may, therefore, be found with those detailed in the "Front Drum Brake" section, above.

BRAKE BACKING PLATE

Removal and Installation

1. Remove both the wheel and the brake drum. Unfasten the backing plate attachment nuts and remove the washers. Withdraw the axle shaft together with its retainer.

2. Detach the hydraulic line from the wheel cylinder.

3. Take the cable off the parking brake lever. To pull the cable out of the support plate, compress the three legs of the cable retainer with a suitable pair of pliers.

4. Detach the brake backing plate from the axle housing.

Installation of the backing plate is performed in the following manner.

1. Attach the brake shoes to the backing plate. Use a small amount of sealing compound (putty) around the back of the holes and openings in the backing plate. This will prevent water and foreign material from entering the brake assembly.

2. Fit the backing plate on the axle housing. Slide the rear axle shaft and retainer into the housing. Install the retainer nuts and washers. Tighten the nuts to 35 ft lbs.

3. Fasten the brake line to the wheel cylinder. Torque the line to 95 in. lbs (1965–70) or to 115 in. lbs (1971–72). Put the brake cable through the support plate and fasten the cable at the parking brake lever.

4. Attach the brake drum and the wheel. Bleed the brakes and adjust them as outlined elsewhere in the chapter.

Handbrake

The handbrake, or parking brake, is part of the rear service brake assembly. A han-

dle or pedal assembly, located beneath the dash panel, operates a flexible steel cable which is connected to an equalizer. Cables, running from the equalizer to each rear brake, operate the lever and strut mechanisms, which, in turn, activate the rear brake shoes.

Adjustment

For the handbrake to be adjusted properly, the service brakes must be adjusted first.

1. Release the handbrake so that the brake is off. Using a wire brush, clean the cable adjustment threads. Lubricate the threads and loosen the cable adjustment nut.

2. Be sure that the handbrake cable is slack, then tighten the adjustment nut until a resistance is felt when the rear wheels are rotated. Back off the cable adjustment nut until both of the rear wheels rotate freely and then loosen the nut two more turns.

3. Set and release the handbrake several times, then check to make sure that the rear wheels will still rotate freely when the handbrake is released.

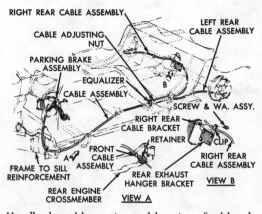

Handbrake cable routing and location of cable adjusting nut

Brake Specifications

(All measurements are given in in.)

| Year | Model | Master Cylinder | | Wheel Cylinder | | | Brake Diameter | | |
| | | Disc | Drum | Front | | | Front | | |
				Disc	Drum	Rear	Disc	Drum	Rear
'65	All 6 Cyl	——	1.00	——	1.00	$\frac{13}{16}$	——	9.0	9.0
	All V8	——	1.00	——	1.00	$\frac{13}{16}$	——	9.0	9.0
'66	All 6 Cyl	——	1.00	——	1.00	$\frac{13}{16}$	——	9.0①	9.0①
	All V8	——	1.00	——	1⅛	$\frac{15}{16}$	——	10.0	10.0
'67	All 6 Cyl	——	1.00	——	1.00	$\frac{29}{32}$	——	9.0	9.0
	All V8	——	1.00	——	1⅛	$\frac{29}{32}$	——	10.0	10.0
	All with disc brakes	1.00	——	$1\frac{41}{64}$	——	$\frac{15}{16}$	11⅞	——	10.0
'68	All 6 Cyl	——	1.00	——	1.00	$\frac{13}{16}$	——	9.0	9.0
	All V8	——	1.00	——	1⅛	$\frac{15}{16}$	——	10.0	10.0
	All with disc brakes	1.00②	——	③	——	$\frac{15}{16}$	④	——	10.0
'69	All 6 Cyl	——	1.00	——	1.00	$\frac{13}{16}$	——	9.0	9.0
	All V8	——	1.00	——	1⅛	$\frac{15}{16}$	——	10.0	10.0
	All with disc brakes	⑤	——	⑥	——	$\frac{15}{16}$	⑦	——	10.0
'70	All 6 Cyl	1.125	1.00	2.750	1.187	0.9375	10.72	10.0	10.0
	All V8	1.125	1.00	2.750	1.187	0.9375	10.72	11.0⑧	11.0
'71	All 6 Cyl	1.03	1.03	1.625	1.187	0.9375	11.04	10.0	10.0
	All V8	1.03⑨	1.03	2.750	1.187	0.9375	10.72⑧	11.0	11.0⑧
'72	All	1.03	1.03	2.751	1¾₆	$\frac{15}{16}$	10.98	10.0	10.0⑩

① 10 in. brakes optional
② Budd—1⅛ in.
③ Kelsey Hayes 1.638 in.
  Bendix 2 in.
  Budd 2.375
④ Kelsey Hayes 11.04 in.
  Bendix 11.19 in.
  Budd 11.88 in.
⑤ Kelsey Hayes 1 in.
  Kelsey Hayes (floating caliper) 1⅛ in.
  Bendix 1⅞ in.

⑥ Kelsey Hayes 1.636 in.
  Kelsey Hayes (floating caliper) 2¾ in.
  Bendix 2 in.
⑦ Kelsey Hayes 11.04 in.
  Kelsey Hayes (floating caliper) 11.75 in.
  Bendix 11.19 in.
⑧ 318, 340, 383 2 bbl engines—10 in.
⑨ 426 Hemi—1.125 in.
⑩ 11 in. optional
—— Not applicable

10 · Body

Doors

Removal and Installation

1. Open the front door fully and support it, using a jack with a block of wood or a pad on the lift-plate, as close to the hinge as possible. This will brace the door as the bolts in the hinge are unfastened.

2. Remove the trim and the hardware from the interior side of the door.

3. To aid in hinge alignment, scribe lines around the upper and lower hinge plates on both the A-pillar and the door panel.

4. Remove the bolts from the door itself. Lift the door clear of the car.

To install the door, proceed in the following manner.

1. Install the inner hardware on the door. Position the door in the opening and support it on the padded jack.

2. Position the hinge plates and hand-tighten the bolts. Align the hinge plates with the scribe marks by moving and adjusting the jack.

3. Align the doors by adjusting one hinge at a time. Movement in and out of the door is made at the door hinge half, while adjustment fore and aft is made on the pillar hinge half. Vertical adjustment is made at either hinge half. Tighten the hinge bolts.

DOOR PANELS

Removal and Installation

1. Remove the window regulator handle by unfastening the allen setscrew which holds it in place.

2. On older models, remove the inside door handle in the same manner as the window regulator. On newer models, i.e., those with the "paddle" type of inside door handles, remove the screw from the inner end.

3. Remove the armrest by unfastening the two screws which retain it, from underneath.

4. Remove the screws from the upper door rail panel. Insert a screwdriver with a wide, flat blade between the trim panel, the door frame, and adjacent to each re-

taining clip. Snap each clip individually out of the door frame.

CAUTION: *Do not try to snap out several clips at once, as damage to the trim panel may result.*

Once all of the clips are unfastened, withdraw the panel.

Before installation of the interior trim panel, check the watershield and be sure that the escutcheon springs are on the regulator shafts. Then proceed as follows:

1. Carefully align each clip with its hole in the door frame. Use the heel of the hand to press them into place.

CAUTION: *Do not use a hammer to fasten the clips, as damage to both the trim panel and the clip may result.*

2. Install the upper door rail panel and fasten its retaining screws.

3. Attach the washers, handles, and the armrest in the reverse order of their removal.

WINDOWS

Adjustment

1965–69 BARRACUDA

1. Remove the trim panel.

2. To correctly adjust the division channel, move it in or out at its base until the vent window frame is aligned with the roof rail.

3. If the window is binding against the division channel, or is too loose in relation to it, move it by using the fore-aft adjuster at the base of the channel.

4. The rear channel may be adjusted to align with the division channel by loosening the attachment screws that are located at the lower end of the rear channel.

5. To stop the glass from binding at the

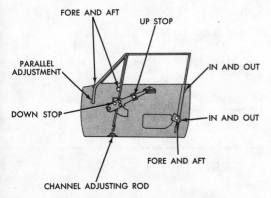

Door glass adjustment—1965–69 Barracuda. Early models do not have a channel adjusting rod

beltline, adjust the upper end of the rear channel.

6. Install the interior trim panel.

1970–72 BARRACUDA AND CHALLENGER

1. Raise the window completely. Remove the door trim panel.

2. Loosen the screw at the upper end of the window front track.

3. Align the front edge of the door glass to the A-pillar and to the top edge of the roof rail weatherstrip. The top edge of the glass should be parallel to the weatherstrip.

4. Tighten the screw at the upper end of the window front track.

5. Loosen the bottom screws at the window front track lower support.

6. Loosen the screw located at the bottom of the rear track lower support. Move the front track lower support outward until the glass contacts the weatherstrip. The rear track will also be moved as the lower support is pushed outward.

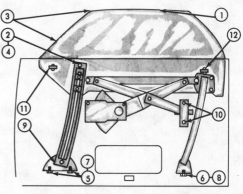

Door glass adjustment—1970–72 Barracuda and Challenger. Numbers refer to the steps of the glass adjustment procedure

7. Tighten the front track lower support screws.

8. Tighten the rear track lower support screw.

9. If further alignment of the window glass to the A-pillar or to the roof rail is necessary, adjust it by moving the idler arm pivot bracket of the window regulator up or down.

10. Attach the regulator arm pivot guide to the door panel.

11. Depress the front up-stop against the bumper on the door glass. Tighten the

screws which secure the assembly to the beltline reinforcement.

12. Repeat the preceding step for the rear up-stop.

13. Install the door trim panel.

Hood

ALIGNMENT

The hood is counterbalanced by means of torsion bars. Adjustments to the hood are made by means of oversize mounting holes in the hinge arms. Adjustments should be performed in the following order.

To Cowl

1. Scribe the position of the hinge plates on the hood.

2. Loosen the hinge attachment bolts. Move the hood until its alignment is correct in relation to the cowl.

3. Torque the attachment bolts to 180 in. lbs.

To Fender

FRONT

After completing the hood-to-cowl adjustment, check the clearance between the front of the hood and the fender. If adjustment is required, perform it in the following manner:

1. Remove the rubber hood bumper stops. The adjustment screw is now exposed.

2. Move the adjustment screw in or out, until the proper alignment is obtained.

3. Install the rubber bumper stop. If the hood-to-fender alignment is still not satisfactory, loosen the fender attachment bolts and move the fender up or down, as required.

NOTE: *On some models, shims are used between the fender and the inner panel. For these models, hood-to-fender clearance may be adjusted by the addition or subtraction of shims.*

REAR

1. Loosen the bolts that attach the hinge to the hood, on both sides.

2. Move the back of the hood in the direction of the wider space. Do this until the spacing is equal on both sides.

3. Tighten the attachment bolts. Lower the hood and check the alignment. If the space is still too large, or too little, on one side, proceed with the following steps:

4. Loosen the hinge to hood bolts on the side that requires adjustment.

5. To move the hood *out*, insert a large screwdriver between the upper hinge plate and the hood flange. Force the hood out with the screwdriver. Maintain the pressure on the screwdriver, while tightening the bolts.

6. If the hood must be moved *in*, push on the outside edge of the hood, until proper alignment is reached. Tighten the attachment bolts. Close the hood, and check for proper fit.

Projection Beyond the Fender

The leading edge of the hood should not project beyond the front fender. If it does, and the fender-to-door spacing is close, align it by loosening the fender bolts, then shifting the fender forward. Tighten the bolts.

Fender Contour

If the contour of the hood does not follow the curve of the fender, align it as follows.

1. Insert a 1 in. square block of wood between the fender flange and the hood, opposite the hood's low spot.

2. Slowly close the hood. Apply hand-pressure to the hood, slightly ahead of the block.

3. Repeat the steps above, every 6 in., until the hood contour matches that of the fender.

Latch

The hood latch is mounted using oversize attachment holes. To adjust it, loosen the adjustment screws, and move it in the desired direction.

Trunk Lid

ALIGNMENT

Testing

To determine if the trunk lid is in proper alignment, place 1 in. wide paper

strips along the edges of the trunk opening. Close the lid. If the pieces of paper
pull out evenly and snugly from the edges,
a good fit is indicated. If, however, the
paper is loose on one side, and tight on the
other, the lid should be aligned, as detailed below.

Centering

1. Loosen the bolts which hold one of
the hinges to the trunk lid.
2. Move the lid in the necessary direction. Tighten the bolt.
NOTE: *On cars built after 1967, only a
very slight amount of movement is possible.*
3. Repeat for the other hinge. Close the
lid and check the alignment. The lid
should be flush with both the body and
the rear quarter panels.

Lock and Striker Plate

1. To adjust the lock vertically, loosen
its attachment bolts and move it in the desired direction. Tighten the bolts.
2. Side-to-side adjustment is made by
loosening the striker plate mounting bolts.
3. The striker plate may also be moved
forward or backward. Doing this lowers or
raises the plate. The lock may be adjusted
in this manner. Tighten the bolts when the
adjustments are completed.

Fuel Tank

CAUTION: *Do not smoke or use an
open flame near the fuel tank, even if it
is empty. Vapors from the tank can ig-
nite, causing an explosion and serious
injury.*

Removal

1965–69 BARRACUDA

1. Disconnect the fuel line at the fuel
pump and use a siphon to drain the tank
completely dry. Collect the fuel in a clean,
dry container. Detach the lead which runs
to the gauge sender, the ground strap, and
the fuel line from the tank.
2. Unfasten the vent pipe from the fuel
filler at its connector. Remove the screws
which attach the fuel filler at its gasket to
the quarter panel. From the inside of the
trunk, unfasten the screws and the washers
that hold the fuel filler seal to the floor of
the trunk. Withdraw the end of the vent
pipe from the seal.
3. Using both hands, rotate the fuel
filler, while forcing it downward, into the
tank. Its upper end must clear the quarter
panel. Detach the gasket.
NOTE: *If the fuel filler is frozen to the
tank, slide the dust shield clear, and*

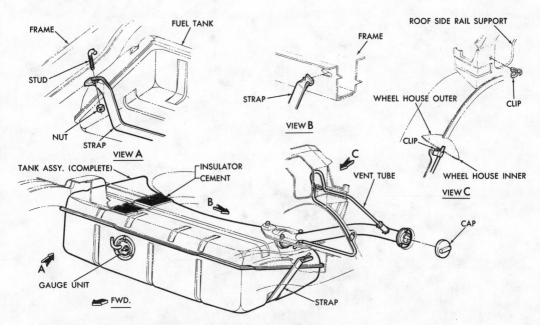

Fuel tank assembly—1965–69 Barracuda

work rubber lubricant into the grommet. Withdraw the filler.

4. Rotate the filler 180 degrees to withdraw it completely from the tank and seal. Lift it clear of the trunk.

5. Unfasten the nut which holds the retaining strap to the J-bolt. Allow the strap to hang down, clear of the tank, and remove the tank from the car.

6. Unfasten the gauge sender unit and slide it out of the tank. Throw away the old gasket.

1970–71 Barracuda and Challenger with Vapor Saver System

The fuel tank removal procedure is similar to that given above, for 1965–69 Barracuda models, except that you must substitute the following step:

2. Unfasten the heat shield from the floor pan. Withdraw the clamps and hoses from the vapor separator.

NOTE: *On cars with dual exhausts, the exhaust pipe and/or the muffler must be lowered in order to remove the heat shield and the vapor separator hoses.*

Take out the screws that attach the fuel filler and its gasket to the quarter panel. Remove the screws and washers that hold the fuel filler to the trunk floor.

1972 Barracuda and Challenger with Evaporation Control System

The fuel tank removal procedure for the 1972 cars is similar to that for the 1965–69 cars outlined above. Be sure, however, to note the following steps, which are different:

2. Unfasten the clamp and the line from the single outlet of the fuel tank vent pipe. Remove the screws which attach the fuel filler and gasket to the quarter panel. Unfasten the fuel filler seal from the floor of the trunk, by removing the nuts and washers that hold it in place.

3. Using both hands, twist the fuel filler, while lifting it upward away from the tank, until it is clear of the quarter panel. Withdraw the gasket.

NOTE: *If the fuel filler is frozen to the tank, slide the dust shield clear, and work rubber lubricant into the grommet, in order to remove it.*

Installation

1965–69 Barracuda

1. Check the condition of the filter at the end of the fuel gauge suction tube. If the filter is clogged, install a new one.

2. Replace the rubber grommet on the tank with a new one. Fit a new gasket into

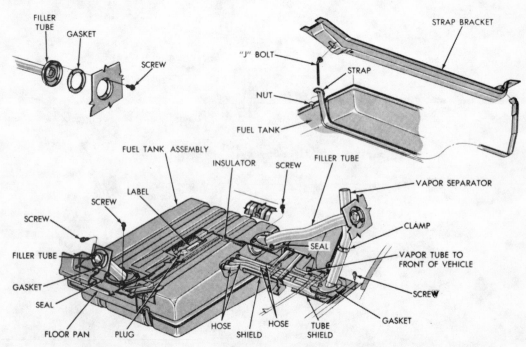

Fuel tank assembly—1970–71 Barracuda and Challenger with Vapor Saver System

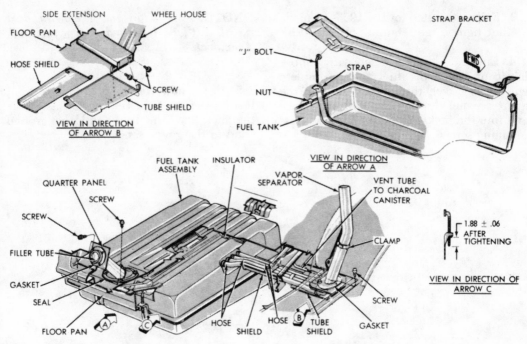

Fuel tank assembly—1972 Barracuda and Challenger with Evaporation Control System

the fuel gauge opening. Slide the gauge into the opening and align its tangs with those on the tank. Attach the lockring and then tighten the gauge.

3. Position the tank under the car. Thread the retaining strap onto the J-bolt, while holding the tank in place. Secure them by tightening their attachment nut to 60 in. lbs, or less.

4. Use rubber lubricant on the grommet. Fit the fuel filler through the dust seal and into the tank. Be sure that it clears the quarter panel. Rotate the filler 180 degrees and line it up with the hole in the quarter panel. Use a new gasket on the end of the filler. Lift the filler from the tank until it is positioned against the quarter panel. Line up the attachment holes, fasten the attachment screws, and fit the vent tube through the seal.

NOTE: *If the dust seal had to be disturbed during removal, align it and fasten its attachment screws.*

5. Attach the vent line to the fuel filler connector. Connect the fuel line, the hot lead, and the ground strap to the fuel gauge sender.

6. Fill up the tank, and test it for leaks.

1970–71 Barracuda and Challenger with Vapor Saver System

Installation of the fuel tank on the 1970–71 Barracuda and Challenger models is the same as that for the 1965–69 Barracuda, except for the following steps:

3. Align the insulation pad on the top of the tank. Position the tank, as above, and tighten the retaining nut to 50 in. lbs, or less.

5. Fit new vent hose clamps and attach the hoses to the vapor separator connectors. Tighten the hose clamps. Attach the heat shield with its retaining screws.

NOTE: *On cars with dual exhausts, install the tail pipe/muffler assembly next.*

Attach the fuel line, the lead, and the ground strap to the gauge sender. Complete the installation and testing, as above.

1972 Barracuda and Challenger with Evaporation Control System

The basic procedures for the fuel tank installation for the 1972 Barracuda and Challenger models follow those for the 1965–69 Barracuda. The following steps, however, should be changed:

2. Follow this step for the 1965–69 models, but tighten the retaining nut to 50 in. lbs.

4. Lubricate the grommet with rubber lubricant. Slide the fuel filler, complete with new gasket, through the hole in the quarter panel through the tank dust seal, and into the tank. Fasten the filler with its retaining screws.

NOTE: *First, align and attach the dust seal, if it was disturbed during fuel tank removal.*

5. Use a new clamp to install the vent line on the gas tank vent outlet. Assemble the fuel line, the lead, and the ground strap to the gauge sender.

Appendix

General Conversion Table

Multiply by	To convert	To	
2.54	Inches	Centimeters	.3937
30.48	Feet	Centimeters	.0328
.914	Yards	Meters	1.094
1.609	Miles	Kilometers	.621
.645	Square inches	Square cm.	.155
.836	Square yards	Square meters	1.196
16.39	Cubic inches	Cubic cm.	.061
28.3	Cubic feet	Liters	.0353
.4536	Pounds	Kilograms	2.2045
4.226	Gallons	Liters	.264
.068	Lbs./sq. in. (psi)	Atmospheres	14.7
.138	Foot pounds	Kg. m.	7.23
1.014	H.P. (DIN)	H.P. (SAE)	.9861
——	To obtain	From	Multiply by

Note: 1 cm. equals 10 mm.; 1 mm. equals .0394″.

Conversion—Common Fractions to Decimals and Millimeters

INCHES			INCHES			INCHES		
Common Fractions	Decimal Fractions	Millimeters (approx.)	Common Fractions	Decimal Fractions	Millimeters (approx.)	Common Fractions	Decimal Fractions	Millimeters (approx.)
1/128	.008	0.20	11/32	.344	8.73	43/64	.672	17.07
1/64	.016	0.40	23/64	.359	9.13	11/16	.688	17.46
1/32	.031	0.79	3/8	.375	9.53	45/64	.703	17.86
3/64	.047	1.19	25/64	.391	9.92	23/32	.719	18.26
1/16	.063	1.59	13/32	.406	10.32	47/64	.734	18.65
5/64	.078	1.98	27/64	.422	10.72	3/4	.750	19.05
3/32	.094	2.38	7/16	.438	11.11	49/64	.766	19.45
7/64	.109	2.78	29/64	.453	11.51	25/32	.781	19.84
1/8	.125	3.18	15/32	.469	11.91	51/64	.797	20.24
9/64	.141	3.57	31/64	.484	12.30	13/16	.813	20.64
5/32	.156	3.97	1/2	.500	12.70	53/64	.828	21.03
11/64	.172	4.37	33/64	.516	13.10	27/32	.844	21.43
3/16	.188	4.76	17/32	.531	13.49	55/64	.859	21.83
13/64	.203	5.16	35/64	.547	13.89	7/8	.875	22.23
7/32	.219	5.56	9/16	.563	14.29	57/64	.891	22.62
15/64	.234	5.95	37/64	.578	14.68	29/32	.906	23.02
1/4	.250	6.35	19/32	.594	15.08	59/64	.922	23.42
17/64	.266	6.75	39/64	.609	15.48	15/16	.938	23.81
9/32	.281	7.14	5/8	.625	15.88	61/64	.953	24.21
19/64	.297	7.54	41/64	.641	16.27	31/32	.969	24.61
5/16	.313	7.94	21/32	.656	16.67	63/64	.984	25.00
21/64	.328	8.33						

Conversion—Millimeters to Decimal Inches

mm	inches	mm	inches	mm	inches	mm	inches	mm	inches
1	.039 370	31	1.220 470	61	2.401 570	91	3.582 670	210	8.267 700
2	.078 740	32	1.259 840	62	2.440 940	92	3.622 040	220	8.661 400
3	.118 110	33	1.299 210	63	2.480 310	93	3.661 410	230	9.055 100
4	.157 480	34	1.338 580	64	2.519 680	94	3.700 780	240	9.448 800
5	.196 850	35	1.377 949	65	2.559 050	95	3.740 150	250	9.842 500
6	.236 220	36	1.417 319	66	2.598 420	96	3.779 520	260	10.236 200
7	.275 590	37	1.456 689	67	2.637 790	97	3.818 890	270	10.629 900
8	.314 960	38	1.496 050	68	2.677 160	98	3.858 260	280	11.032 600
9	.354 330	39	1.535 430	69	2.716 530	99	3.897 630	290	11.417 300
10	.393 700	40	1.574 800	70	2.755 900	100	3.937 000	300	11.811 000
11	.433 070	41	1.614 170	71	2.795 270	105	4.133 848	310	12.204 700
12	.472 440	42	1.653 540	72	2.834 640	110	4.330 700	320	12.598 400
13	.511 810	43	1.692 910	73	2.874 010	115	4.527 550	330	12.992 100
14	.551 180	44	1.732 280	74	2.913 380	120	4.724 400	340	13.385 800
15	.590 550	45	1.771 650	75	2.952 750	125	4.921 250	350	13.779 500
16	.629 920	46	1.811 020	76	2.992 120	130	5.118 100	360	14.173 200
17	.669 290	47	1.850 390	77	3.031 490	135	5.314 950	370	14.566 900
18	.708 660	48	1.889 760	78	3.070 860	140	5.511 800	380	14.960 600
19	.748 030	49	1.929 130	79	3.110 230	145	5.708 650	390	15.354 300
20	.787 400	50	1.968 500	80	3.149 600	150	5.905 500	400	15.748 000
21	.826 770	51	2.007 870	81	3.188 970	155	6.102 350	500	19.685 000
22	.866 140	52	2.047 240	82	3.228 340	160	6.299 200	600	23.622 000
23	.905 510	53	2.086 610	83	3.267 710	165	6.496 050	700	27.559 000
24	.944 880	54	2.125 980	84	3.307 080	170	6.692 900	800	31.496 000
25	.984 250	55	2.165 350	85	3.346 450	175	6.889 750	900	35.433 000
26	1.023 620	56	2.204 720	86	3.385 820	180	7.086 600	1000	39.370 000
27	1.062 990	57	2.244 090	87	3.425 190	185	7.283 450	2000	78.740 000
28	1.102 360	58	2.283 460	88	3.464 560	190	7.480 300	3000	118.110 000
29	1.141 730	59	2.322 830	89	3.503 903	195	7.677 150	4000	157.480 000
30	1.181 100	60	2.362 200	90	3.543 300	200	7.874 000	5000	196.850 000

To change decimal millimeters to decimal inches, position the decimal point where desired on either side of the millimeter measurement shown and reset the inches decimal by the same number of digits in the same direction. For example, to convert .001 mm into decimal inches, reset the decimal behind the 1 mm (shown on the chart) to .001; change the decimal inch equivalent (.039" shown) to .000039".

Tap Drill Sizes

National Fine or S.A.E.				National Coarse or U.S.S.		
Screw & Tap Size	Threads Per Inch	Use Drill Number		Screw & Tap Size	Threads Per Inch	Use Drill Number
No. 5	44	37		No. 5	40	39
No. 6	40	33		No. 6	32	36
No. 8	36	29		No. 8	32	29
No. 10	32	21		No. 10	24	25
No. 12	28	15		No. 12	24	17
$\frac{1}{4}$	28	3		$\frac{1}{4}$	20	8
$\frac{5}{16}$	24	1		$\frac{5}{16}$	18	F
$\frac{3}{8}$	24	Q		$\frac{3}{8}$	16	$\frac{5}{16}$
$\frac{7}{16}$	20	W		$\frac{7}{16}$	14	U
$\frac{1}{2}$	20	$\frac{29}{64}$		$\frac{1}{2}$	13	$\frac{27}{64}$
$\frac{9}{16}$	18	$\frac{33}{64}$		$\frac{9}{16}$	12	$\frac{31}{64}$
$\frac{5}{8}$	18	$\frac{37}{64}$		$\frac{5}{8}$	11	$\frac{17}{32}$
$\frac{3}{4}$	16	$\frac{11}{16}$		$\frac{3}{4}$	10	$\frac{21}{32}$
$\frac{7}{8}$	14	$\frac{13}{16}$		$\frac{7}{8}$	9	$\frac{49}{64}$
$1\frac{1}{8}$	12	$1\frac{3}{64}$		1	8	$\frac{7}{8}$
$1\frac{1}{4}$	12	$1\frac{11}{64}$		$1\frac{1}{8}$	7	$\frac{63}{64}$
$1\frac{1}{2}$	12	$1\frac{27}{64}$		$1\frac{1}{4}$	7	$1\frac{7}{64}$
				$1\frac{1}{2}$	6	$1\frac{11}{32}$

Decimal Equivalent Size of the Number Drills

Drill No.	Decimal Equivalent	Drill No.	Decimal Equivalent	Drill No.	Decimal Equivalent
80	.0135	53	.0595	26	.1470
79	.0145	52	.0635	25	.1495
78	.0160	51	.0670	24	.1520
77	.0180	50	.0700	23	.1540
76	.0200	49	.0730	22	.1570
75	.0210	48	.0760	21	.1590
74	.0225	47	.0785	20	.1610
73	.0240	46	.0810	19	.1660
72	.0250	45	.0820	18	.1695
71	.0260	44	.0860	17	.1730
70	.0280	43	.0890	16	.1770
69	.0292	42	.0935	15	.1800
68	.0310	41	.0960	14	.1820
67	.0320	40	.0980	13	.1850
66	.0330	39	.0995	12	.1890
65	.0350	38	.1015	11	.1910
64	.0360	37	.1040	10	.1935
63	.0370	36	.1065	9	.1960
62	.0380	35	.1100	8	.1990
61	.0390	34	.1110	7	.2010
60	.0400	33	.1130	6	.2040
59	.0410	32	.1160	5	.2055
58	.0420	31	.1200	4	.2090
57	.0430	30	.1285	3	.2130
56	.0465	29	.1360	2	.2210
55	.0520	28	.1405	1	.2280
54	.0550	27	.1440		

Decimal Equivalent Size of the Letter Drills

Letter Drill	Decimal Equivalent	Letter Drill	Decimal Equivalent	Letter Drill	Decimal Equivalent
A	.234	J	.277	S	.348
B	.238	K	.281	T	.358
C	.242	L	.290	U	.368
D	.246	M	.295	V	.377
E	.250	N	.302	W	.386
F	.257	O	.316	X	.397
G	.261	P	.323	Y	.404
H	.266	Q	.332	Z	.413
I	.272	R	.339		

ANTI-FREEZE CHART

Temperatures Shown in Degrees Fahrenheit
+32 is Freezing

Cooling System Capacity Quarts	Quarts of ETHYLENE GLYCOL Needed for Protection to Temperatures Shown Below													
	1	2	3	4	5	6	7	8	9	10	11	12	13	14
10	+24°	+16°	+ 4°	−12°	−34°	−62°								
11	+25	+18	+ 8	− 6	−23	−47								
12	+26	+19	+10	0	−15	−34	−57°							
13	+27	+21	+13	+ 3	− 9	−25	−45							
14			+15	+ 6	− 5	−18	−34							
15			+16	+ 8	0	−12	−26							
16			+17	+10	+ 2	− 8	−19	−34	−52°					
17			+18	+12	+ 5	− 4	−14	−27	−42					
18			+19	+14	+ 7	0	−10	−21	−34	−50°				
19			+20	+15	+ 9	+ 2	− 7	−16	−28	−42				
20				+16	+10	+ 4	− 3	−12	−22	−34	−48°			
21				+17	+12	+ 6	0	− 9	−17	−28	−41			
22				+18	+13	+ 8	+ 2	− 6	−14	−23	−34	−47°		
23				+19	+14	+ 9	+ 4	− 3	−10	−19	−29	−40		
24				+19	+15	+10	+ 5	0	− 8	−15	−23	−34	−46°	
25				+20	+16	+12	+ 7	+ 1	− 5	−12	−20	−29	−40	−5…
26					+17	+13	+ 8	+ 3	− 3	− 9	−16	−25	−34	−4…
27					+18	+14	+ 9	+ 5	− 1	− 7	−13	−21	−29	−3…
28					+18	+15	+10	+ 6	+ 1	− 5	−11	−18	−25	−3…
29					+19	+16	+12	+ 7	+ 2	− 3	− 8	−15	−22	−2…
30					+20	+17	+13	+ 8	+ 4	− 1	− 6	−12	−18	−2…

For capacities over 30 quarts
vide true capacity by 3. Find qu
Anti-Freeze for the ⅓ and mul
by 3 for quarts to add.

For capacities under 10 quarts multiply true capacity by 3. Find quarts Anti-Freeze for the tripled volume and divide by 3 for quarts to add.

To Increase the Freezing Protection of Anti-Freeze Solutions Already Installed

Cooling System Capacity Quarts	Number of Quarts of ETHYLENE GLYCOL Anti-Freeze Required to Increase Protection													
	From +20°F. to					From +10°F. to					From 0°F. to			
	0°	−10°	−20°	−30°	−40°	0°	−10°	−20°	−30°	−40°	−10°	−20°	−30°	−40°
10	1¾	2¼	3	3½	3¾	¾	1½	2¼	2¾	3¼	¾	1½	2	2½
12	2	2¾	3½	4	4½	1	1¾	2½	3¼	3¾	1	1¾	2½	3¼
14	2¼	3¼	4	4¾	5½	1¼	2	3	3¾	4½	1	2	3	3½
16	2½	3½	4½	5¼	6	1¼	2½	3½	4¼	5¼	1¼	2¼	3¼	4
18	3	4	5	6	7	1½	2¾	4	5	5¾	1½	2½	3¾	4¾
20	3¼	4½	5¾	6¾	7½	1¾	3	4¼	5½	6½	1½	2¾	4¼	5¼
22	3½	5	6¼	7¼	8¼	1¾	3¼	4¾	6	7¼	1¾	3¼	4½	5½
24	4	5½	7	8	9	2	3½	5	6½	7½	1¾	3½	5	6
26	4¼	6	7½	8¾	10	2	4	5½	7	8¼	2	3¾	5½	6¾
28	4½	6¼	8	9½	10½	2¼	4¼	6	7½	9	2	4	5¾	7¼
30	5	6¾	8½	10	11½	2½	4½	6½	8	9½	2¼	4¼	6¼	7¾

Test radiator solution with proper hydrometer. Determine from the table the number of quarts of solution to be drawn off from a full cooling system and replace with undiluted anti-freeze, to give the desired increased protection. For example, to increase protection of a 22-quart cooling system containing Ethylene Glycol (permanent type) anti-freeze, from +20°F. to −20°F. will require the replacement of 6¼ quarts of solution with undiluted anti-freeze.